Adopting a Territorial Approach to Food Security and Nutrition Policy

This document has been prepared by the staff of OECD, FAO and UNCDF. This document was approved by the Regional Development Policy Committee by written procedure on April 11th 2016 and prepared for publication by the OECD Secretariat. The views expressed and conclusions reached in this report do not necessarily correspond to those of the United Nations, including FAO, UNCDF or their Member States. The mention of specific companies or products of manufacturers, whether or not these have been patented, does not imply that these have been endorsed or recommended by FAO, OECD or UNCDF in preference to others of a similar nature that are not mentioned.

This document and any map included herein are without prejudice to the status of or sovereignty over any territory, to the delimitation of international frontiers and boundaries and to the name of any territory, city or area.

Please cite this publication as:
OECD/FAO/UNCDF (2016), *Adopting a Territorial Approach to Food Security and Nutrition Policy*, OECD Publishing, Paris.
http://dx.doi.org/10.1787/9789264257108-en

ISBN 978-92-64-25709-2 (print)
ISBN 978-92-64-25710-8 (PDF)

The statistical data for Israel are supplied by and under the responsibility of the relevant Israeli authorities. The use of such data by the OECD is without prejudice to the status of the Golan Heights, East Jerusalem and Israeli settlements in the West Bank under the terms of international law.

Photo credits: Cover Illustration © Jeffrey Fisher.

Corrigenda to OECD publications may be found on line at: *www.oecd.org/about/publishing/corrigenda.htm*.

Foreword

The calls for action are numerous: at the United Nations Rio+20 Conference on Sustainable Development in September 2012, governments reaffirmed the fundamental right of everyone to be free from hunger. The same year, the UN Secretary General launched the "Zero Hunger Challenge" campaign to end hunger globally. The United Nations 2030 Agenda for Sustainable Development, endorsed in September 2015, confirms the importance of achieving food security, and eradicating hunger is the second Sustainable Development Goal (SDG 2).

Since 1990, much progress has been made in reducing hunger. Yet, challenges to food security and nutrition remain as pressing as ever. Around 800 million people remain food insecure, although the world produces enough food to feed everyone. Food insecurity primarily affects the rural poor. Three-quarters of the world's extreme poor live in the rural areas of developing countries. This marks not only the scope of the problem, but also identifies a territorial divide. And, not all rural areas are alike. Most rural poor and food insecure live in sub-national regions that are disadvantaged in many other ways: they lack adequate infrastructure and basic services and are more vulnerable to adverse climatic conditions. Continued population growth brings added pressure to these challenges and, through migration and urbanisation, food insecurity may also become an increasingly urban problem.

Tackling high levels of food insecurity calls for innovative policy approaches that recognise that geography matters. Different territories need different policy responses to account for their particular challenges. Food security issues in remote rural areas are not the same as those in metropolitan areas, nor are the problems in one rural area the same as those faced by adjacent rural areas. Territorial specificities, including the institutions, infrastructure, education, health, natural resources, and human and social capital, strongly influence food security and nutritional outcomes. Policies must be grounded in a coherent, multidimensional framework to address the problem's inherent complexities. To this end, the Food and Agricultural Organization (FAO), the Organisation for Economic Co-operation and Development (OECD) and the United Nations Capital Development Fund (UNCDF) have launched a joint initiative to promote a territorial approach to food security and nutrition policies.

Indeed, this study presents a framework for a territorial approach to food security and nutrition based on five case studies in Cambodia, Colombia, Côte d'Ivoire, Morocco and Peru and two national workshops held in Mali and Niger. It was conducted by the OECD Regional Development Policy Committee (RDPC) through its Working Party on Rural Policy (WPRP), a unique forum for international exchanges and debates. The case studies were carried out in close collaboration with national and/or local governments.

The study proposes a shift from a sectoral, top-down and "one-size-fits-all" approach to one that is multisectoral, bottom-up and context-specific. It highlights the importance of a well-functioning multi-level governance system. It stresses that achieving sustainable food security and nutrition requires improving development conditions and accessing income-generating activities. The most efficient way of doing this is to tailor interventions to specific local conditions and to tap underutilised local assets and potential by means of a territorial approach. Governments, multilateral agencies, the private sector, philanthropic foundations and the media each have a critical role to play.

Ensuring that policies tackle each region's specific challenges confronting food security and nutrition will bring us closer to realising the call to action to eradicate hunger.

Rolf Alter	Judith Karl	Mario Pezzini	Rob Vos
Director, Directorate of Public Governance and Territorial Development, OECD	Executive Secretary, UNCDF	Director, OECD Development Centre	Director, Agricultural Development Economics Division, UN FAO

Acknowledgements

This publication is the outcome of the joint FAO, OECD, UNCDF project on the Territorial Approach to Food Security and Nutrition Policy. The project was co-ordinated by Raffaele Trapasso (OECD Directorate of Public Governance and Territorial Development) and Stefano Marta (first FAO and then OECD) under the direction of Joaquim Oliveira Martins (OECD) and Rob Vos (FAO) and the supervision of Enrique Garcilazo (OECD) and Vito Cistulli (FAO). Special thanks go to Stina Heikkila (FAO) for her valuable contributions to the report and the preparation of the case studies. The OECD Development Centre participated in the research and the co-ordination of the Côte d'Ivoire case study, led by Vicente Ruiz, under the direction of Federico Bonaglia. The UNCDF working group, composed of Christel Alvergne, Katiella Mai Moussa, Simona Santoro and Tara Sharafudheen, organised country diagnostics and national workshops in Mali and Niger. Important contributions to the drafting of the report were provided by Andres Rodriguez-Pose (London School of Economics) and David Freshwater (University of Kentucky).

We are particularly grateful to Nicola Crosta (Epic Foundation) and to a number of experts who provided valuable input and comments to the report, in particular: Bill Below (OECD), Nina Brandstrup (FAO Representative in Cambodia), Carmel Cahill (OECD), Mark Cropper (European Commission), Daniel Daumgartner (Switzerland), Elodie De Oliveria (OECD), Guillaume Lecaros de Cossio (OECD), Luiz De Mello (OECD), Ebba Dohlman (OECD), Jared Greenville (OECD), Michael Hage (FAO Representative in Morocco), Hassan Kordass (CGDA Morocco), Tamara Krawchenko (OECD), Karen Maguire (OECD), Chris McDonald (OECD), Kosal Oum (FAO), John Preissing (FAO Representative in Peru), Oriana Romano (OECD), Seung Soy (FAO), William Tompson (OECD), Andrea Uhrhammer (OECD) and Rafael Zavala (FAO Representative in Colombia).

We would like to thank all the people and institutions involved in the country case studies, in particular: the Council for Agriculture and Rural Development (CARD) and the Ministry of Agriculture in Cambodia, Prosperidad Social (DPS) in Colombia, the Conseil Général du Développement Agricole (CGDA) and the Haut Commissaire au Plan (HCP) in Morocco, the Ministry of Agriculture and Irrigation and CEPLAN in Peru, the Haut-Commissariat à l'Initiative 3N (HCI3N) in Niger, and the Commissariat à la Sécurité Alimentaire (CSA) in Mali, as well as to the FAO country offices in Cambodia, Colombia, Morocco and Peru. We are also grateful to the participants of the conference organised during Expo Milan (19-20 October 2015) for their contribution to the discussion and to the report.

We are especially thankful to the Ministry of Food and Agriculture of Germany for the financial contribution to publish the report and to the city of Milan for their support during the Expo Milan Conference.

We would also like to thank delegates of the OECD Working Party on Rural Policy (WPRP) for valuable discussions during their meeting in November 2015 and written comments.

Pilar Philip co-ordinated the publication process and Jennifer Allain, Victoria Elliott and Kate Lancaster provided editorial support.

Table of contents

Tables

Figures

Boxes

Executive summary

Main findings

Food security and nutrition (FSN) policies have been dominated by top-down approaches

To date, food security and nutrition (FSN) policies have been developed mainly through traditional, "top-down" approaches; that is, they are designed and implemented at the national level, often without sufficiently taking into account the priorities and needs of local stakeholders, and without involving them in the policy-making process. This lack of co-ordination and stakeholder engagement is exacerbated when policies are the result of project-based international co-operation efforts; the short timelines and narrowly targeted nature of such projects can lead to fragmented policy and programme interventions and generate local dependency on external aid. The need for a "bottom-up" approach – where different levels of government work together – is increasingly recognised by the countries covered in this report (Cambodia, Colombia, Côte d'Ivoire, Mali, Morocco, Niger and Peru).

Geography matters for food security and nutrition policy

Disparities in FSN levels are increasing, both among countries and *within* countries. For example, food insecurity and rural poverty usually go hand-in-hand and are often concentrated in specific geographic areas. National averages typically mask these pockets of poverty and food insecurity. The country case studies in this report highlight the importance of targeting policies to fight food insecurity in very specific regions, in addition to existing national-level policies. Such targeted policies are better placed to address the causes and possible solutions to hunger and malnutrition, which can differ significantly across metropolitan, adjacent rural and remote rural areas.

To date, food security and nutrition policies have largely taken a sectoral approach

Policies tackling hunger and malnutrition have traditionally focused on the agriculture sector and on temporary relief interventions. These interventions have produced modest results in reducing food insecurity and disparities among people and across geographic areas. Efforts have focused mainly on food production without sufficiently taking into account the other dimensions of FSN, namely availability, access, utilisation and stability. The case studies show that poverty is often the main cause of food insecurity, and addressing it is critical to finding a sustainable solution. Consequently, promoting off-farm employment opportunities can have a positive income effect on individuals who are suffering from hunger and can improve the access dimension of FSN. In addition to low incomes, other causes of food insecurity include unemployment, natural resources degradation, low health and education status, weak institutions and governance systems, and lack of co-ordination across different policies and levels of government.

Key recommendations

A territorial approach is needed for better food security and nutrition policy

Current food security and nutrition policies are characterised by a sectoral, top-down and "one-size-fits-all" approach that has been unable to deliver appropriate long-term responses to food insecurity. The regional and context-specific nature of FSN has been broadly overlooked. There is a need for a paradigm shift in addressing FSN policy that embraces multisectoral, bottom-up and place-based interventions. This can be achieved through a territorial approach to FSN. In this framework, aligning objectives and actions across levels of government is critical. Doing so improves the vertical and horizontal co-ordination of FSN policies and interventions. Similarly, a territorial approach allows the diversity of different territories to be taken into account, and leads to a better understanding of differences in development opportunities that are so often missed with one-dimensional or one-size-fits-all policies. A territorial approach also recognises and capitalises on the benefits of urban-rural linkages, instead of addressing urban and rural areas through different, often disconnected, policies.

A territorial approach can help food security and nutrition policy and should focus on four key domains:

1. **Enhancing strategies and programmes beyond agriculture.** Agricultural interventions are important, but not sufficient, to adequately address food insecurity and malnutrition. Most countries now recognise FSN as a multidimensional issue, but implementation is still very sectoral, and the opportunities offered by the off-farm rural economy are often unexploited. There is also insufficient attention paid to differences in geographic conditions and to income inequalities
2. **Promoting multi-level governance systems to strengthening horizontal and vertical co-ordination.** The case studies show that lack of vertical and horizontal co-ordination at the central level and weak, decentralised government bodies and stakeholders are a major obstacle to the implementation of FSN strategies and policies. Improving capacity at the local and regional levels is a key priority since it can help with the implementation of FSN policy. It is also a necessary condition to promote a bottom-up approach that can scale-up innovations undertaken at the local level.
3. **Increasing the availability of data and indicators at the local and regional levels to support evidence-based FSN policy.** The case studies highlight the lack of reliable data as one of the main constraints for effective FSN policy, particularly at the sub-national level. More information at the local and regional levels can help identify the bottlenecks that are hampering food security and establish areas of priority.
4. **Linking social policies with economic growth policies.** FSN is usually addressed through social policies and programmes (e.g. social protection) that are key to supporting people facing food insecurity. These policies could be made more sustainable and have a much stronger impact if they were better co-ordinated and integrated with growth policies.

Assessment and recommendations

Reducing food security and nutrition (FSN) problems is a global development priority and a territorial approach is a key to making progress in addressing it. This report provides a set of lessons that can help implement this agenda. It summarises the main findings of the research project jointly implemented by the Food and Agriculture Organization of the United Nations (FAO), the Organisation for Economic Co-operation and Development (OECD) and the United Nations Capital Development Fund (UNCDF) between 2013 and 2015 to examine the usefulness of adopting a territorial approach to addressing food security and nutrition (FSN) problems. According to the definition adopted by the Committee on World Food Security (CFS), FSN "exists when all people at all times have physical, social and economic access to food, which is safe and consumed in sufficient quantity and quality to meet their dietary needs and food preferences, and is supported by an environment of adequate sanitation, health services and care, allowing for a healthy and active life" (CFS, 2012). Persistent food insecurity, malnutrition, poverty and regional disparities are major international concerns, and addressing them is central to the recently adopted 2030 Agenda for Sustainable Development,[1] including its sustainable development goals (SDGs). Sustainable Development Goal 2 (SDG 2) calls on countries to "end hunger, achieve food security and improved nutrition, and promote sustainable agriculture". These concerns are pressing in both urban and rural areas of developing countries, but have different dimensions. This report suggests that a place-based, territorial approach can be an effective analytical and policy framework for tackling these issues.

Typically, FSN is discussed at either the national or at the household level, but both of these approaches are problematic, because they ignore the territorial distribution of food insecurity. The national approach tends to ignore geographic variability within a country and instead focuses on broad groups such as the poor or minorities, without considering their location in space. Household-based analysis has paid more attention to geographic location, but tends to focus on household-specific coping strategies. However, many of these ultimately hinge upon the economic performance of the region in order to be successful. A territorial approach addresses both of these weaknesses. Not only does food security vary by region, but the nature and magnitude of the problems also vary by type of region – urban, rural adjacent and remote rural. As a result, policies to address food insecurity must recognise these differences if they are to be fully effective. Evidence is provided from five country case studies – Cambodia, Colombia, Côte d'Ivoire, Morocco and Peru – and two national workshops, in Mali and Niger, to support the argument for this territorial approach. The evidence suggests that adopting a territorial approach can greatly enhance the effectiveness of policies aiming at food security and nutrition.

1 *Transforming our world: The 2030 Agenda for Sustainable Development*, Resolution adopted by the UN General Assembly on 25 September 2015, A/RES/70/1.

Since the turn of the century, territorial approaches have become more mainstreamed. Pathways to development should recognise the great diversity across territories, and their varying capacities to develop and respond to problems and opportunities. In the past, many development policy approaches were place-neutral and centrally driven, and policies to address food insecurity focused mainly on a single dimension of FSN: increasing domestic food production. By contrast, a territorial approach focuses on the specific drivers and inhibitors of growth and development in a particular territorial setting, and uses this information to define broad-based development goals. The approach requires policy makers to design coherent, complementary action across sectors and areas of intervention, appropriate for the conditions and needs of different territorial settings.

While concerns over food security and nutrition adequacy are important in certain areas of all OECD member countries, the problem is much more pressing in the lower- and middle-income developing nations. In many of these countries, the level of development is unevenly distributed, and urban and coastal regions are typically better integrated into market economies than more remote rural regions. For FSN, differences in the degree of market integration matter. In urban regions, markets are typically able to provide an adequate supply of food, although often not at a price affordable for the urban poor. Conversely, in rural regions, self-supply is more common, due to weak transport infrastructure and incomplete markets of all types. Subsistence and semi-subsistence farm households rely to a great extent on the limited variety of food they directly produce, which is one of the factors that can make them susceptible to production shortfalls. And in these regions, any constraints on local food production are exacerbated by the low level of economic activity, which in turn limits opportunities to earn the income that would allow market purchases of food. This suggests that strengthening regional economies may be the most effective way to combat food insecurity, because higher incomes and better integration of markets strengthen the availability of food and access to it.

However, because the concept of food security has mainly been discussed either at the national level, where it largely relates to the ability to produce, store or purchase sufficient food for the population, or at the household level, where it focuses on the ability of specific households to obtain enough food of various types to meet caloric and nutritional requirements, this regional approach has not been typical. In terms of geography, FSN interventions often focus on the global or national level, as well as on the community/household level, overlooking the importance of the subnational (regional) level. In addition, FSN is a complex issue linked to food supply and demand, the functioning of factor markets, social policies, the role of different national and local actors and institutions, asset and income distributions, and myriad other subjects across several disciplines. These topics are the precise focus of regional analysis and regional policy, which further suggests that adopting a territorial approach to the study of food security issues can offer a useful understanding of the issues and a better perspective on ameliorative policies.

There are growing challenges in attaining FSN. These include population growth, rapid urbanisation, climate change, increasing demand for energy and food, natural resources deterioration, land and water degradation, and economic and financial market volatility. Policies to mitigate food insecurity must also take into account the interaction of these factors with FSN. The territorial approach can be a helpful entry point for exploring the complexity of FSN and identifying possible solutions.

The territorial approach proposed in this report provides a conceptual and operational framework to address the multidimensional (availability, access, utilisation and stability), multi-actor and multi-level nature of FSN. This framework puts emphasis on new dimensions, such as: 1) a shift from a sectoral (mainly agricultural) to a multisectoral approach in addressing food insecurity; 2) more emphasis on bottom-up approaches and their alignment with top-down priorities; 3) the elaboration of context-specific policies and interventions to capture the regional diversity of FSN, as opposed to "one-size-fits-all" approaches; 4) recognition of the importance of a well-functioning multi-level governance system, in order to align national objectives and strategies with regional and local priorities and needs and to improve policy coherence and complementarities across the various sectors influencing FSN.

Assessment

The analysis developed in the five case studies, in Cambodia, Colombia, Côte d'Ivoire, Morocco and Peru, as well as the outcomes of two national workshops in Mali and Niger, confirms that the territorial approach can be a very useful tool to support the design of effective FSN policies and inclusive governance systems. It provides a useful framework to understand, analyse and capture: 1) the multidimensional, multisectoral and multi-actor nature of food security and nutrition; 2) the geographic socio-economic and FSN inequalities and disparities; 3) the interdependencies between the various levels of policy making and the opportunities to encourage integration and ensure overall coherence with the institutional systems in place; 4) the need for cross-sector coherence of FSN policies; 5) the territorial dynamics and development potential (expressed and latent), notably endogenous potential based on local assets; 6) the importance of social participation in the implementation of FSN policies.

Another finding emerging from the case studies is that it is possible to outline a territorial approach to improving food security and nutrition that provides a general framework for understanding the varying regional dimensions of food security in a country. More specifically, the approach allows for a clear differentiation of the problems that emerge in large metropolitan regions, in rural regions that are adjacent to metropolitan regions, and in more remote rural regions that are not well connected to large urban agglomerations. Moreover, the approach can be refined to account for how differences in the stages of national development can affect both the most common types of food insecurity and the way these differences are distributed across the three types of regions. It is also important to recognise that FSN challenges are also faced by developed and developing countries, and while geographic differences exist in all countries, the nature of the problem varies with the stage of development.

Appropriate investments in rural regions that stimulate economic growth, thereby raising incomes and reducing risk, represents one of the main solutions to food insecurity. In some cases, agricultural investments will be a particular focus, as a means to increase food availability and to provide higher incomes for farm households. But increasing agricultural productivity (SDG Target 2.4 calls on countries to "double agricultural productivity by 2030") is only one part of a rural development strategy. In addition, investments are needed in network services, including transport, electrification and broadband, that connect communities to markets. Investments in improving levels of basic education and access to new technologies and finance for business development are also important for effective rural development, because they allow for the diversification of the rural regional economy, which can facilitate growth in local employment and mitigate risk.

Central governments increasingly recognise the multidimensional nature of food security and nutrition. Many countries, including those considered in the analysis of this report, have created inter-ministerial commissions and institutions to enhance co-ordination across interventions to deal with one or other of the dimensions of FSN. Most of these co-ordination mechanisms only focus on tackling FSN at the national level, however.

The wide territorial disparities in most developing countries put into question whether nationwide strategies suffice to address the problems of food insecurity and malnutrition. Good progress in bringing down national averages may hide the persistence of pockets of food insecurity and poverty in specific areas of the country. As indicated in the case studies, food insecurity and poverty are mainly concentrated in marginal and remote rural areas, signalling persistent urban-rural divides and other territorial disparities. The barriers to development, as well as the opportunities for tackling food insecurity, are context-specific and may strongly vary from one sub-national region to another.

In response, an increasing number of developing country governments are facilitating stronger roles for sub-national and local levels in policies and decision making. Greater political commitment to a "decentralisation" or "regionalisation" process is evident in four of the five countries considered in the analysis (Cambodia, Colombia, Morocco and Peru). Colombia and Peru are working in sub-national fiscal reforms to better match the responsibilities of sub-national governments with the funding they receive (OECD, 2014; forthcoming). Morocco is advancing towards a reform regionalising a number of sectoral policies. Finally, Cambodia is advancing in the creation of national institutions that can better co-ordinate cross-sectoral policies at the sub-national level, but still faces challenges on vertical forms of co-ordination with sub-national governments.

Although the decentralisation of FSN policies has taken different forms across the case study countries, there are common traits such as the weaknesses in implementation. For instance, the multidimensionality of FSN formulated at national level often risks getting lost where implementation follows a so-called "silo approach", with different government bodies and agencies acting independently from one another and limiting the potential for both horizontal and vertical co-ordination. Individual ministries and agencies have their own priorities, monitoring systems, operational and budgeting mechanisms, and, with a few exceptions, financial resources. Moreover, centrally led strategies and priorities, without a clear consideration for local needs and specificities, still dominate the implementation processes. Finally, lack of capacity and financial resources at sub-national level can undermine local authorities' contribution to the policy-making process, in particular in implementation, monitoring and evaluation.

Sectoral interventions for addressing FSN predominate. When it comes to enhanced household access to food, for instance, attention often remains focused on the domestic agriculture sector. As a result, opportunities for promoting off-farm income and employment other than agriculture in rural areas are often underexploited. While the case study analysis shows that developing countries have considerable potential to promote rural development by adopting an integrated approach, these opportunities are often left unexplored. This is the case, for example, in Cambodia, where it would be possible to tap into the potential of energy and tourism as catalysts for broader rural development. This is also true in Peru for the mining sector, and in Colombia and Morocco for rural tourism and local market development.

Moreover, other aspects of FSN, such as health and nutrition, are usually addressed through social policies, which are disconnected from economic development policies. As a consequence, the impact of social policies on economic development is weakened by a failure to exploit synergies with the competitiveness agenda. Some of the case study countries – in particular Colombia, Morocco and Peru – have invested strongly in social programmes (e.g. basic services, conditional cash transfer programmes and public work programmes) with the aim of reducing food insecurity and poverty. These policies are usually implemented by the Ministries of Welfare (the Prosperidad Social in Colombia, the Ministry of Interior in Morocco, and the Ministry of Development and Social Inclusion, or MIDIS, in Peru), but are not co-ordinated with economic development policies implemented by other ministries (e.g. the Ministry of Economy and Finance or Ministry of Planning). Such a lack of co-ordination can be true both at the national and particularly at the sub-national level. Broader and more flexible policy frameworks promoting synergies between the social and competitiveness dimensions of public policies could not only deliver better results in terms of tackling FSN problems, but also for generating sustainable development.

The lack of sub-national data – both related to the four FSN dimensions and to the socio-economic dynamics that impact food security – is another key obstacle for the effectiveness of territorial approaches for FSN. Regional and local statistics and indicators are generally poorly developed and in some cases absent altogether, which undermines the possibility of developing territorial monitoring systems and evidence-based policies. The importance of developing territorial information systems is increasingly recognised, and some countries have engaged in the production of detailed GIS-based maps, such as in Morocco. These efforts have, nevertheless, not so far found much success. The lack of co-ordination, harmonisation of approaches and communication between line ministries often leads to fragmentation of information and duplication issues. In other cases, as in Cambodia, the development of regional information is largely left in the hands of international partners. As a result, data tend to be project-focused and no comprehensive data collection process covers all regions over time in a coherent manner.

In addition, the territorial approach is not always fully understood. In some cases, a distinction is not always made between "regionalisation" of sectoral policies and the multisectoral and integrated approach to FSN policies envisaged by a territorial approach. In other cases, a territorial approach is meant merely as local development, without considering the key role of multi-level governance in territorial policies and processes. It may also be confused with community-based development, overlooking the importance of linking grassroots interventions at the community level to policy frameworks at national and sub-national levels. This can promote their sustainability and capitalise on the information and learning they may have generated.

In sum, the main implementation challenges identified in the five case studies for a more effective territorial approach to FSN are the following:

- the need to go beyond policies that strengthen agriculture, since agricultural interventions are important, but not sufficient, to adequately address food insecurity and malnutrition
- the need to promote multi-level governance systems by strengthening policy co-ordination at the central level and empowering decentralised government bodies and stakeholders
- the need to improve territorial information systems for an evidence-based FSN policy

- the need to link social policies with the competitiveness agenda in place-based, comprehensive rural development strategies.

Recommendations

This section extracts the key findings of the case study analysis conducted in five countries and the two national workshops on a territorial approach to FSN. The case studies confirmed the importance and value-added of adopting a territorial approach to FSN, and also identified a number of barriers and bottlenecks that need to be overcome to successfully adopt such an approach. Notably, four common implementation challenges appear to emerge in all five case studies, at different orders of magnitude.

1. Sectoral versus multisectoral and integrated approaches

As stressed above, most of the countries recognise FSN as a multidimensional issue and are developing strategies or creating institutions/co-ordination mechanisms accordingly. The main issue is the implementation of those strategies using a cross-sectoral and co-ordinated approach. In most of the countries considered, despite this multidimensional concept of FSN, policies and interventions still tend to be focused on the agricultural sector, and the opportunities related to off-farm activities are often underexplored.

In Peru, the two main sectors that could represent the main engines of growth in rural areas are agriculture and mining, including in poor regions such as in the department of Cajamarca. Agriculture is the main source of employment, while mining is the sector with the highest potential for promoting rural development, given the vast reserves of gold and copper in the soil. This could have a positive impact on FSN by increasing the incomes of the local population and improving access to FSN. However, the use of mining for rural development is underexploited. Public policies focus mainly on the agricultural sector, while mining is left to the private sector. The absence of policies integrating the two sectors in a single holistic vision for development means that agriculture and mining compete with one another, undermining the opportunities for development in rural areas.

In Colombia, farming is considered the only business opportunity for addressing food insecurity. As a result, most of the FSN policies and programmes promote small-scale or subsistence agriculture. This neglects the potential of income-enhancing opportunities offered by other sectors, in particular manufacturing, as a means of raising household incomes to reduce food insecurity. Currently, the richest departments in Colombia are those with a strong manufacturing element in addition to agriculture.

The sectoral approach to FSN policies is also dominant in Cambodia. The main priority has been the development of a rice-based farming system. The focus on rice production, however, limits incentives to diversify the rural economy that could lead to greater off-farm income and employment opportunities, including for part-time farm households. The consequence has been increased migration from rural areas to Phnom Penh and abroad. Eco-tourism and renewable energy sectors could present fruitful alternatives for developing Cambodia's rural areas. A more integrated approach is therefore needed in order to exploit these opportunities and improve FSN.

In Morocco, agriculture is the key sector of the rural economy and the source of between 75% and 80% of rural employment. However, it alone is not sufficient to promote sustained growth and development in Morocco's rural areas. Based on this evidence, diversification of the rural economy, off-farm income and employment opportunities outside agriculture have recently moved to the top of the government's agenda. The Moroccan government is trying to adopt a more balanced approach to rural development. The aim is to co-ordinate policy actions with the development of social services, targeted social protection schemes and infrastructure.

The evolution of rural development policies in the Côte d'Ivoire highlights the shortcomings of the sectoral approach to rural development and FSN. Rural development initiatives have focused almost exclusively on agricultural value chain development. However, the gains from this process have mainly been enjoyed by actors involved in the value chains who were already doing well. Other important rural challenges have been left unattended. Existing sectoral policies have prioritised agricultural production, resulting in haphazard, piecemeal investment in rural infrastructure and services. Progress in improving FSN has been unsatisfactory as a result.

The national workshops in Mali and Niger confirmed that food security has been approached sectorally, overlooking opportunities for improving employment and incomes of people in off-farm activities that could improve access to FSN.

2. Multi-level governance and institutions

Co-ordination across national and sub-national authorities

The ability to co-ordinate FSN policies horizontally across sectors, as well as vertically across national and sub-national levels of government, is key to delivering effective rural development strategies addressing the multidimensional nature of FSN. Case study countries offer some examples of policy co-ordination mechanisms for co-ordinating policies across line ministries at the national level. These mechanisms have taken the form of an inter-ministerial council or commission, involving not just government agencies, but also other national stakeholders, such as citizen organisations, non-governmental organisations (NGOs), trade unions and, in some cases, sub-national governments. The majority of the countries considered, as mentioned earlier, also had in place a national FSN strategy reflecting the different dimension of food security and nutrition. Nevertheless, the role of these fora has often remained vague, since most were set up without executive powers and lacked the authority to influence policy making. Their recommendations have thus frequently had to depend on the capacity and willingness of the various line ministries to implement cross-sectoral strategies.

Another common problem that emerges in the case studies is a lack of co-ordination between national and sub-national priorities and programme delivery. This has resulted in misalignment of objectives and intervention in policy implementation, due chiefly to the governance gaps in information, capacity, fiscal, administrative capacity and policy (Charbit and Michalun, 2009). First, involvement of sub-national stakeholders in formulating national FSN priorities appears to have been infrequent. Co-ordination across national and sub-national levels of government generally suggests that although sub-national authorities are in charge of implementing national policies, they have little input in their formulation. In most cases, the capacity and resources at sub-national level have not been able to ensure the effective delivery of a territorial approach to FSN, even where comprehensive national policies and strategies are in place and decentralisation is relatively advanced.

In Cambodia, the Council of Ministries for Agriculture and Rural Development (CARD) was set up in 2004, specifically to co-ordinate national-level FSN policies, and involve international development partners in its working group on FSN and Social Protection. However, CARD does not have its own budget for implementing FSN programmes. This, in combination with the limited resources and capacity at sub-national level, means that effective implementation will remain a challenge for the foreseeable future.

A similar national structure exists in Peru. The Commission for Food Security responsible for the FSN plan formulated for 2015-21 brings together different policy sectors. The commission further functions as a key forum for FSN stakeholders, involving several ministers, technical bodies, NGOs and representatives from sub-national governments. The system does have drawbacks in terms of co-ordination. First, it lacks the authority to co-ordinate different ministries and policies, and has limited ability to directly influence the implementation of government FSN programmes. Second, the ministry that could potentially have a lead role in co-ordinating programme delivery is the Ministry for Social Inclusion, the MIDIS. This agency, however, lacks the capacity, and the power, to co-ordinate a broad FSN agenda. As a result, most policy actions and programmes focus on immediate hunger relief and do not take into account the range of factors affecting food security, despite the advanced multidimensional definition elaborated in the national plan.

In Colombia, the inter-sectoral commission for FSN, the *Comisión Intersectorial de Seguridad Alimentaria y Nutricional* (CISAN), was created in 2009 to offer national stakeholders a forum to discuss key challenges related to FSN, and to enhance co-ordination and collaboration. This commission appears to be much needed, given the lack of co-ordination among ministries and government agencies involved in FSN. Different agencies use various definitions and narratives of FSN, which range from subsistence to a more holistic understanding of access to food, including the income dimension. This discrepancy across ministries has led to a lack of policy coherence, further complicated by the complex delivery structure, especially at the local level.

No specific government body has been set up to co-ordinate FSN policies in Morocco and the Côte d'Ivoire, implying that no single strategy draws together the FSN challenges to be addressed. In Morocco, this has resulted in a predominantly sectoral approach to FSN. Agricultural, social, health and economic dimensions of FSN are addressed separately, by different ministries, with very limited interaction and co-ordination. Only recently has the government started trying to adopt a more integrated policy approach. In the Côte d'Ivoire, a rather narrow approach is taken to rural development in general, focusing strongly on developing selected agricultural value chains, namely cocoa, cotton and cashew production. While there has been an attempt to engage public and private stakeholders in multistakeholder platforms, only occasional support is provided to local governments engaging in a more holistic approach. Rural development and territorial planning are still mainly seen as by-products of agricultural growth. This lack of appreciation of FSN as a cross-sectoral issue may have serious implications for the country's long-term food security. Not only does it put considerable pressure on natural resources, but inadequate attention has been paid to the employment prospects of the growing population of working age. Moreover, civil conflict and social unrest (2002-11) have disrupted development and government functions, including the building of stable and democratic institutions. Focusing too strictly on value chain development may be a missed opportunity to build institutional capacity at national and sub-national levels, encouraging sustainable FSN policies with local ownership.

In Niger, the *Haute Autorité à la Sécurité Alimentaire* (HASA) was created in 2010 to co-ordinate FSN policies. In addition, it launched the 3N Initiative (Nigériens Nourish Nigériens), which became the reference framework for all FSN interventions. This is an ambitious programme based on a strong political commitment to eradicate hunger, boost incomes and guarantee the conditions for full participation of citizens in national policy making.

In addition to the set of issues experienced in the co-ordination of policies across ministries, one problem identified in several instances was the lack of co-ordination with non-governmental stakeholders. Without a clear vision and co-ordination mechanism at the sub-national level, the work of development partners and national and local NGOs has sometimes led to a duplication of efforts and a fragmented, project-based approach. A strategic, holistic approach is often missing, both at the national and the sub-national level.

In Cambodia and Colombia, the presence of international development partners has frequently led to a duplication of efforts and *ad hoc* solutions. It is not rare to find that development partners have even set up their own separate institutional arrangement for delivering FSN projects and programmes, creating a structure separate from the one put in place by the national government.

A lack of vertical and horizontal co-ordination is also a major problem for implementing FSN policy in Mali and Niger. There, as in Cambodia, there is a strong dependency on external aid from international co-operation and a project-based approach to food insecurity. The workshop also revealed the importance of improving capacity, particularly at the local level, to implement an effective territorial approach to FSN policy.

The role of sub-national institutions

Recent decentralisation reforms provide an opportunity to create a multi-level governance framework more suitable than the existing mechanisms to apply a territorial approach to FSN. However, decentralisation alone cannot be viewed as a panacea. Enough capacity and resources have to be in place to ensure that policies can be effectively formulated, made coherent and implemented at the local level. Decentralisation also involves a greater risk of lack of co-ordination, as well as a host of other problems, including enhanced potential for corruption and for the local elite to capture the benefits of policies. If these risks are to be avoided, especially in the initial stages of decentralisation, greater monitoring of the process is required to ensure full transparency and democratic governance. The countries included in this report have reached various stages of decentralisation, and their multi-governance structures vary enormously from country to country. Nevertheless, the most common problems appeared to be lack of capacity and resources at sub-national level. Moreover, the involvement of sub-national stakeholders in national policy making – especially in relation to FSN – appeared to be rare.

In Colombia, for instance, the capacity of regional governments to design, implement and monitor public policies varies considerably from department to department, both in financial and institutional terms. Economic and institutional capacity tend to go hand in hand. In places with more favourable economic conditions, such as the department of Antioquia, local authorities have demonstrated a strong capacity to implement a multidimensional FSN policy, including programmes like school meals, but also direct support to small-scale farming. These represent a more holistic territorial approach to FSN. The success of the Antioquian approach to FSN – called MANA (*Mejoramiento Alimentario y Nutricional de Antioquia*) – has further influenced national policy making. Some key features of its success are continuous political support and budget stability, as well as its mainstreaming into local policies.

In Morocco, many policies dealing with FSN have been largely decentralised, as part of the broader "*Régionalisation Avancée*" agenda. Increasing power is granted to sub-national authorities, including finance and planning. In 2015, the first elections of regional and municipal authorities were held. Nevertheless, the case study analysis showed that, with regards to FSN, the regionalisation process in Morocco has so far resulted in "territorialised sectoral strategies". In other words, while policies are being decentralised and brought closer to the territories, they are still not coherent and hence do not fully reflect the cross-cutting nature of FSN. More effective horizontal co-ordination mechanisms to maximise the potential synergies between actors and across sectors at the local level have been put in place. Institutional capacity and human resources available at the decentralised level nevertheless remain relatively weak, partly due to the lack of experience of the actors involved.

While Cambodia has also put decentralisation on a legal footing recently, a lot remains to be done in terms of building the capacity and empowering the sub-national level of government to deal with FSN challenges. Lack of budget allocation and involvement of local stakeholders in national-level policy making have been identified as key issues in the creation of a multi-level governance framework to address local FSN problems. As things stand, a significant disconnect is found between national and sub-national planning. Development plans prepared by sub-national authorities are mainly formulated based on national policies and strategies, without any involvement of sub-national stakeholders. Moreover, since the national co-ordination body for FSN is further limited to horizontal co-ordination at the national level, co-ordination across sectors does not seem to trickle down to the provincial level. This appears to result in a largely sectoral approach in practice, with provincial departments receiving funds based on national sectoral priorities.

The case of Peru further highlights the importance of informal institutions for the smooth implementation of FSN programmes. The peer-to-peer learning initiative *Mi Chacra Emprendedora*, led by the Ministry of Social Inclusion, promotes the introduction of innovations in farming through a network of local leaders and a system of peer-to-peer learning. In the department of Cajamarca, for instance, local leaders, *yachachiq*, have helped small-scale farmers introduce new crops with a high value added on the international market, such as quinoa and *aguaymanto* (or *physalis*), based on their knowledge of the local *milieu* and their cultural proximity to beneficiaries. This has provided better income for the local population and has had a positive effect on access to food. Nevertheless, the programme is so far of limited geographical reach, covering only 5 out of 12 departments in the country.

3. Improving territorial information systems for evidence-based food security and nutrition policies

Introducing an integrated and territorial approach can increase the effectiveness of responses to rural poverty and food insecurity. However, it requires information, tools and approaches that can help to describe and analyse the different dimensions and territorial assets of rural areas. This can shed light on territorial dynamics and the implications for rural development. In several of the case study countries, territorial information systems are either weak or absent altogether. FSN statistics are thus gathered in an unsystematic, uncoordinated way, with little or no continuity in the collection of sub-national data. In others, a failure to use territorial data in an integrated way to support evidence-based policies appeared to be the main shortcoming, rather than the availability of information *per se*.

In Peru, collecting statistics to back evidence-based policy making needs to become a priority, especially given the relative abundance of territorial statistics. Better co-ordination of data collection and use is needed. The same appears to be true for Morocco. While local information is collected and processed by various government agencies and ministries, as well as mainstreamed through most programmes and initiatives, no clear vision appears to guide the use of data across sectors.

The Colombian government is working to improve its territorial information system, since, as things currently stand, public authorities often lack basic information about rural communities in particular, including the number of inhabitants, *desplazados* (displaced people) and land titles. One of the key aspects that needs attention includes consolidation of baseline data. First, Census data is not mandated at regular intervals. Data collection at the sub-national level is typically carried out by a multitude of actors as a result of their programme deliveries or management, and could benefit from improved co-ordination and oversight. Use and dissemination of the data collected could be improved if it was shared between FSN stakeholders. Further review of the definitions of urban and rural that are used in policy formulation and delivery could enhance the utility of geographical data for such purposes. For example, the *Familia in Acción* programme which provides 3 million households with conditional cash transfers does not take account of the beneficiaries' local context. Finally, capacity to analyse territorial data needs to be built both at the national and the local level. The government's commitment to create a "territorial observatory" is a welcome move in this direction.

In Cambodia, a centralised effort has been mounted to produce FSN statistics at the sub-national level. An FSN Info Task Force has been set up, but the availability of reliable data at sub-national level has presented a challenge. So far, intra-national disparities in FSN have been estimated through statistical modelling. This provides an aggregate picture, but does not give precise information at the province or district level. Moreover, territorial information has mainly been produced by international development organisations, and tends to be issue-specific, and tied to the timeframe of their operations. Better capacity and awareness among sub-national governments could help address this barrier to evidence-based policies.

4. Linking social policies with competitiveness agendas

Food security and nutrition policies tend to be disconnected from growth policies

While it is not a sufficient remedy in itself, economic growth is a critical part of the fight against hunger and malnutrition. In all the case studies, economic growth and job creation have been important in reducing poverty and hunger. Despite this evidence, FSN and social policies appear not to be connected with the policy framework for stimulating growth and investments. At least three factors seem to lie at the root of this disjuncture:

- First, ministries in charge of investment policy (the pro-growth agenda) do not participate in institutions where social policy and/or FSN policy are designed. Even in countries such as Colombia, where the government makes the effort to produce a multi-year national development strategy (the National Development Plan), the connection between the social dimensions and growth is tenuous.
- Second, cultural constraints are also at play. Poor citizens are not so much considered an untapped asset, but as in need of social assistance. This cultural constraint may depend on several factors, including the way in which the constituencies are formed, and the educational background of operators and

policy makers dealing with FSN policies. Last but not least, the policy packages and funding made available by donor agencies and international organisations are not designed to be integrated with national pro-growth policies.

- Third, institutional volatility disrupts continuity in policy making. Short political cycles, a poorly developed civil service and the changing priorities of influential international stakeholders, such as donor agencies and international organisations, may explain the lack of consistency in policy making. On occasion, funds allocated by international stakeholders – and their agendas – may contribute to the creation of *ad hoc* institutions, often at the community level, that do not necessarily co-ordinate with national stakeholders and may represent an element of complexity within the multi-level governance framework of a given country.

Conditional cash transfer programmes can inform investment policy

The information collected through conditional cash transfers policies and the institutional networks that administer such policies represent an untapped resource. Not only could they promote policy complementarities, but they could be used to help guide a pro-growth investment strategy. In Peru, for instance, the national programme *Juntos* provided approximately 1 million households (in 2014) with conditional cash transfers. The programme is delivered through a mechanism that collects a large amount of information about these households and the place in which they live, and also involves local communities to select beneficiaries. Local governments are responsible for the delivery of the health care and/or education services that beneficiaries must use if they are to be eligible for receiving the cash transfers. This system has already achieved a high degree of co-ordination and integration among the different policy actors involved that could be used to inform an investment policy that creates job opportunities in poor communities.

Scaling-up small investment implemented by programmes

In some cases, the social and economic dimensions in small-scale programmes at the local level are complementary. These programmes are usually delivered by sub-national governments, deconcentrated national agencies or NGOs. They provide poor households both with relief and with small sums of capital to be used to create a stable income. Often, the experience gathered in their design and implementation remains at the local level. It may not be transmitted to due to poor multi-level governance, or it may end if a programme is discontinued because of a lack of funds or changes in the political/institutional context. This represents a lost opportunity that could be used to inform policy at the regional or national level. Small-scale investments in infrastructure, service delivery, education or in other areas can result in disconnected initiatives with fragmented outcomes. A territorial, place-approach integrating local initiatives into a common, multi-annual agenda can benefit from economies of scale and deliver opportunities in the medium and long term.

References

Charbit, C. and M. Michalun (2009), "Mind the gaps: Managing mutual dependence in relations among levels of government", *OECD Working Papers on Public Governance*, No. 14, OECD Publishing, Paris, http://dx.doi.org/10.1787/221253707200.

OECD (forthcoming), *OECD Territorial Review of Peru 2016*, OECD Publishing, Paris.

OECD (2014), *OECD Territorial Reviews: Colombia 2014*, OECD Publishing, Paris, http://dx.doi.org/10.1787/9789264224551-en.

Chapter 1.

Why a territorial perspective is useful for food security and nutrition policy

This chapter argues that all too often, policies to combat food insecurity have neglected to take into account the territorial dimension of this issue. The nature of food insecurity varies significantly across urban and rural regions as well as across different territories. If policies are to be effective, they must also reflect regional differences. This chapter argues that food security and nutrition (FSN) is a multidimensional issue that has instead often been addressed through a sectoral, top-down and "one-size-fits-all" approach. Drawing on the OECD New Rural Paradigm, the chapter proposes a holistic territorial approach as an alternative framework for tackling this issue. A territorial approach to FSN policy is also needed to facilitate co-ordination among different sectoral policies and levels of government. This can help make the FSN policy framework broader and more flexible. Following a territorial approach is complex but crucial for policy making that connects the objectives of equity, economic efficiency and environmental sustainability – each indispensable in the fight against food insecurity and malnutrition.

Introduction

In a world that is growing ever richer, more globalised and increasingly productive, the benefits of these advances have been highly uneven. A striking feature of contemporary economic development is unprecedented regional disparities, not only *across* but even more *within* countries. Within OECD countries, inequities between regions within countries are larger than inequalities between countries (OECD, 2016). Across developing countries, many have experienced limited progress in economic development, especially in rural regions. These gaps reinforce the notion of a dual economy first advanced by Arthur Lewis in the 1950s (Lewis, 1954). The discussion of regional disparities tends to focus on mainstream economic concepts, including levels of gross domestic product (GDP) per capita, employment rates and types of economic specialisation. There are often also large differences in access to food between more developed urban regions and less developed rural regions.

Problems of food insecurity and malnutrition continue to face all nations, whether in low-income developing countries or high-income industrialised ones. It is easy to find sub-populations in any country where chronic hunger and an unhealthy diet limit the growth of children and their ability to learn, and make adults less effective workers. Moreover, while severe problems of famine and acute hunger are less common than in previous centuries, there are still places in the world where hunger either leads directly to death or leaves people too weak to be able to fight off disease.

Hunger and malnutrition have a clear geographic concentration, whether in low-income inner-city neighbourhoods in large metropolitan regions or in isolated subsistence farming communities in remote rural regions. Both types of regions exist in the developed OECD member countries and in developing countries. Food insecurity and malnutrition within a country tends to occur in geographical clusters, and the forces that lead to food insecurity can vary by type of geography. Consequently, a place-based or territorial approach to food insecurity can potentially improve current food security and nutrition (FSN) policies in all types of countries.

In facing the many dimensions of FSN, and poverty, it is often acknowledged that it is in rural areas where the battle will be "won or lost" (Anríquez and Stamoulis, 2007: 6). This reflects two important realities. The first is that it is in rural areas where food is mainly produced, and to the extent that shortages in supply contribute to food insecurity, they must be addressed through improvements in agricultural productivity. The second, and less acknowledged, reality is that food insecurity can be much higher in rural areas because of a far greater reliance on a narrow range of locally produced foodstuffs whose yields are unstable. Limited access to national and global food markets, and high levels of poverty can price rural people out of food markets.

The international track record in alleviating persistent issues of food insecurity and rural poverty has been lacklustre (World Bank, 2007). In the last decade, greater focus has been placed on integrating rural regions into the national and global economies, broadening the economic base of rural regions and improving agricultural productivity. In many respects, the pursuit of competitiveness, productivity and income generation (regional development) are necessary to sustain progress in the effort to reduce hunger, malnutrition and poverty. However, they are far from sufficient on their own. As "[r]ural people make up a high percentage of the hungry and malnourished in developing countries [...] efforts to promote growth in agriculture and the rural sector can be an important component of a strategy for promoting inclusive growth and improving food security and nutrition" (FAO, IFAD and WFP, 2015: 42).

We currently lack frameworks, tools[1] and policies that target FSN challenges and poverty across all types of regions, particularly rural regions. To be effective, FSN initiatives need to be integrated into broader economic development strategies, since development reduces vulnerability to a broad range of individual and social problems, nutrition included. With these challenges in mind, the central thesis of this report is that a territorial, place-based approach is needed to address FSN challenges and that such an approach should be integrated into broader regional development strategies in both urban and rural territories. Further, improving the level of economic development in rural areas is central to addressing the challenges of FSN and poverty. Development strategies are needed that focus on "mechanisms which build on local capabilities and promote innovative ideas through the interaction of local and general knowledge, and of endogenous and exogenous actors in the design and delivery of public policies" (Barca, McCann and Rodríguez-Pose, 2012: 149).

Similarly, implementing the Sustainable Development Goals (including SDG 2) requires whole-of-government and integrated approaches. The 17 goals, incorporating economic, social and environmental aspects, are indivisible and recognise the interlinkages in achieving sustainable development. The territorial approach of this study has much in common with the cross-cutting approach called for by the Agenda 2030.

The context: Territorial trends and challenges in the developing world

Global objectives of eradicating hunger, malnutrition and poverty are proving stubbornly resistant to change. It is estimated that just under 1 billion people live in extreme poverty worldwide (i.e. on less than USD 1.25 per day – at PPP-adjusted, 2005 prices). Three-quarters of them live in rural areas (UNDP, 2015), and two-thirds earn their living from agriculture (Olinto et al., 2013). These estimates of the rural-urban disparity may be somewhat low. Indicators of multidimensional poverty – a measure that utilises more inclusive dimensions of acute poverty in health, education and living standards – put the rural-urban poverty divide as high as 85% (Alkire et al., 2014). From a food security standpoint, of the global population that is food insecure (795 million people), 94% live in the rural regions of low- and middle-income countries (UN, 2013). The precarious and volatile nature of this picture is also worth emphasising. The global food price spike of 2011, for example, pushed a further 44 million people into hunger (Ivanic, Martin and Zaman, 2012) and brought the issue of food insecurity back as a more acute concern.

The case for intervention to address food insecurity, malnutrition and poverty in rural areas is a strong one. It is also a message that tends to get lost in the dominant development discourse, which focuses on national macroeconomic conditions and is largely spatially blind. In particular, while it is clear that urban populations are expanding at an unprecedented rate, the absolute number of people living in rural areas has also expanded significantly – by 70% in the last 50 years and by 120 million people since the

1. The OECD is working to develop a screening tool for policy coherence for sustainable development and food security [SG/PCD(2016)4]. It aims to support governments and stakeholders in designing, promoting, implementing and assessing policies that have a potential impact on food security.

turn of the millennium. Rural populations are projected to expand in absolute numbers until at least 2030. Importantly, for the vast majority of low- and middle-income countries (LMICs), rural inhabitants still outnumber city dwellers (Figure 1.1). Finally, it is worth noting that rapid urbanisation can largely be attributed to rural-urban migration, because rural areas are failing to provide suitable livelihoods, particularly for younger people. These migrants typically become part of the urban underclass, with limited job prospects and low incomes, which in turn increases the number of urban residents with food insecurity problems.

Figure 1.1. **Percentage of global rural population, 1961-2011**

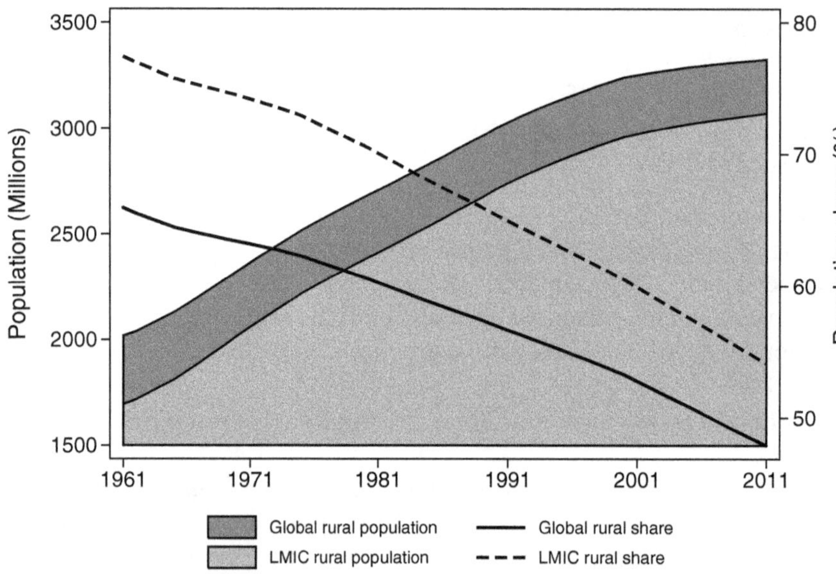

Note: LMIC, Low-and middle-income country.

Source: Own elaboration based on World Development Indicators, http://data.worldbank.org/data-catalog/world-development-indicators.

Food insecurity, malnutrition and poverty: Spatial correlation

As outlined by the Committee on World Food Security in 2012, FSN is defined as a condition that "exists when all people at all times have physical, social and economic access to food, which is safe and consumed in sufficient quantity and quality to meet their dietary needs and food preferences, and is supported by an environment of adequate sanitation, health services and care, allowing for a healthy and active life" (CFS, 2012). In practice, however, a lack of clarity and consistency in the way food security (Pinstrup-Andersen, 2009) as well as rural development (van der Ploeg et al., 2000) have been defined has resulted in "many fads … but few satisfying economic evaluations" (Hewings, 2004; cited in Valdés et al., 2005). In particular, development efforts typically address one dimension – the adequacy of domestic food production – and have largely neglected to address the dynamics of access, utilisation and stability of food availability, as summarised in Table 1.1. As such, it is now commonplace for the domestic food supply within a country to be more than adequate, but for its distribution to be constrained to a subset of regions, typically metropolitan regions, where incomes are higher, market forces are more prevalent and there is political pressure to maintain a general access to food. The remainder of this section surveys the state of FSN and poverty globally, and for rural populations in particular, and how these factors relate to additional challenges in increasing food production and encouraging vibrant rural economies.

Table 1.1. **Dimensions of the food security and nutrition problem**

Availability	Achieved when an adequate supply of food is at a population's disposal.
Access	Guaranteed where all households and all individuals within those households have a sufficient economic and physical capability to obtain appropriate food (through production, purchase or donation) for a nutritious diet.
Utilisation	Refers to the biological and social constraints on food security, related to the ability of the human body to ingest and metabolise food (i.e. through proper health care and culturally sensitive food provision, to ensure that disease and illness are avoided and food is adequately utilised).
Stability	Refers to the temporal dimension of food security and nutrition and affects all three physical elements. Chronic food insecurity (i.e. repeated food shortages) should be distinguished from transitory food insecurity (i.e. linked to a natural or man-made disaster).

Source: Adapted from FAO (2012a), *The State of Food Insecurity in the World 2012: Economic Growth is Necessary but not Sufficient to Accelerate Reduction of Hunger and Malnutrition*, available at: www.fao.org/docrep/016/i3027e/i3027e.pdf.

While urban regions – where food production is limited – have better access to food, rural regions – where most food is produced – have more limited and variable access to food. This basic contradiction is one of the driving forces militating in favour of a territorial approach to food insecurity. Clearly, geographic proximity to the supply of domestic food is not enough to ensure access to food. Urban regions have greater access to food, in part because they are better connected to national and international markets, and able to source food from multiple locations, whereas in more remote rural regions, there may be few alternatives to local production, due to limited connections to other food sources. Urban regions also tend to be richer, which provides them with the income to purchase food even at times of shortage, when higher prices ration demand. Finally, rural regions tend to rely on the few varieties of food that can be locally produced, and production may be difficult to increase due to limited land or an inability to modernise production methods. In addition, the volume of the local food supply may also be highly variable, leading to a higher frequency of food insecurity episodes in rural regions.

In most countries, the supply of agricultural land is fixed or declining. This means that increases in output have to come from improved productivity. Meanwhile, population has grown, and shifted towards higher calorific intake, as developing and emerging countries grow economically. Demand for the food supply is projected to increase by 50% in the next two decades (Figure 1.2). Since the 1960s, the global arable land surface has only increased by 9% (Pretty, 2008), with population growth of more than 110%. Competing demands for farmland, including urban conversion and the increasing production of non-food crops, such as textiles and biofuels, further complicate the picture. Consequently, the United Nations Food and Agriculture Organization (FAO) stresses that close to 80% of future increases in food production will have to come both from intensification of production in low-yield regions, and from innovation in all regions, but particularly in those where yields are already high and likely to stagnate.

Environmental concerns, including natural resource deterioration, soil and water degradation (SDG 15) and climate change (SDG 13), also pose great risks to agricultural yields – which have already plateaued in many countries after steady increases throughout the 20th century (Grassini, Eskridge and Cassman, 2013). There are multiple causes for yield decline or increases in yield variability. Several climate change models suggest that the effects of changes in global temperatures and rainfall intensities will be experienced differently across the world, but crucially, that developing regions are likely to experience some of the most adverse effects, both in terms of average yield and variability in yield over time. Research to improve agricultural productivity, except in the case of a few large crops, has been a low priority in recent decades. Traditional farming practices in some rural regions can also contribute to low output and high variability in output if soil fertility is depleted due to erosion, failure to maintain nutrient levels or the adverse consequences of monoculture. "Simply put, poor farmers have passed on their suffering to the land through extractive practices. They cultivate marginal soils with marginal inputs, produce marginal yields, and perpetuate marginal living and poverty" (Lal, 2004).

Figure 1.2. **Agricultural land per rural inhabitant in low- and middle-income countries by region**

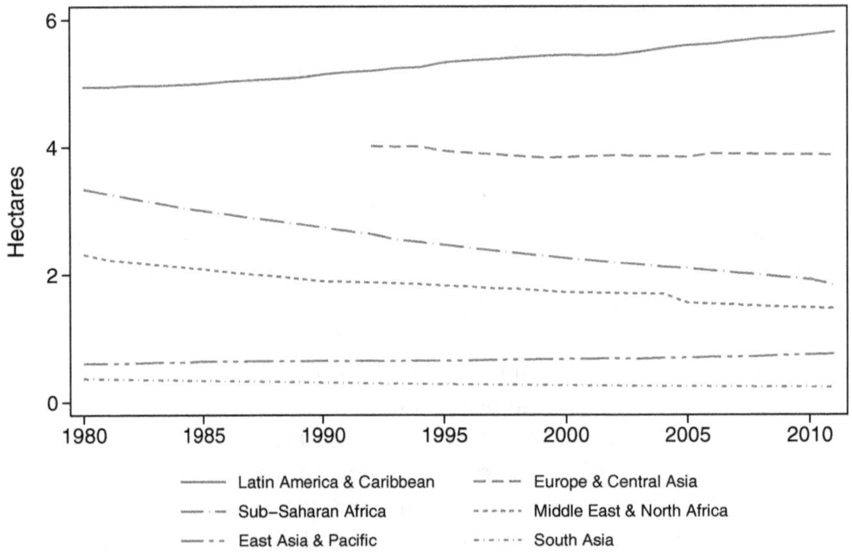

Note: Consistent data for Europe and central Asia only available from 1992.

Source: Own elaboration based on World Development Indicators, http://data.worldbank.org/data-catalog/world-development-indicators.

The geographical unevenness of these effects is worth re-emphasising. Countries with larger rural populations, in general, tend to be more food insecure (Figure 1.3). Considerable variation in agricultural yields exists across many regions, many producing well below their potential (Tilman et al., 2011). Linking farms into globalised production and supply chains, and helping to disseminate new, more productive practices, thus becomes necessary to meet future demand. To a great extent, this implies the use of more capital-intensive, more sophisticated farming practices involving new technologies. Agricultural modernisation inevitably leads to farm consolidation and the release of labour, which creates a clear employment problem for current small farm operators and farm workers. These points to the need for broader rural development initiatives that can provide a more diversified regional economy in rural areas, to absorb these released workers. This has been the experience of OECD countries over the last 100 years, as they increased agricultural output, reduced the number of farm workers and increased the financial well-being of farm households to close to, or even above, the level of their urban population.

Agricultural modernisation and a failure to address broader approaches to rural development only serve to push ever greater numbers of the rural poor and food insecure into urban regions. The trouble is, however, that many cities are simply unable to absorb current rates of natural population growth, let alone more rural emigration. Thus, although a great deal of focus is placed on reducing the ills of rapid urbanisation – including overburdened social services, expanding slums, pollution, crime, poverty and hunger – a greater emphasis is also needed on rural areas to stem the tide of rural-urban migration. This means developing many more employment opportunities, including in new non-agricultural industries, with an emphasis on jobs attractive to the rural youth – those most likely to leave and most needed to rejuvenate rural areas economically and demographically (OECD, 2006).

Figure 1.3. **Rural population and food supply adequacy**

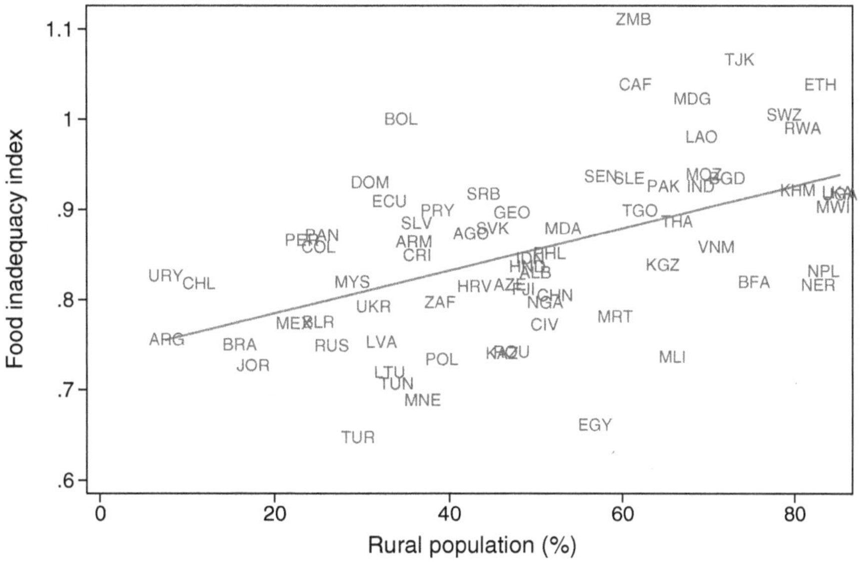

Note: The food insecurity index is the inverse of the Food and Agriculture Organization's Average Dietary Energy Supply Adequacy (ADESA) indicator.

Source: Own elaboration based on World Development Indicators, http://data.worldbank.org/data-catalog/world-development-indicators; FAOSTAT.

Rural poverty has, however, shown signs of improvement in recent decades – as is well documented in progress reports concerning the Millennium Development Goals (MDGs). Yet, even allowing for the general progress made in reducing poverty, the persistence of strong pockets of rural poverty ought to keep rural development high on national and international agendas (Dercon, 2009). It is also possible that the scale of these issues is underestimated. Between 1993 and 2001, for example, estimates suggest that 100 million fewer people were classified as rural poor. Over the same period, estimates of the urban poor increased by 50 million (Ravallion, Chen and Sangraula, 2007). It is certainly conceivable that some portion of the fall in rural poverty could simply be the result of rural-urban migration, representing a displacement of the issue to urban areas. In this respect, tackling the causes of rural poverty at their source could be all the more significant for addressing poverty in broader terms.

Regional disparities in food security and nutrition and poverty

Traditionally, regional disparities in FSN and poverty have been construed in terms of the global North and South or across an urban-rural dimension. However, recent data highlight a new element within these global figures: the highly uneven geographical distribution of incomes, food security and poverty *within* countries. As illustrated in Figures 1.4 and 1.5, sub-national income disparities are not only at their highest in developing countries, they have also tended to widen in recent decades. On the first point, the right-hand side of Figure 1.4 indicates a concentration of LMICs with the widest levels of territorial inequality. Of the 20 LMICs with the highest levels of regional disparities, only 5 have levels of GDP per capita in excess of USD 10 000 (Bulgaria, Hungary, Kazakhstan, Mexico, Panama). Those middle- and high-income countries with high levels of regional disparities tend to be located in Central and Eastern Europe – including Croatia, Latvia, the Russian Federation and the Slovak Republic – all having undergone post-socialist transitions. Others include Chile and the United Arab Emirates, both natural resource-dependent countries, but with economic activity highly concentrated in metropolitan regions – Santiago, Abu Dhabi and Dubai, respectively. By contrast, of the 20 countries with the lowest level of internal disparities, almost all are high-income OECD member countries. The few LMICs with relatively low disparities tend to be small economies, such as El Salvador or Nicaragua, to fall into the upper middle-income bracket (as in the case of Jordan), or are more exceptional, as in the cases of Bolivia and Morocco.

Figure 1.4. **Differences in interpersonal and territorial income inequalities among selected countries**

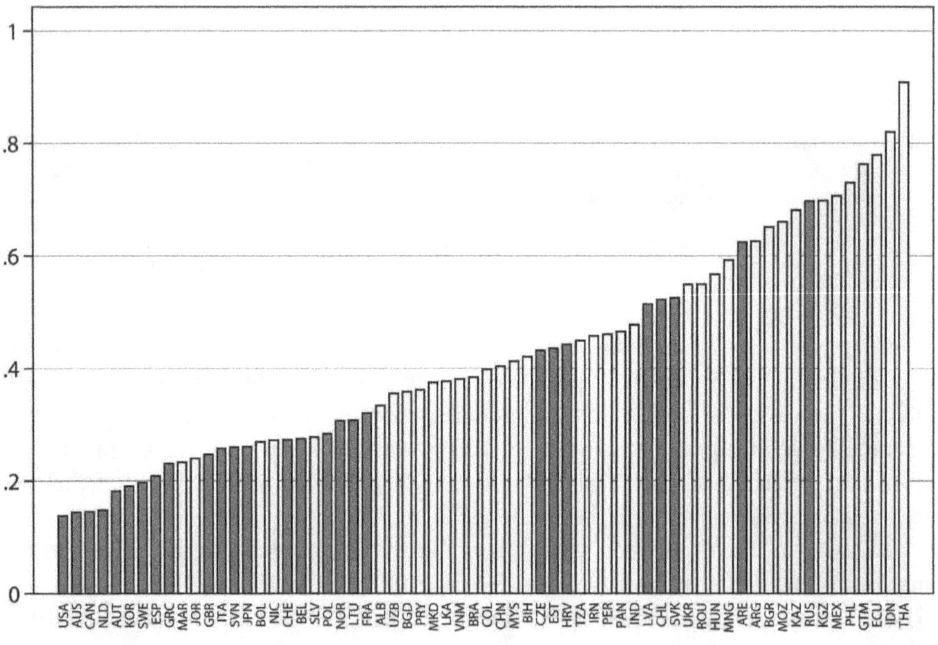

Note: White bars indicate low- and middle-income countries; blue bars indicate high-income countries.

Source: Own calculations based on World Development Indicators, http://data.worldbank.org/data-catalog/world-development-indicators; data appendix in Gennaioli et al. (2014), "Growth in regions", http://dx.doi.org/10.1007/s10887-014-9105-9.

Figure 1.5 presents additional information on the association of the degree of regional income disparity (based on regional GDP per capita) on the horizontal axis, with four core measures of economic structure and performance – GDP per capita, share of employment in agriculture, household poverty rate and a food inadequacy index that measures the share of households without secure access to food. Countries are grouped by income level – high, middle and low – and a linear trend line is fit to the data to suggest the relationship with higher levels of regional disparity. Note that only a limited number of low-income countries are included in the analysis.

Figure 1.5. **Regional disparities and their association with incomes, agricultural employment, poverty and food security**

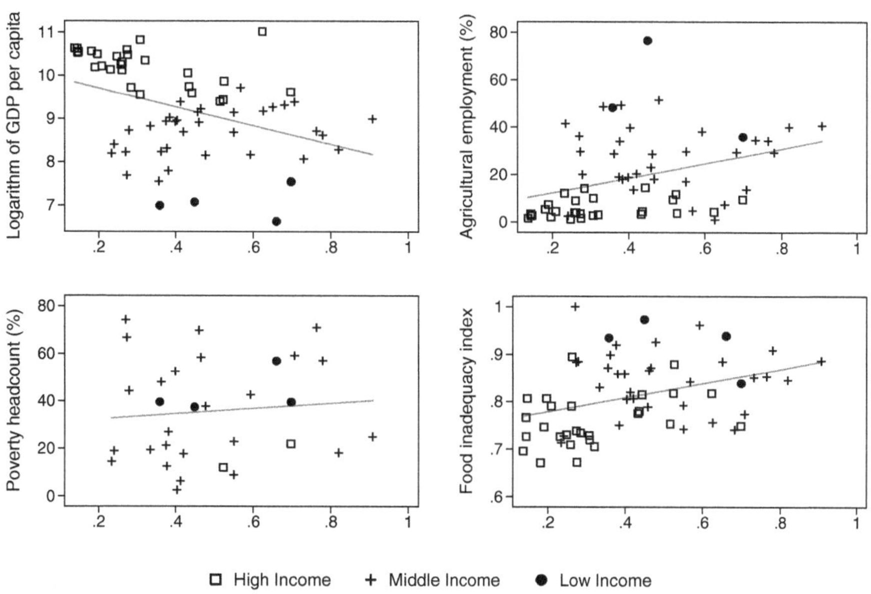

Source: Own calculations based on World Development Indicators, http://data.worldbank.org/data-catalog/world-development-indicators; data appendix in Gennaioli et al. (2014), "Growth in regions", http://dx.doi.org/10.1007/s10887-014-9105-9.

First, the correlation between GDP per capita and its degree of internal spatial disparity is plain when both are plotted against one another in the upper left figure. High-income countries (represented with a square indicator) are mostly clustered in the upper left of the graph (high incomes, low inequalities). The figure does, however, show considerable variation within each income grouping. For example, LMICs like Bolivia, Morocco and Nicaragua (all with levels of GDP per capita below USD 4 000), have levels of regional inequality above, or on par with, several high-income economies, including Belgium, Italy, Japan and the United Kingdom (each with levels of GDP per capita of USD 28 000 and above).

Second, a greater dependence on agriculture is positively associated with higher internal spatial disparities – albeit less markedly so than with levels of per capita GDP. For example, countries where a high percentage of the population is engaged in agricultural employment – including Bangladesh, the People's Republic of China (hereafter "China"), India, Indonesia and Thailand – feature at the top end of our regional inequality scale. Countries with low agricultural employment tend to be clustered in the bottom left of the figure, indicating lower levels of regional inequality.

Third, the data suggest that the degree of regional income disparity appears to be only weakly associated with poverty levels. While this association is drawn from a small sub-sample of countries, it does suggest that poverty is found in all countries, irrespective of their level of development or the degree of regional disparity in incomes. However, there is a stronger association with regional disparities and levels of food insecurity. Notably, while most upper-income countries are clustered in the low spatial inequality portion of the graph, with low food insecurity, several have considerable regional income inequality and relatively high levels of food insecurity. Both the middle- and low-income countries tend to have both high levels of regional inequality and high levels of food insecurity.

These data largely support the notion that there are regional differences within countries that affect the spatial distribution of food security. They also indicate that the spatial distribution of food insecurity is relevant to low-, middle- and high-income countries, although the territorial dimensions will vary with the stage of development of a specific country and its ability to produce food throughout its various regions. Moreover, given the well-established importance of increasing global food supplies to deal with a growing and wealthier population, it is clear that the historical focus on addressing food insecurity by increasing agricultural output in all countries remains relevant. The agricultural shift from subsistence and semi-subsistence smallholder farming to more modern commercial farming is likely in lower-income developing countries. However, it will be less likely to result in the impoverishment of those squeezed out of farming if a parallel investment in broadening the economic development of rural regions accompanies investments in agricultural modernisation. In particular, public investments in building transport and communication infrastructure, and investments in education and training for the least skilled can facilitate the transformation to an integrated market economy (OECD, 2011).

A territorial approach to food security and nutrition policy

The world produces enough food to feed everyone. Yet, about 800 million people suffer from hunger and malnutrition. This "paradox" – which His Holiness Pope Francis I called "intolerable" when he addressed the delegates of the FAO Conference at the Vatican on 20 June 2013 – is caused by multiple factors. As of now, policies to confront hunger have been based principally on centrally led and short-term relief approaches, with a focus mainly on increasing food production through sectoral policies. The overall result has had only a modest effect on reducing hunger and malnutrition.

There is increasing recognition that territorial approaches provide an appropriate framework to address the structural and emerging issues of FSN, including widening within-country inequalities and disparities in so far as they allow the exploration of the multidimensional, multi-actor and multi-level nature of food security and nutrition. In recognising the diversity of geographic spaces (metropolitan, rural adjacent, remote rural) and their capacity to react to shocks (external and internal), such approaches are also suited to tackling the sources of food insecurity. This involves strengthening local institutions and putting them at the forefront of the battle against food insecurity, to ensure the achievement of FSN in its multiple dimensions (availability, access, utilisation and stability).

This section develops a conceptual framework for a territorial approach to food insecurity and nutrition. It recognises that food availability, access, utilisation and stability can differ significantly across three types of regions – metropolitan, rural adjacent and rural remote. This provides the context for connecting the various forms of food insecurity to types of regions and for better understanding the importance of policies spatially sensitive to the various dimensions of food insecurity across regions. Crucially, a country's stage of development – lower-income developing through higher-income developed – also influences the territorial dimensions of food insecurity.

Regional diversity and territorial characteristics are increasingly acknowledged as both potential drivers of food security and development and factors responsible for the reproduction of hunger and inequalities. These shape the social, economic, institutional and environmental characteristics, as well as the socio-economic and policy dynamics, of a country's geographic areas. A territorial approach can thus be a helpful entry point from which to explore the complexity of economic and social diversity in a country and to formulate FSN strategies able to respond to diverse needs.

Food security and nutrition is the result of a dynamic interaction of economic, social, institutional and environmental policies. These policies, reflecting the heterogeneity of metropolitan, rural adjacent and rural remote societies, aim to reduce risks, increase rural households' resilience to shocks, promote development and boost livelihoods. Addressing rural poverty and inequalities requires a holistic approach acknowledging the diversity of regional spaces. While a sectoral approach to FSN policy and strategy is necessary, it is not a sufficient condition to impact rural livelihoods and reduce inequalities (between rural and urban areas, across rural areas or across individuals).

FSN is a complex, multidimensional issue. In addition to the availability dimension, there is a need to address the issues of access to food (both economic and physical), the nutritional quality of food (utilisation), and the stability of both the availability and access dimensions in the long run. Other causes of food insecurity are generally attributed to low incomes, unemployment, health, education, nutrition status, natural resource degradation and weak political commitment, which exacerbate vulnerability to risk. As noted by the FAO, fighting rural poverty and food insecurity will require resilient and diversified rural economies that offer employment and income opportunities. Helping small farmers improve farm productivity can help, but in most contexts, it is not enough to lift all rural poor out of poverty (FAO, 2013).

Raising the income of the poor is thus one of the main challenges of ensuring food security and nutrition. The basic requirement for poverty reduction is broad-based development, whose underpinnings include political stability; sound policy at the global, national and sub-national level; strong institutions; well-defined property rights; and good governance (OECD, forthcoming *a*). In addition, territorial capital and assets (natural, human, manmade, organisational, relational and cognitive capital) play a key role in the fight against hunger.

Ensuring food security and nutrition is a global challenge that calls for a cross-sectoral, coherent approach at local, national, regional and international levels. However, interconnectedness between different sectors increases the risk that action in one area may undermine efforts in another. Breaking down the silos that separate policy sectors requires co-operation among political institutions and other stakeholders in promoting cross-sectoral synergies for achieving food security (OECD, forthcoming *a*).

The underlying assumption of this research is that an effective approach to food security and nutrition in rural areas should recognise the multidimensionality of FSN. If food security objectives are to be realised, all four dimensions must be recognised. While agricultural development plays a key role in the achievement of food security in developing countries, a sectoral approach is not enough. Agriculture is an important activity in rural areas of developing countries, yet its relative weight is generally declining. In Africa and Latin America, 30-60% of rural household incomes are from non-farm sources. Livelihoods of rural communities increasingly depend on identifying and exploiting diverse new local economic drivers, which can be connected with the agricultural sector. This is supported by the evidence that the incidence of poverty is, in general, less severe in off-farm or multi-activity households than in families dependent on agriculture. Many of the world's food insecure people are low-income, small-scale farmers who are not integrated into larger productive networks and are exposed to food price shocks, natural catastrophes and climate change.

There is wide recognition (FAO, 2006; World Bank, 2007; UCFA, 2010; OECD and FAO, 2010) that sector-wise policies are not sufficient to set a sustainable path out of poverty and food insecurity. Cross-sectoral and place-based policies aiming at integrating the agricultural sector with upstream and downstream markets, as well as with non-farm activities, may be potentially more effective for improving rural livelihoods and FSN. Evidence obtained from a series of OECD policy reviews, as well as research conducted by both the FAO and the United Nations Capital Development Fund (UNCDF), suggests that there is need for a shift towards a broader and more holistic approach to FSN and rural development.

The regional dimension of food security and malnutrition

Within-country variability among regions tends to be greater than across-country variability for almost any socio-economic indicator (OECD, 2012). However, within a country, extremes in regional conditions tend to be "averaged out" in constructing the national average measure. A national average can be a somewhat misleading descriptor of how well typical citizens are doing. Where regional variability is high, the national average may be accurate in only a very small number of regions, and the majority either far better or worse off than the average would suggest. This phenomenon is true for basic socio-economic indicators such as per capita income, employment rates, educational attainment, poverty levels, and for hunger and malnutrition levels.

The *OECD Regional Database* provides a comprehensive overview of many socio-economic indicators for member countries at the sub-national level, provided for various regional categories. Diversity at the regional level is the main motive for the OECD's emphasis on territorial policy in the Regional Development Policy Programme. In particular, the programme recognises the distinct differences between highly urbanised regions and rural regions, even in the most advanced industrialised democracies, where there is a high degree of connectivity across regions. Given these regional differences, it is important that development policies of any kind incorporate differences in conditions and opportunities across regions, to ensure that regions of all types benefit and that national welfare is maximised.

Food insecurity and malnutrition fall into this situation, with significant differences in both the frequency and degree of FSN problems across regions. If there are large differences among different types of regions within a country, there would seem to be *prima facie* evidence for a territorial approach to improving food security and nutrition levels. For example, if large urban regions have low levels of food insecurity while rural regions have high levels, there may be grounds for policies that differentiate between urban and rural regions. However, this may be too simplistic an approach.

If the example is pushed further and the regional populations are subdivided by income level, it may appear that that the urban poor are as food insecure as the rural poor. This might suggest that geography is not the issue for FSN policy, but that poverty is. However, deeper analysis indicates that the well-functioning food distribution and marketing system in urban areas ensures that food is available to those with sufficient funds – a true poverty problem. In rural regions, poverty is clearly an issue, but households rely on self-supply, a more limited set of markets for food and limited scope for food imports due to weak transport links. Moreover, strategies to address poverty in urban and rural regions will differ significantly.

This suggests that addressing FSN problems can benefit from a territorial approach for precisely the same reasons that other forms of economic development policy benefit if more carefully tailored support is offered to different types of regions. A large body of literature suggests the best way to address food insecurity and malnutrition is to strengthen food markets and increase household incomes. Thus, strengthening the link between policies supporting economic prosperity and food security is crucial.

A conceptual framework for a territorial approach to food security and nutrition policies

The preceding discussion has highlighted the many interlinked dimensions of FSN as well as its context-specific nature. To date, while most approaches to FSN problems acknowledge the need for extensive rural transformations to compete in the global economy, few factor in provisions to explicitly design pathways that link food security and poverty. The critical issue is that many factors generate, and co-evolve alongside, FSN challenges. Some are environmental conditions that affect the availability and quality of agricultural land; inadequate land tenure systems; limited economic opportunities for growing populations; disparities linked to the remoteness of rural communities; poor policy making and the presence of institutions that exacerbate issues of crime, corruption, clientelism and conflict. A critical question is how to connect efforts to improve agricultural productivity while also promoting new employment opportunities that can provide alternative sources of income and improve the access dimension of FSN.

The most common rural development policies used currently fall into three categories. The first is a single-sector approach, typically agriculturally oriented, that focuses on using a leading sector to pull development forward. The second approach is to try to encourage diversification to create multiple sources of income and employment, largely through small-scale enterprises. A third approach is to concentrate efforts in urban areas and rely on spread effects to pull rural areas along, using spatially blind policies. None of these approaches looks explicitly at the problems and opportunities for specific rural regions, and none has a focus on connecting various policy initiatives into a package that provides a co-ordinated and coherent approach. The remainder of this chapter seeks to outline competing themes in rural development in the form of policies centred on the promotion of single sectors (usually agriculture or primary commodities) and others on diversification (OECD, 2006). Prevailing approaches are considered that adopt spatially blind strategies (i.e. concentrating on sectors or people). This contrasts with the new, territorially sensitive, place-based paradigm, which tries to get to grips with the drivers and inhibitors of growth in a particular territorial setting, and uses this information to define development goals.

Single-sector approaches

Agriculture-centred policies are the archetypal single-sector approach to rural development. Indeed, rural development practice has long been regarded as synonymous with agricultural development in many contexts (Pisani and Franceschetti, 2011; OECD, 2010). Three reasons lie behind this. First, more is known about the promotion of agricultural growth than the promotion of alternative, non-agricultural activities (Valdés and Foster, 2010). Second, the responsibility for rural development has often fallen to government departments responsible for agriculture, farming and related activities (Rojas-Caldelas et al., 2010). Third, in most developing countries, the vast majority of the rural population is engaged in agriculture, and improving farm incomes is often seen as an obvious first step. It is not that approaches based on single sectors in isolation are necessarily ineffective or undesirable, but simply that an approach to development with too narrow a focus is unlikely to recognise the full complexity, externalities and opportunities that affect the development potential of a given region.

However, most rural communities in developing contexts rely upon primary activities – including agriculture, forestry and fishing. According to the most recently available World Development Indicator on the subject, over 30% of global employment is concentrated in agriculture, rising to 38% in middle-income countries and 46% in lower middle-income countries. Ignoring the potential to develop the agricultural sector would be a missed opportunity to make a real difference to food security and rural poverty (Hazell et al., 2010). An expanding agrarian sector can also induce strong urban-rural and forward linkages that can pull non-agricultural sectors with it, increasing both farm and non-farm opportunities in rural areas (Anríquez and Stamoulis, 2007). However, an inevitable consequence of agricultural modernisation is that greater productivity substitutes capital investment for labour and involves larger farms. The supply of food may increase and food prices may decline, but additional efforts will have to be made to introduce new employment opportunities for households leaving agriculture, or food insecurity problems will increase.

Diversification approaches

Where single-sector approaches focus largely on specialisation, diversification approaches emphasise multi-functionality and diversity. This reduces the risks inherent in overt specialisation in rural regions, and helps develop an economic base for future growth. In light of such constraints as a limited supply of agricultural land and the declining potential for agriculture to employ a growing rural population, it has often been argued that farming and the agrarian economy alone will not be able to provide a way out of poverty for a significant proportion of the rural poor (IFAD, 2010; Brooks, Cervantes-Godoy and Jonasson, 2009). This represents the central tenet of the OECD's "New Rural Paradigm" (2006), as outlined in Table 1.2. The New Rural Paradigm, endorsed in 2006 by OECD member countries, proposed a conceptual framework that positioned rural policy as an investment strategy to promote competitiveness in rural territories. This represented a radical change from the typical subsidy programmes of the past aimed at specific sectors.

Table 1.2. **The OECD's 2006 "New Rural Paradigm"**

	Old approach	New approach
Objectives	Equalisation, farm income, competitiveness of rural areas, valorisation of local assets, farm competitiveness	Competitiveness of rural areas, valorisation of local assets, exploitation of unused resources
Key target sector	Agriculture	Various sectors of rural economies (i.e. rural tourism, manufacturing, ICT industry, etc.)
Main tools	Subsidies	Investments
Key actors	National governments, farmers	All levels of government (supra-national, national, regional and local), various local stakeholders (public, private, non-governmental organisations)
Target geography	Dichotomy between urban and rural areas	Focus on the importance of urban-rural linkages

Source: OECD (2006), *The New Rural Paradigm: Policies and Governance*, http://dx.doi.org/10.1787/9789264023918-en.

Subsequent studies highlight the role of multisectoral approaches, with emphasis on non-agricultural development as "decisive to fight rural poverty" (Ambrosio-Albalá and Bastiaensen, 2010: 9). Two classic rationales for diversifying farming household incomes exist. The first is to mitigate risk associated with output shocks and the seasonal availability of food (Lohmann and Liefner, 2009: 143). The second is to provide an alternative to farming as a source of household income by introducing new activities in rural regions.

To embrace the new FSN and rural policy challenges faced by many countries, innovative governance mechanisms have been developed to enhance co-ordination across sectors and levels of government, as well as between public, private and non-profit stakeholders. Moreover, new policy instruments with a significant territorial and place-based focus are being created to identify and capitalise on rural areas' competitiveness, local assets and knowledge, as well as to tap into diverse potential for development. The OECD has described this evolution as a paradigm shift in rural development policies. The defining characteristics of the 2006 New Rural Paradigm are a focus on places rather than sectors and an emphasis on investments rather than national transfers and subsidies.

Recent work of the OECD builds on the New Rural Paradigm in order to propose a new toolkit for addressing the challenges, while reaping the opportunities, faced by rural areas in developing countries today (OECD, 2016). Challenges include a more demanding competitive international environment, rapidly growing rural populations, increased pressure on limited environmental resources and climate change. Opportunities include advances in information and communications, agricultural, energy, and health technologies that can help address some of these challenges. The toolkit for developing countries stresses the need for multisectoral and multi-level strategies, which should be context-specific. Being focused on developing countries, the toolkit pays particular attention to key development areas such as demography, basic infrastructure and the role of secondary cities for strengthening positive urban-rural linkages. Moreover, enhancing governance and capacity building appear as key factors for the development of any rural or territorial development strategy in developing countries. Indeed, in contrast to OECD member countries, developing countries are characterised by weak institutions, which hinders the establishment of well-functioning co-ordination mechanisms, which further limits the effectiveness of any territorial development strategy.

The OECD's rural policy approach is now evolving – from the New Rural Paradigm in 2006 to the current Rural Policy 3.0 (OECD, forthcoming b), which puts more emphasis on implementation. The new dimensions in the Rural Policy 3.0 include the recognition of rural and urban linkages, and a general focus on building capacity at the local level in order to encourage participation and bottom-up development strategies. It maintains that a key objective of rural policy should be to increase rural competitiveness and productivity in order to enhance the social, economic and environmental well-being of rural areas. Within this approach, policies should focus on enhancing comparative and absolute advantages in rural communities and should draw on integrated investments and delivery of services that are adapted to the needs of rural areas and benefit from potential complementarities. The Rural Policy 3.0 describes a partnership-driven approach that builds capacity at the local level to encourage participation and bottom-up development. Partnerships between different levels of government, between rural and urban locales, and among rural communities are critical for community and economic development.

Few would question the importance of developing new sectors of employment to offset static growth or decline in agricultural employment as a basis for sustainable development (Dirven, 2011; Reardon and Timmer, 2007; Barrett, Reardon and Webb, 2001; Berdegué et al., 2000). Indeed, for many developing and emerging countries, the rural non-farm sector is already a source of considerable employment. In India, in particular, the rural non-agricultural activities sector employs the largest percentage of people in the country (Reddy et al., 2013). More broadly, studies increasingly emphasise how a growing percentage of rural incomes are now derived from rural non-agricultural employment (Lanjouw and Lanjouw, 2001; Haggblade, Hazell and Reardon, 2007). Approximately 35-50% of employment in the rural developing world now falls within this category (de Janvry and Sadoulet, 2001; Barrett, Reardon and Webb, 2001; Bryceson, 2002; Rigg, 2006), ranging from 34% of rural incomes in Africa to 47% in Latin America, and 51% in Asia (Imai, Gaiha and Thapa, 2013).

In principle, diversification approaches are highly attractive. However, in practice, in rural regions they face significant geographical challenges: long distances, low density and lack of critical mass. Distance from markets increases transport costs for purchased inputs and outputs. Low density increases the cost of commuting for workers and distributing goods and services. Lack of critical mass means small home markets and a small labour force, which limits the number and size of firms. Consequently, while diversification may be able to supplement a primary resource sector, it will typically be unable to replace it.

Approaches to safeguard food security and reduce poverty should recognise the interplay between incomes, skills and socio-economic deficits and the dynamics of employment opportunities in the rural economy (Chawanote and Barrett, 2011). However, despite the growth and development potential of non-agricultural activities, governments and donors have often paid relatively little attention to approaches that explicitly promote non-agricultural opportunities. Considerable scope thus remains to shape the development of non-agricultural activities in the interests of sustainable development and poverty reduction (IFAD, 2010; Babatunde and Qaim, 2010; Chang and Mishra, 2008).

The "spatially blind" paradigm

> "Unless there are spatial barriers that limit adjustment, economists argue that policies to alleviate poverty should focus on poor people, not poor places." (Partridge and Rickman, 2008: 1).

Although the stance of the World Bank has shifted since, the 2009 *World Development Report* prominently advocated the ascendancy of a spatially blind approach to development. The report diagnosed the three D's – density, distance and division – as the foremost impediments to regional development, and proposed the three I's – institutions, infrastructure and integration – as the treatment for each. From this perspective, the principal problem that impoverished rural areas face is a lack of agglomeration related to sparsely populated areas with few connections to more densely settled towns and cities. From this perspective, rural areas face considerable physical, institutional and transactional cost barriers to accessing and engaging in trade with domestic and international markets. The more remote and sparsely populated – where poverty is coincidentally at its highest – the lower the development potential. These are precisely the areas of the world most at risk of facing food insecurity issues. Remote and poorly endowed regions may thus enter into a vicious cycle of underdevelopment and food and nutrition insecurity: lack of agglomeration, poor integration and distance to markets curtails their capacity to develop, and poor development prospects raise the risk of food insecurity, which, in turn, further undermines the potential for development.

"One-size-fits-all" policies are the mainstay of a spatially blind approach. They are designed around the noted 3 I's: institutions (to promote density), infrastructure (to encourage agglomeration) and integration (to reduce division) (World Bank, 2009). The first, establishing sound and effective institutions for development, emphasises the significance of formal institutions, such as legal and regulatory frameworks, for protecting private assets and facilitating market access and trade flows to unlock the agglomeration potential of the country or region (North, 1990; Tabellini, 2010). Second, problems related to distance can be overcome by the building of infrastructure. Infrastructure investments have been a central component of rural development strategies, and development more generally. Infrastructure such as road and rail investments reduces distance between places and promotes agglomeration, reduces transaction costs, and induces flows of labour, resources and capital to regions where higher returns can be yielded. Finally, the importance of integration implies the formation of larger internal markets, which, in part, serve to facilitate the further expansion and densification of urban cores. Thus, in contrast to traditional approaches to development, all components emphasise policy designs geared towards the promotion of further expansion and densification in more agglomerated core regions, with little or no emphasis on increasing the potential for development in peripheral areas.

Economic agglomeration in a spatially blind approach is regarded as a basic step for economic development. If countries want to develop, they must inevitably go through an agglomeration stage during which territorial disparities increase (World Bank, 2009). In the process, greater agglomeration will generate powerful externalities, resulting in higher economic growth, which, in later stages, will spread out first to neighbouring regions before reaching more peripheral areas. However, as was first noted by Myrdal in 1957, the spread effects of urban growth can be offset by backwash effects that pull resources out of rural regions, leaving them worse off.

Large agglomerations clearly generate positive externalities, which are beneficial to firms, sectors and to the region as a whole, but these externality effects may not spread far beyond the urban agglomeration. Consequently, the outcome of greater agglomeration is just as likely to be even greater agglomeration (Rodríguez-Pose, 2010). Any spread effects from the core will thus be insufficient to compensate for the presence of very powerful backwash forces (McCann, 2008). In this situation, a more spatially sensitive balanced growth approach may increase total national well-being by allowing rural regions to make a positive contribution to national growth. This requires a rural development policy that is compatible with urban development policies, in that it seeks to improve rural-urban linkages, but also recognises that urban policy and rural policy should not be identical, because rural opportunities and constraints are fundamentally different from those in urban regions.

The importance of a holistic approach to food security and nutrition policies

None of the three standard approaches to economic development in rural regions has proven to be satisfactory. This suggests that an integrated approach, as proposed in the New Rural Paradigm, might offer a better way to manage development challenges in developing countries, including FSN issues. Most intermediate and peripheral areas have economic potential which runs the risk of being neglected by a paradigm that favours "one-size-fits-all-policies" in the agglomerated cores of a country (Parkinson et al., 2012). Leaving economic potential untapped is not only pernicious for those places being overlooked, but also for the overall efficiency of policy and for the growth of a country. The discussion of agricultural and diversification approaches is illuminating in this respect. It is clear that there is an important role for both agriculture and non-agricultural activities in the secondary and tertiary sectors for eradicating food security and poverty. Contrary to the one-sided discussions that are typical of the relevant streams of literature, they are both needed for rural development and complement each other. They comprise two important pillars of the rural economy and are strongly inter-connected.

Similarly, urban-rural interactions, including links with local urban towns as well as more major medium and large cities, offer a vital conduit for instigating development, if channelled appropriately (OECD, 2013a). If connections can be encouraged that expand market access and create additional opportunities for enterprise and employment, while also improving access to health care and education, this can instigate positive externalities, build a more diverse portfolio of economic activities and generate employment – while also reducing food insecurity and poverty locally. However, to generate these benefits, it will be necessary to avoid inducing capital flight and skilled migration, by building local assets and resources.

Most importantly, it is critical that economic development strategies be explicitly connected to social development strategies and to FSN concerns. All three issues have clear territorial differences, in terms both of the magnitude of the challenges and the potential approaches to resolve them. Moreover, they are linked policy concerns. FSN is best addressed by improving incomes, education and health care. Workers are more productive if they are not malnourished. Public services, including health care, are more effective if people have incomes and access to nutritious food.

Robust institutions and multi-level governance can help promote policy coherence

Challenges to any FSN and rural development strategy are multifold. The competitiveness and nature of social exclusion in rural areas is conditioned by a variety of factors, many already alluded to, such as levels of urban demand for rurally produced products and services. More specifically, from a policy perspective, effective rural development strategies rely on considerations related to the quality of government, the ability to co-ordinate complementary approaches across sectors – as well as vertically across national and sub-national authorities – and to make provisions for the localised capacity of sub-national governments, including their authority and legitimacy.

Policy coherence for sustainable development (PCSD) can support governments in their efforts to design policies that consider the various dimensions of FSN. It can be particularly useful for identifying synergies and trade-offs and minimising negative spill-overs, including from a spatial perspective. The OECD defines PCSD as "an approach and policy tool to integrate the economic, social, environmental and governance dimensions of sustainable development at all stages of domestic and international policy making".

There is strong evidence that food security and nutrition levels are influenced by territorial capital or assets, including human capital, infrastructure, local institutions as well as natural resources and environment, which vary across geographic areas. This diversity is, however, often overlooked in policy making, which is generally centralised and does not take into account specific local opportunities and issues. Integrated territorial approaches do rely on good, effective governance at multiple tiers of government, but particularly at the local level, to instigate sustainable regional development. The term "good governance" has ascended to the forefront of development debates as they have become increasingly place-based and community-centred (Meso et al., 2006).

Many of these problems are most pertinent to territorial settings that are divided, with significant regional cleavages based on conflict, social movements and structural differences that call into question the accountability and legitimacy of sub-national governments to pursue local goals and priorities (Ambrosio-Albalá and Bastiaensen, 2010). The risk is that low-quality governments – at all levels in fact – have a tendency to push zero- and negative-sum initiatives based on redistribution, rather than more integrated, sustainable and positive-sum modes of development (Bebbington, Abramovay and Chiriboga, 2008). As such, where local institutions are of questionable quality, decentralisation cannot be viewed as a panacea. There are many well-known risks to decentralisation when implemented ineffectively or inappropriately, including corruption and local elite capture of policies (Bardhan and Mookherjee, 2006). A strong role from central governments is, in this respect, essential for the design, co-ordination and regulation of effective policies, particularly at the outset, to compensate for weak local capacities. Strong multi-level co-ordination, interaction and commitment between national and sub-national authorities can then, over time, raise local capacities, which can then incrementally and commensurably increase their own levels of responsibility (De Ferranti et al., 2005).

The fundamental importance of (formal and informal) institutions and capacity building for development strategies is no longer a mystery (Rodríguez-Pose, 2013). What can be done to alter institutional frameworks and cultural conditions is, however, another story altogether. Little is available in the way of strong evidence to show how many institutional forms can be augmented over the short to medium term. They represent, nevertheless, one of the key pillars of a place-based approach to FSN and poverty in developing countries. Informal institutions in particular play a critical role for FSN and its determinants, and include components such as norms, traditions, social capital and culture. Under a spatially blind approach, the importance and context-specific nature of informal institutions is frequently overlooked – due to the partial, incomplete comprehension of institutions in such approaches, which tend to over-emphasise formal dimensions.

Place-based approaches are thus needed to understand, and account for, how institutional and related territorial features can be accommodated in policy practice.

Moreover, institutional reforms play a key role even in the debates between place-based and spatially blind approaches in emerging and developing countries. Spatially blind approaches prefer to promote agglomeration and urban expansion in order to overcome institutional weaknesses inherent in developing contexts. By contrast, place-based proponents counter that "the ability of urbanisation to overcome rather than to exacerbate institutional problems is not at all clear, because it depends on their interactions, which in turn may also depend both on the level of development and also on the existing limited institutional arrangements" (Barca, McCann and Rodríguez-Pose, 2012: 145). A holistic, place-based approach instead allows for the formulation and implementation of policies that aim to utilise and enhance the institutional capacity of a given place (Barc, McCann and Rodríguez-Pose, 2012). This can be achieved through external actors, such as international organisations and donor agencies, via conditionality arrangements, where parts of aid programmes could be made conditional upon appropriate packages of institutional capacity building.

Another key role within the scope of place-based approaches is the ability to establish mechanisms that allow for a combination of long-term strategies and short-term needs. In other words, developmental success stories frequently involve institutions, such as regional development agencies, that are able to go beyond the political pressures of short-term policy cycles and provide greater consistency and autonomy to develop and maintain a more long-term vision or strategy. In the words of Tomaney, "institutions which are separated but linked to the political structures […] allow you to take a long term view", without this and because of "the way in which accountability is instituted, that is the way in which the political class is refreshed and so on […] you are destined towards sclerosis" (interview in Cistulli et al., 2014).

Therefore, given these and the previous considerations, both the strong influence of territorial capital and the key role of institutions (formal and informal), it appears clear that any FSN strategy based entirely on a spatially blind approach – which neglects the highly context-specific nature of FSN – would prove highly ineffective and very likely to fail in addressing any future iterations of MDG 1 on poverty and hunger reduction. A place-based approach that considers the territorial place-specific features of rural regions can establish both the constraints and obstacles to achieving FSN and reducing poverty in a given place. In doing so, it can present possible solutions to improve and tackle these issues, and, by adopting a multi-level governance orientation, integrate these approaches into a macroeconomic FSN policy regime that promises to be much more effective.

Integrating social policies and competitiveness agendas

Traditional policies to address FSN and poverty have tended to follow a decontextualised, individual approach. The limitation of the traditional sectoral and assistance-led approach to food security is not only that it does not address and consider the complexity of the process of development, but it creates, even without the intent to do so, a passive approach to development. Yet, it seems statistically that beyond the peculiar attributes of the people in the territory, the territorial attributes themselves also have some impact in terms of poverty and inequalities. These illustrate the limits of prevailing approaches – based on a national competitiveness paradigm – to issues of FSN and poverty.

By treating populations as recipients rather than pro-active participants in development, opportunities are missed to develop a better understanding of the determinants of local food insecurity, poverty and underdevelopment, and thus to devise more effective policies to remedy these ills. Holistic, territorial approaches offer a different line of attack. Not only do they aspire to extract the utmost from the internal assets of each and every region, like local firms and regional infrastructure endowments, but they also emphasise the need to develop the softer, more intangible factors within a region, such as its social and institutional fabric. As Barca (2009) stresses, social policies (and therefore also FSN policies) must be place-based, because both the conditions and the well-being of any individual, and the effectiveness of the policy actions to address inequalities, are highly context-specific and influenced by social, economic, cultural and institutional forms of capital typical of their territorial context. Like one weakness of the inequality literature – the treatment of social exclusion at the household level with little regard for the territorial features influencing it – the issue of FSN needs to be addressed beyond the household level and with an eye towards its territorial determinants. In the words of Barca (2009: 36), "[t]he social agenda needs to be 'territorialised', the territorial agenda 'socialised'. The place-based approach to social inclusion should be the result of these two shifts".

In a more general sense, these sentiments reflect a change in orientation from an emphasis on "national" competitiveness to the regional level. All territories have development potential and, as such, policies should be aimed at exploiting each and every region's endogenous potentials. Research by Rodríguez-Pose and Tjimstra (2007) shows that even in sub-Saharan Africa – where it is typical to concede that exceptional solutions are needed to address development issues – there is still clear potential for local economic development strategies to instigate progress. Their specific conclusions for sub-Saharan Africa echo the main thrust of this chapter's argument, that two, rather limited, lines of attack left the territorial dimension as overlooked. First is the tendency for "a combination of macroeconomic stability packages with supply-side sectoral measures applied throughout the continent with little regard for specific local conditions"; and the second, for a prevalence of "piecemeal development projects aimed at guaranteeing the survival of individuals, often in extremely precarious conditions" (Rodríguez-Pose and Tjimstra, 2007: 532.). Community development approaches, in particular, suffer from the latter shortcoming, tending to be disconnected from broader and extra-regional development strategies and institutional frameworks (Mansuri and Rao, 2004). This emphasises the need for approaches that integrate the meso level – i.e. between the national level and the neighbourhood or village level – where there is a patent need for sustained and integrated approaches to maximise the efficacy of relatively scarce development funds.

In terms of socially geared policy instruments, territorial approaches emphasise the importance of investing in hard and soft modes of infrastructure – such as improving the business environment, building social capital, providing public goods, creating and maintaining networks, ensuring the smooth functioning of labour markets, and promoting connectivity through appropriate infrastructure – as opposed to the prevailing preoccupation with packages of subsidies and state aid. In terms of governance processes, the territorial paradigm stresses the need to shift from the typical model based on imperious central government rule towards more even-handed, multi-level governance systems in which different governmental tiers (national, regional and local) and stakeholders (both public and private) are involved in the decision-making process. In a similar vein, policy makers need to target interventions beyond the (arbitrary) borders of administrative jurisdictions and seek to formulate and implement regional development policies over more meaningful functional economic areas.

Food security and nutrition in different regional typologies and stages of development

Addressing food security and nutrition in different regional typologies

The three types of region, irrespective of the stage of national development, have some clear differences in terms of their ability to produce food, their ability to supply food and the territorial development opportunities.

Metropolitan regions

The large population of metropolitan regions, their relatively compact size and competing demands for land result in a low capacity for food self-supply. Food that is produced tends to be of high value and often perishable, such as dairy products, fresh fruits and vegetables, and other specialty crops. Basic commodities, including most meat, grains, and fruits and vegetables produced for processing, are imported. Some metropolitan regions may have a significant food-processing sector, but mainly rely on raw materials from outside the region. While locally produced food is limited in quantity, these regions have good access to a wide variety of imported food, either from other regions in the country or imports from other countries.

Supply of food is rarely a problem in large cities because they have well-functioning food markets that are connected to global suppliers. In developing countries, connectivity to foreign markets happens first in large cities, and these urban agglomerations have the densest networks of connections, largely because markets develop first and in greater complexity in cities. Further, relatively high average incomes mean that food expenditure is a manageable share of household income for all but the poor, so food price increases in times of shortage may be unpleasant, but not threatening. Finally, because city residents tend to be better organised politically and government institutions are based in cities, there is a general tendency for political regimes to ensure that cities are reasonably well supplied with food even in times of national shortages.

For the poor, who may account for a large share of the regional population, food insecurity is a major challenge. The major challenge in large cities, however, involves access to food for those with low and unstable income. Even for the very poor, there is a relatively high likelihood of having sufficient access to food through local relief organisations, because these are easier to organise and operate in an urban setting, where surplus food may be readily available. Thus, in these instances, hunger may be a chronic problem, but may not be immediately life-threatening.

Territorial development opportunities in metropolitan regions are closely tied to the benefits of economies of agglomeration. A growing body of evidence and analysis confirms that, other things being equal, larger cities make their residents more productive (OECD, 2015). In part, this can be explained by the characteristics of the workforce and the firms in cities. Larger cities tend to attract highly educated and experienced residents, who would have high levels of productivity wherever they choose to work and live, and they also attract more productive firms. However, the evidence is now clear that cities themselves can contribute significantly to their residents' productivity. Residents of larger cities are more productive than if they were living in smaller cities due to "agglomeration benefits", the positive productivity spill-overs that arise when highly productive firms and people are brought closer together. Typically, these benefits are created through shared inputs, better "matching" between firms and employees, and mutual learning among firms and residents (Box 1.1). "Knowledge spill-overs", in particular, are considered critical in explaining the benefits of cities in modern service-oriented economies.

Adjacent rural

These rural regions are characterised by large areas, relatively low population density and a fairly limited range of economic functions. However, they do have relatively strong connections to larger urban regions in the form of: good transport links, access to urban services and considerable market interactions, including supply chain linkages, wholesale and retail functions. While these regions have autonomous labour markets, which means that workers do not have ready access to urban jobs, local employers are connected to urban markets. This can provide greater levels of employment and higher wages than would otherwise be the case. OECD research shows that rates of growth in output, productivity, GDP per capita and population are relatively high, even when compared to metropolitan regions (OECD, forthcoming *b*).

The development opportunities in these types of regions highly depend on their ability to take advantage of the positive complementarities between rural and urban areas (OECD, 2013a). Rural-urban partnerships help achieve better regional conditions. First, such partnerships facilitate the production of public goods that are useful for economic development. Second, rural-urban partnerships make it possible to achieve greater economies of scale in the provision of public services. Partnerships aggregate the limited local resources of rural governments with more plentiful urban resources, to provide services more efficiently to the entire region. Third, rural-urban partnerships help account for cross-border effects of decisions taken by single urban and rural local authorities.

Box 1.1. **Agglomeration economies**

Three main mechanisms work to produce agglomeration economies:

1. Mechanisms that deal with sharing of:

- Indivisible facilities such as local public goods or facilities that serve several individuals or firms. Examples, other than public goods, include facilities such as laboratories, universities and other large goods that do not belong to a particular agent but where some exclusion is implicit in providing them.
- The gains from the wider variety of input suppliers that can be sustained by a larger final goods industry. In other words, the presence of increasing returns to scale, along with forward and backward linkages, allow firms to purchase intermediate inputs at lower costs.
- The gains from the narrower specialisation that can be sustained with higher production levels. Several firms specialise in producing complementary products, reducing overall production costs.
- Risks. This refers to the idea that an industry gains from having a constant market for skills. If there are market shocks, firms can adjust to changes in demand if they have access to a deep and broad labour market that allows them to expand or contract their demand for labour.

2. Matching mechanisms by which:

- Agglomeration improves the expected quality of matches between firms and workers, so both are better able to find a good match for their needs.
- An increase in the number of agents trying to match in the labour market also improves the probability of matching.

Box 1.1. **Agglomeration economies** *(cont.)*

- Delays are alleviated. There is a possibility that contractual problems arising from renegotiation among buyers and suppliers will result in one of the parties losing out to the other party in a renegotiation. However, if the agglomeration is extensive enough, agents can find an alternative partner.

3. Learning mechanisms based on the generation, diffusion and accumulation of knowledge. This refers not only to the learning of technologies, but also the acquisition of skills.

OECD metropolitan regions benefit from agglomeration effects and thus tend to display higher levels of productivity, higher rates of employment and higher levels of GDP per capita than other regions. These benefits, however, are limited by congestion costs, diseconomies of scale and oversupply of labour, among other potential negative elements, and many metro regions have in recent decades tended to underperform national economies.

Source: Duranton and Puga (2004), "Micro-foundations of urban agglomeration economies"; OECD (2009a), How Regions Grow: Trends and Analysis, http://dx.doi.org/10.1787/9789264039469-en.

OECD research has identified five key factors as having a positive effect on rural-urban partnerships, based on analysis in 11 case studies (OECD, 2013a):

1. understanding the interdependence of rural and urban areas
2. mutual understanding and the need to act in concert
3. clearly defined objectives
4. representational membership and democratic participation
5. leadership

Among the cases studies, clearly defined objectives, representational membership and democratic participation were important across almost all communities' studies (10 out of 11 and 9 out of 11 respectively). Meanwhile, the most common obstacles to partnership were identified as a lack of private sector involvement (in 5 out of 11 cases) or incentives to partner (in 4 out of 11 cases).

Agriculture typically plays an important role in these regions. It tends to be the dominant land use and can provide a significant share of regional GDP. In more developed countries, the role of agriculture in local employment may be low due to the mechanisation of farming, but the value of agricultural production can be high. Conversely, in less developed countries, agriculture may account for a large share of regional employment but due to limited productivity, the value of production is low. In these regions, development is associated with an increase in average farm size, with increased agricultural productivity and with a declining share of the regional workforce employed in agriculture. Farming that is conducted in this type of region tends to produce far more output than can be consumed by the local population. Because of the strong connections to the adjacent urban area, the surplus production tends to go to the urban region for consumption, processing or re-export.

The local economy of adjacent rural regions is relatively diversified, with multiple sources of income and employment available. This provides not only higher incomes, but more stable incomes, and with good market connections and high levels of self-supply of food, the more extreme forms of food insecurity are of only limited concern. Poverty rates are highly variable across adjacent rural regions, some with relatively low rates and others with high rates. In some cases, urban poor relocate to adjacent rural regions to find cheaper housing, while in other cases, the poor in adjacent rural regions relocate to urban regions where social support is more readily available. In addition, there may be a higher rate of economic insecurity in rural regions than in metropolitan regions, which leads to periods of high unemployment that expose households to intermittent food insecurity.

Food may be more expensive than in urban areas, except for those items that are produced locally. On average, incomes are lower than in urban regions, so the percentage of income spent on food can be higher. This reflects the fact that there is less competition among food sellers and that transport costs are higher for importing relatively small volumes of food from external suppliers. Local shortfalls in agricultural production have three main effects: 1) less local food is available, so food prices rise as more imports are brought in; 2) the range of available food types is reduced, which affects nutrition; 3) incomes fall for farmers and farm workers, leading to higher poverty and less food being consumed (increasing hunger).

Remote rural regions

These regions are located far from major urban agglomerations, with tenuous connections to urban centres and global markets. They typically cover large areas, with scattered, small settlements and a narrow economic base highly specialised in natural resource production for export. While the natural resource sector may be well integrated into global markets, the rest of the regional economy and society has only weak ties to the external economy and society. These regions tend to be divided into those that are highly dependent on farming as a source of livelihood and those where farming is a minor activity. The farming-dependent regions show a further dichotomy between poorly integrated regions where farming remains either a subsistence or semi-subsistence activity and regions where farming is highly specialised in the production of a major export crop that has little or no food potential, such as cotton, or is limited in its food value, such as coffee.

All three types of remote rural regions are potentially at risk of food insecurity. Those that produce non-agricultural products rely on imported food, and access to food can be limited by transport restrictions, weak connectivity to external markets or by a decline in incomes if the resource price falls. Those that produce a single agricultural commodity for export have the same problem as the previous group. Those that have a subsistence or semi-subsistence agriculture that provides a variety of foods face the problem of supply shocks that can reduce production. Meanwhile, they have few connections to the market economy and little ability to purchase food, even if it can be made available. By definition, subsistence farms tend to produce little more than the household's immediate needs, even when output is close to the expected level.

In remote rural regions, food imports are expensive, due to weak transport links, the limited quantities sold (high fixed costs) and lack of competition among food vendors. Unless incomes are high in the resource industry, the share of food in household budgets can be large even in good economic times. With limited food choices, malnutrition can be a problem even if food is sufficient to meet caloric requirements. In remote rural regions, food supply can be a major challenge, as can access to food. Moreover, because these regions have small populations that tend to be politically disenfranchised, they are not a high-priority constituency for national governments when food insecurity challenges emerge.

Linking food security, the stage of development and territorial differences

As the food security of households is explicitly linked to income (OECD, 2013b), by extension, the stage of development of a country or region will be an important consideration in developing appropriate FSN policy responses. For poor households, food consumption typically accounts for around half of all expenditures, making them particularly susceptible to price increases. Further, in rural areas, many of the households that are food insecure are also involved in agriculture, meaning that food markets have a dual role in providing both income and food for them. The development process for individual countries often involves expanding the role of markets and improving their functioning in several ways: improving framework institutional conditions (including strengthening property rights and the rule of law), and improving the functioning of markets, by improving the availability of information and enhancing competition. These developments, in turn, help provide more predictable and efficient price signals and better allow for the adjustment process to occur. Such developments can benefit both consuming households and agricultural producers. If such market developments are limited or weak, then countries and regions are, in turn, more likely to experience greater levels of food insecurity and malnutrition. The focus on promoting development includes strengthening networks of all types between urban and rural regions, and moving the rural economy from its reliance on subsistence agriculture to a broader range of economic functions that provide higher and more stable household incomes and greater access to purchased food. Other social and cultural factors are also important causes of food insecurity, in addition to the role of markets.

It is important to recognise that food insecurity and malnutrition are problems whose magnitude and consequences vary widely. It is precisely because there are many forms of FSN that it remains a problem in all countries, irrespective of their degree of development or the size of their agricultural sector. But the specific forms of food insecurity and malnutrition can vary systematically depending on the stage of development of a country and by the type of region within a country. In general, the frequency and intensity of food shortages declines as a country develops. This reflects better-functioning markets that are able to move food from region to region and higher levels of income that allow families to purchase enough food to survive. Similarly, Sen is famously quoted as saying that famines – the most severe form of food insecurity – do not occur in functioning democracies (Sen, 1999). His argument is that elected governments face electoral pressures, including criticism from the press, which prompts them to act to offset food shortfalls.

If famine is the most severe form of food insecurity, acute or severe hunger is the next most significant form. While not directly life-threatening, acute hunger leads to weakness that can impair the ability to work or study, affect the physical development of children and increase the adverse consequences of various diseases. Acute hunger is also accompanied by malnutrition because not only is the quantity of food inadequate, but the composition of the food available may be lacking in the specific attributes of a proper diet. Acute hunger is strongly associated with low incomes, whether in the form of earned income, some share of farm production or self-supply. And chronic hunger tends to reduce earning potential, because it is debilitating and restricts the ability to work.

Minor or chronic hunger and periodic hunger remain relatively common among the poorest in all countries, and can be more common in periods when food is expensive or scarce and when incomes are low and employment rates fall at times of economic crisis. What distinguishes the two is the duration of the event. Chronic hunger persists for an extended period, while periodic hunger is episodic and can be caused by seasonal food shortages, bouts of unemployment or when food prices rise. At times of periodic hunger, individuals may not be able to consume all the calories they need and are almost certain to have an unbalanced diet that can lead to longer-term adverse health consequences if food remains in short supply.

Finally, malnutrition refers to a diet that while providing sufficient calories for human survival does not provide the appropriate nutrients and other requirements to meet human needs. Increasingly, malnutrition is associated with obesity. It may reflect poor food choices made either out of necessity (the available mix of food is inadequate, or some foods are too expensive) or it may reflect poor choices by individuals (lack of understanding or concern with a balanced diet).

For OECD countries, famine has not been a problem in the recent past. It is rare for severe hunger to affect a large share of the populations of OECD member countries. However, chronic hunger and malnutrition remain significant issues in OECD countries. In most developing countries, even those with low income, famine is a rare phenomenon. When famine now occurs in the world, it largely reflects either a failed state where civil war or other conflict has destroyed both the economy and the ability of governments to respond to major food shortages (Gráda, 2010). However, severe hunger remains relatively common in many lower-income countries, as does chronic and episodic hunger and malnutrition.

Tables 1.4 and 1.5 provide a stylised perspective on how the various forms of food insecurity can be associated with the three standard OECD regional types. Table 1.3 examines the relationships for a lower-income developing economy where there are clear differences in the degree of market penetration and the role of market income between urban and more remote rural regions. Table 1.4 presents a typical high-income OECD country where market forces are relatively strong everywhere, but rural regions continue to face problems of food availability and access due to distance, density and lack of critical mass. This can lead to more truncated local economies, greater vulnerability to income and employment shocks, more limited and costly access to public services, and higher transport costs.

Table 1.3. **Forms of food insecurity in a low-income developing country**

Forms of food insecurity	Type of region		
	Metropolitan	Adjacent	Remote
Malnutrition	Common among those with lower incomes, whether due to financial constraints, limited choices or bad nutritional choices	Very common – diet can be limited in quality and quantity due to high reliance on locally produced food	Very common – diet can be limited in quality and quantity due to high reliance on locally produced food
Minor hunger	Common among the very poorest – low-income	Common among the very poorest – low-income Farm families of limited resources are regularly exposed	Common among the very poorest – low-income Farm families of limited resources are regularly exposed
Severe hunger	May exist on a seasonal basis or in a period of low income	May exist on a seasonal basis or during periods of low income	May exist on a seasonal basis or during periods of low income Hunger can be exacerbated by weak market connections that limit food imports
Famine	Extremely rare	Rare – mainly due to civil disruption	Less rare, but not common – due to civil disruption or natural disaster that blocks imports

Note: The forms of food insecurity described in the table are qualitative descriptions based on the literature, not statistical ones.

Source: Own elaboration.

The metropolitan column of Table 1.3 suggests that the most debilitating forms of food insecurity – famine and acute or severe hunger – are not common in large urban regions of lower-income countries. However, less acute forms of food insecurity – minor or chronic hunger and malnutrition – are common among the poorer urban population. In adjacent rural regions, the relatively high level of connectivity with the market economy of nearby urban regions and the existence of good transport infrastructure allows food imports in almost all periods. With a fairly strong local economy, most people have sufficient earned income to ensure that acute hunger is rare, even though there may be significant intervals of chronic hunger if the regional economy declines. In remote rural regions, food insecurity can be common, including periods of acute hunger. This largely reflects a weak rural economy that offers a narrow range of employment opportunities and is subject to considerable income instability. When markets for food, labour and other items are limited in scope and transport infrastructure is weak, households become isolated from buffering mechanisms and can face periods of hunger and extended periods of malnutrition.

Table 1.4. **Forms of food insecurity in a high-income developed country (OECD)**

Forms of food insecurity	Type of region		
	Metropolitan	Adjacent	Remote
Malnutrition	Common among the poor – due to low incomes, lack of choice (food deserts) and bad choices	Common among the poor – due to low incomes, lack of choice (food deserts) and bad choices	Common among the poor – due to low incomes, lack of choice (long transport distance) and bad choices
Minor hunger	Common among the very poorest – low income	Common among the very poor – low income limits purchases Farm families of limited resources can be exposed	Common among very poorest – low income limits purchases Farm families of limited resources can be exposed
Severe hunger	Rare	Rare	Rare
Famine	Extremely rare	Extremely rare	Rare – politically generated

Note: The forms of food insecurity described in the table are qualitative descriptions based on the literature and not statistical.

Source: Own elaboration.

The columns of Table 1.4 correspond to the columns of Table 1.3, but the main difference is that the incidence of the various forms of food insecurity is lower, especially for rural remote regions. Arguably, the process of economic development involves expansion of the market economy and increasing access to employment and earned income that makes it consistently possible to purchase food. Income diversification, coupled with other aspects of development, such as improved government service provision (in terms of health, education and sanitation, for example), are all critical elements in improving food security (OECD, 2013b). In Table 1.3, these benefits were in place for most urban households, but were limited in rural remote regions. By contrast, in OECD countries, market integration has largely occurred in all regions. One aspect of this is that self-supply plays a minor role in almost all households, and the prevalence of food markets makes restricted access to food an income problem and not an availability problem. Thus, food security concerns are in all regions highly correlated with income levels, not just for individual households, but also at the community level.

The range of food varieties and the level of food prices can vary considerably between richer and poorer communities. In rich communities, the presence of people with high incomes induces greater competition among food retailers and thus, more variety and lower prices. Conversely, in poor communities, low household incomes lead to few providers of food and limited choices at high prices. This problem is exacerbated by the high share of income spent on food in low-income households and the competing needs of buying food and paying for other major household expenses such as rent, health care costs and transport to work.

Integrated policies to address food security and nutrition

Policies to address FSN depend strongly on the ability to increase the availability of locally produced food, to encourage stronger connections to import food and to increase incomes to allow greater access to food. All three can be seen as components of a broader economic development strategy that has an explicit food dimension. Importantly, the basic principles for defining a territorially based food security programme should follow the framework of the OECD New Regional Policy.

For lower-income countries in both types of rural regions, increasing the availability of locally produced food can provide some useful food availability improvements. However, the main benefit of increasing the supply of locally produced food is that it improves the incomes of farm households, and can allow them to move from a subsistence form of agriculture to one that is integrated into markets. With greater market income, the family has income to buy other goods and services and to deal with seasonal shortages of food. Higher levels of farm income make it potentially possible to expand into other sectors, including retail, services and rural manufacturing, and to improve trade flows into and out of the region. In short, bringing farmers deeper into the market economy can offer both food security benefits and help achieve broader rural development goals.

Increasing access to imported food is vital for all types of regions, since a broader range of food sources offers both greater certainty that food can be obtained and increases competition among potential suppliers, which can lead to lower prices for imported food. For the poor, lower-priced food offers an important benefit, given that a higher share of their income is spent on food. Increasing access to external food supplies requires improvements in transport infrastructure, strengthening of external market relations and improvements in local incomes. Physical connectivity improvements can lower the cost of shipping food, which lowers its local price, and can also improve the response to food shortages, making temporary supply interruptions uncommon. Creating a strong network between external food providers and local retailers is also important to ensure a responsive system that operates with efficient prices. Finally, higher local incomes are needed to create the incentive to construct a food supply system with strong linkages to external markets. While it may be possible to provide emergency food relief through NGOs or governments in regions with low incomes, there will be no incentive for traders to establish markets that are linked to external suppliers without the possibility of being able to profit from strong sales.

Higher incomes for both food producers and for other residents in a region are vital for addressing food insecurity and malnutrition in all its forms. In market economies, "effective demand" rations goods and services to those with the capacity to pay for them. Over time, higher incomes are signals to increase the supply of goods, including food, since they lead to higher prices, which in turn lead to decisions to increase production. In urban regions in particular, the main factor in FSN problems is low income that limits access. However, in rural regions, low incomes result not only in a lack of access to imported food, but, in the case of farm households, deter investments that could increase the local supply of food. Clearly, the best way to increase local incomes is by expanding opportunities for employment, whether self-employment or wage employment. In this respect, broad rural development strategies linked to agricultural development strategies, where appropriate, can lead to greater food security and to a region's improved economic performance.

The role of policy: Towards a territorial approach to food security and nutrition

In the last few decades, greater awareness of the changes affecting emerging and developing economies, and their rural regions, have led to renewed attempts to formulate more effective development strategies. A clear convergence is emerging in which more holistic, territorial approaches to FSN and rural development have become a bigger part of the discussion (Schejtman and Berdegué, 2008). This growing acceptance of territorial, place-based approaches can be seen as a response to growing recognition of the diversity of FSN and poverty challenges globally, nationally, and, importantly, across regions. Development policies should more fully account for heterogeneous characteristics across territories and communities. This implies mobilising the local endogenous potential of places, actors and activities, and building broader and deeper linkages beyond the boundaries of the system (Ambrosio-Albalá and Bastiaensen, 2010). Territorial approaches place the functioning of institutions (formal and informal) at the core of development initiatives and require strong local participation and representation in the policy process. This calls for strong vertical and horizontal co-ordination in the formulation of local priorities.

This new conjuncture requires policy responses that are multidimensional in character, principally in three key areas. First, addressing FSN requires an approach that views the term comprehensively, taking into account the four dimensions of availability, access, utilisation and stability. Second, there is a need to integrate agendas for both competitiveness and social inclusion at the level of economic regions, to target these issues in the most inclusive and efficient ways possible. Third, these policies should be spatially integrated, allowing sub-national authorities to be pro-active in the design and delivery of development strategies, but in ways that do not ignore the importance of multi-level co-ordination and the regulatory role of central governments.

In short, this means broadening the focus of contemporary economic development strategies beyond urbanisation to include local economic development in rural regions, with a strong emphasis on understanding the interconnections among urban and rural regions. One of the principal virtues of a territorial approach to development is that it can be applied to virtually every territory, regardless of initial conditions. Thanks to its bottom-up nature, it may then generate social and economic benefits.

The linkages between food insecurity and malnutrition and conventional economic development objectives are strong and flow in both directions. A food-insecure population results in a workforce that has difficulty in carrying out its tasks, and children who have difficulty in learning. Similarly, in the absence of a strong and diversified local economy with good connections to other markets, the local populations will have difficulty in purchasing food. In many cases it will be difficult to move emergency food supplies into the region, because transport connections and market links are weak. Moreover, the four key challenges for implementing a spatially nuanced policy to address food insecurity and malnutrition are precisely the challenges facing efforts to implement a bottom-up regional policy. This requires identifying local impediments and opportunities for growth and engaging the local population as key actors in bringing about change.

Table 1.5. **The territorial approach to food security and nutrition policy**

	Traditional (old) approach to food security and nutrition	"New" territorial approach to food security and nutrition policy
Objectives	Providing relief to citizens suffering from food insecurity and malnutrition	A sustainable development solution to food insecurity and malnutrition
Key target sector	Increasing food production and improving productivity of (small-scale) agriculture	Various sectors of rural economies (i.e. rural tourism, manufacturing, ICT industry, etc.)
Main tools	Subsidies – (e.g. conditional cash transfers)	Investment in development opportunities (knowledge pooling, piloting, policy complementarities between social and competitiveness agenda)
Key actors	National governments and donor agencies	All levels of government (national, regional and local), various local stakeholders (public, private, non-governmental organisations), international co-operation
Target geography	Urban and rural areas are addressed by different policy approaches and are often disconnected.	Recognises and capitalises on the benefits of urban-rural linkages

Source: Own elaboration.

References

AfDB/OECD/UNDP (2015), *African Economic Outlook 2015: Regional Development and Spatial Inclusion*, OECD Publishing, Paris, http://dx.doi.org/10.1787/aeo-2015-en.

Akpan, N.S. (2012), "Rural development in Nigeria: A review of pre- and post-independence practice", *Journal of Sociological Research*, Vol. 3/2, pp. 146-159, http://dx.doi.org/10.5296/jsr.v3i2.2302.

Alkire, S. et al. (2014), "Poverty in rural and urban areas: Direct comparisons using the global MPI 2014", *OPHI Brief*, No. 24, Oxford Poverty & Human Development Initiative, Oxford, www.ophi.org.uk/poverty-in-rural-and-urban-areas.

Alvergne, C. (2008), "Le défi des territoires: Comment dépasser les disparités spatiales en Afrique de l'Ouest et du Centre", Karthala, Paris.

Ambrosio-Albalá, M. and J. Bastiaensen (2010), "The new territorial paradigm of rural development: Theoretical foundations from systems and institutional theories", *IOB Discussion Paper 2010-02*, University of Antwerp, Belgium, available at: www.ua.ac.be/objs/00251118.pdf.

Anríquez, G. and R. López (2007), "Agricultural growth and poverty in an archetypical middle-income country: Chile 1987-2003", *Agricultural Economics*, Vol. 36/2, pp. 191-202, http://dx.doi.org/10.1111/j.1574-0862.2007.00198.x.

Anríquez, G. and K. Stamoulis (2007), "Rural development and poverty reduction: Is agriculture still the key?", *ESA Working Paper*, No. 07-02, Food and Agriculture Organization, Rome, available at: www.fao.org/3/a-ah885e.pdf.

Babatunde, R.O. and M. Qaim (2010), "Impacts of off-farm income on food security and nutrition in Nigeria", *Food Policy*, Vol. 35/4, pp. 303-311, http://dx.doi.org/10.1016/j.foodpol.2010.01.006.

Barca, F. (2009), "An agenda for a reformed cohesion policy: A place-based approach to meeting European Union challenges and expectations", independent report prepared at the request of Danuta Hübner, Commissioner for Regional Policy, available at: www.europarl.europa.eu/meetdocs/2009_2014/documents/regi/dv/barca_report_/barca_report_en.pdf.

Barca, F., P. McCann and A. Rodríguez-Pose (2012), "The case for regional development intervention: Place-based versus place-neutral approaches", *Journal of Regional Science*, Vol. 52/1, pp. 134-152, http://dx.doi.org/10.1111/j.1467-9787.2011.00756.x.

Bardhan, P. and D. Mookherjee (2006), "Decentralization, corruption, and government accountability", Chapter 6 in: Rose-Ackerman, S. (ed.), *International Handbook on the Economics of Corruption*, Edward Elgar Publishing Limited, UK, pp. 161-188.

Barrett, C.B., T. Reardon and P. Webb (2001), "Nonfarm income diversification and household livelihood strategies in rural Africa: Concepts, dynamics, and policy implications", *Food Policy*, Vol. 26/4, pp. 315-331, http://dx.doi.org/10.1016/S0306-9192(01)00014-8.

Bebbington, A., R. Abramovay and M. Chiriboga (2008), "Social movements and the dynamics of rural territorial development in Latin America", *World Development*, Vol. 36/12, "Special Section: Social Movements and the Dynamics of Rural Development in Latin America", pp. 2 874-2 887, http://dx.doi.org/10.1016/j.worlddev.2007.11.017.

Berdegué, J.A. et al. (2000), "Policies to promote non-farm rural employment in Latin America", *Natural Resource Perspectives*, No. 55, June, ODI, available at: www.odi.org/sites/odi.org.uk/files/odi-assets/publications-opinion-files/1953.pdf.

Bezemer, D. and D. Headey (2008), "Agriculture, development, and urban bias", *World Development*, Vol. 36/8, pp. 1 342-1 364, http://dx.doi.org/10.1016/j.worlddev.2007.07.001.

Bommarco, R., D. Kleijn and S.G. Potts (2013), "Ecological intensification: Harnessing ecosystem services for food security", *Trends in Ecology and Evolution*, Vol. 28/4, pp. 230-238, http://dx.doi.org/10.1016/j.tree.2012.10.012.

Brenner, N. (2004), *New State Spaces: Urban Governance and the Rescaling of Statehood*, Oxford University Press, Oxford, United Kingdom.

Brooks, J., D. Cervantes-Godoy and E. Jonasson (2009), "Strategies for smallholders in developing countries: Commercialisation, diversification and exit", European Association of Agricultural Economists 111th seminar, "Small Farms: Decline or Persistence", 26-27 June, University of Kent, Canterbury, United Kingdom, available at: http://purl.umn.edu/52867.

Bryceson, D.F. (2002), "The scramble in Africa: Reorienting rural livelihoods", *World Development*, Vol. 30/5, pp. 725-739, http://dx.doi.org/10.1016/S0305-750X(02)00006-2.

Byerlee, D., A. de Janvry and E. Sadoulet (2009), "Agriculture for development: Toward a new paradigm", *Annual Review of Resource Economics*, Vol. 1/1, pp. 15-31, http://dx.doi.org/10.1146/annurev.resource.050708.144239.

CFS (2012), "Coming to terms with terminology", Committee on World Food Security, 39th Session, 15-20 October, Rome, available at: www.fao.org/fsnforum/sites/default/files/file/Terminology/MD776(CFS___Coming_to_terms_with_Terminology).pdf.

Chang, H.H. and M. Mishra (2008), "Impact of off-farm labor supply on food expenditures of the farm household", *Food Policy*, Vol. 33/6, pp. 657-664, http://dx.doi.org/10.1016/j.foodpol.2008.02.002.

Charbit, C. and M. Michalun (2009), "Mind the gaps: Managing mutual dependence in relations among levels of government", *OECD Working Papers on Public Governance* No. 14, OECD Publishing, Paris, http://dx.doi.org/10.1787/221253707200.

Chawanote, C. and C.B. Barrett (2011), "Rural non-farm dynamics: Occupational ladders and earnings mobility in Thailand", Agricultural and Applied Economics Association, 2011 Annual Meeting, 24-26 July, Pittsburgh, Pennsylvania, http://purl.umn.edu/103879.

Christiaensen, L., L. Demery and J. Kuhl (2011), "The (evolving) role of agriculture in poverty reduction: An empirical perspective", *Journal of Development Economics*, Vol. 96/2, pp. 239-254.

Cistulli, V. et al. (2014), "Addressing food security and nutrition by means of a territorial approach", *Food Security*, Vol. 6/6, pp. 879-894, http://dx.doi.org/10.1007/s12571-014-0395-8.

De Ferranti, D.M. et al. (2005), *Beyond the City: The Rural Contribution to Development*, World Bank, Washington, DC, available at: https://openknowledge.worldbank.org/bitstream/handle/10986/7328/32333.pdf;jsessionid=C25602BCCCF171AE857017211DE3FF01?sequence=1.

De Janvry, A. and E. Sadoulet (2001), "Income strategies among rural households in Mexico: The role of off-farm activities", *World Development*, Vol. 29/3, pp. 467-480, http://dx.doi.org/10.1016/S0305-750X(00)00113-3.

De Luca, L. et al. (2012), *Unleashing the Potential for Rural Development through Decent Work: Building on the ILO Rural Work Legacy 1970s-2011*, International Labour Organization, Geneva, available at: www.ilo.org/employment/units/rural-development/WCMS_176668/lang--en/index.htm.

Dercon, S. (2009), "Rural poverty: Old challenges in new contexts", *The World Bank Research Observer*, Vol. 24/1, pp. 1-28, available at: http://elibrary.worldbank.org/doi/abs/10.1093/wbro/lkp003?journalCode=wbro.

Dercon, S. and J. Hoddinot (2005), "Livelihoods, growth, and links to market towns in 15 Ethiopian villages", *FCND Discussion Paper*, No. 194, International Food Policy Research Institute, Washington, DC, available at: http://ebrary.ifpri.org/cdm/ref/collection/p15738coll2/id/62391.

Dirven, M. (2011), "Non-farm rural employment and rural poverty reduction: What we know in Latin America in 2010", paper presented at the International Fund for Agricultural Development Conference on New Directions for Smallholder Agriculture, available at: www.ifad.org/documents/10180/3ce3eed2-8aa4-45b6-b878-fd8e8d934a6c.

Duranton, G. and D. Puga (2004), "Micro-foundations of urban agglomeration economies", Chapter 48 in: *Handbook of Regional and Urban Economics*, Vol. 4, pp. 2 063-2 117.

Duranton, G. and D. Puga (2000), "Diversity and specialisation in cities: Why, where and when does it matter?", *Urban Studies*, Vol. 37/3, pp. 533-555.

Ellis, F. and S. Biggs (2002), "Evolving themes in rural development 1950s-2000s", *Development Policy Review*, Special Issue: Rethinking Rural Development, Vol. 19/4, pp. 437-448, http://dx.doi.org/10.1111/1467-7679.00143.

Ezcurra, R. and A. Rodríguez-Pose (2013), "Does economic globalization affect regional inequality? A cross-country analysis", *World Development*, Vol. 52, pp. 92-103, http://dx.doi.org/10.1016/j.worlddev.2013.07.002.

Faiguenbaum, S., J.A. Berdegué and T. Reardon (2002), "The rapid rise of supermarkets in Chile and its effects on the dairy, vegetable and beef chains", *Development Policy Review*, Vol. 20/4, Special Issue: Supermarkets and Agrifood Systems: Latin American Challenges, pp. 459-471, http://dx.doi.org/10.1111/1467-7679.00183.

FAO (2013), "Our priorities: The FAO strategic objectives", Food and Agriculture Organization, Rome, available at: www.fao.org/docrep/018/mi317e/mi317e.pdf.

FAO (2012a), *The State of Food Insecurity in the World 2012: Economic Growth is Necessary but not Sufficient to Accelerate Reduction of Hunger and Malnutrition*, Food and Agriculture Organization, Rome, available at: www.fao.org/docrep/016/i3027e/i3027e.pdf.

FAO (2012b), *Proceedings: International Scientific Symposium on Food and Nutrition Security information: From Valid Measurement to Effective Decision Making*, 17-19 January 2012, Food and Agriculture Organization, Rome, available at: www.fao.org/docrep/017/i3244e/i3244e.pdf.

FAO (2010), *The State of Food Insecurity in the World: Addressing Food Insecurity in Protracted Crises*, Food and Agriculture Organization, Rome, available at: www.fao.org/docrep/013/i1683e/i1683e.pdf.

FAO (2006), "Food security", *Policy Brief*, June, Issue 2, Food and Agriculture Organization, Rome, available at: www.fao.org/forestry/13128-0e6f36f27e0091055bec28ebe830f46b3.pdf.

FAO, IFAD and WFP (2015), *The State of Food Insecurity in the World 2015: Meeting the 2015 International Hunger Targets: Taking Stock of Uneven Progress*, Food and Agriculture Organization, Rome, available at: www.fao.org/3/a-i4646e.pdf.

Frenken, K., F. Van Oort and T. Verburg (2007), "Related variety, unrelated variety and regional economic growth", *Regional Studies*, Vol. 41/5, pp. 685-697.

Freudenburg, W.R. (1992), "Addictive economies: Extractive industries and vulnerable localities in a changing world economy", *Rural Sociology*, Vol. 57/3, pp. 305-332, http://dx.doi.org/10.1111/j.1549-0831.1992.tb00467.x.

Gennaioli, N. et al. (2014), "Growth in regions", *Journal of Economic Growth*, Vol. 19/3, pp. 259-309, http://dx.doi.org/10.1007/s10887-014-9105-9.

Glaeser, E.L. (1999), "Learning in cities", *Journal of Urban Economics*, Vol. 46/2, pp. 254-277.

Grassini, P., K.M. Eskridge and K.G. Cassman (2013), "Distinguishing between yield advances and yield plateaus in historical crop production trends", *Nature Communications*, Vol. 4, pp. 2 918-2 928, http://dx.doi.org/10.1038/ncomms3918.

Gutman, G.E. (1999), "Desregulación, apertura commercial y reestructuracion industrial: La industria lacteal en argentina en la decada de los noventa", in: *La desregulación de los mercados: Paradigmas e inequidades de las politicas del neoliberalismo*, edited by D. Aspiazu, G.E.

Haggblade, S., P. Hazell and T. Reardon (eds.) (2007), *Transforming the Rural Non-Farm Economy*, John Hopkins University Press, Baltimore, Maryland.

Harrison, A. (2006), "Globalization and poverty", *NBER Working Paper*, No. 12 347, http://dx.doi.org/10.3386/w12347.

Hazell, P. (2007), "Transformations in agriculture and their implications for rural development", *Journal of Agricultural and Development Economics*, Vol. 4/1, pp. 47-65.

Hazell, P. and S. Wood (2008), "Drivers of change in global agriculture", *Philosophical Transactions of the Royal Society B*, Vol. 363/1 491, pp. 495-515, http://dx.doi.org/10.1098/rstb.2007.2166.

Hazell, P. et al. (2010), "The future of small farms: Trajectories and policy priorities", *World Development*, Vol. 38/10, pp. 1 349-1 361, http://dx.doi.org/10.1016/j.worlddev.2009.06.012.

Hewings, G. (2004), "Overview of regional development issues", paper presented at the 10th annual World Bank conference on development in Latin America and the Caribbean, San Jose, Costa Rica.

Hirschman, A.O. (1958), *The Strategy of Economic Development*, Yale University Press, New Haven, Connecticut.

IFAD (2010), *Rural Poverty Report 2011*, International Fund for Agricultural Development, Rome, available at: www.ifad.org/documents/10180/c47f2607-3fb9-4736-8e6a-a7ccf3dc7c5b.

Imai, K.S., R. Gaiha and G. Thapa (2012), "Does non-farm sector employment reduce rural poverty and vulnerability? Evidence from Vietnam and India", *Economics Discussion Paper Series*, EDP-1226, University of Manchester.

Ivanic, M., W. Martin and H. Zaman (2012), "Estimating the short-run poverty impacts of the 2010-11 surge in food prices", *World Development*, Vol. 40/11, pp. 2 302-2 317.

Jerve, A.M. (2001), "Rural-urban linkages and poverty analysis", Chapter 4 in: UNDP (eds.), *Choices for the Poor: Lessons from National Poverty Strategies*, CMI/UNDP, New York.

Justino, P., J. Litchfield and Y. Niimi (2004), "Multidimensional inequality: An empirical application to Brazil", *PRUS Working Paper*, No. 24, Poverty Research Unit at Sussex, Department of Economics, University of Sussex, Brighton, United Kingdom, available at: www.sussex.ac.uk/webteam/gateway/file.php?name=wp24.pdf&site=260.

Kaur, S. et al. (2011), "Prospects of non-farm employment and welfare in rural areas", *Handbook of South Asian Economics*, Routledge, London and New York.

Kraybill, D. and M. Kilkenny (2003), "Economic rationales for and against place-based policies", AAEA-RSS Annual Meeting, Montreal, pp. 27-30.

Lal, R. (2004), "Soil carbon sequestration impacts on global climate change and food security", *Science*, Vol. 304/5 677, pp. 1 623-1 627, http://dx.doi.org/10.1126/science.1097396.

Lanjouw, P. (2001), "Nonfarm employment and poverty in rural El Salvador", *World Development*, Vol. 29, No. 3, pp. 529-547.

Lanjouw, J. and P. Lanjouw (2001), "The rural non-farm sector: Issues and evidence from developing countries", *Agricultural Economics*, Vol. 26/1, pp. 1-23, http://dx.doi.org/10.1016/S0169-5150(00)00104-3.

Lewis, W.A. (1954), "Economic development with unlimited supplies of labour", *The Manchester School*, Vol. 22/2, pp. 139-191, http://dx.doi.org/10.1111/j.1467-9957.1954.tb00021.x.

Lohmann, C. and I. Liefner (2009), "Location, non-agricultural employment, and vulnerability to poverty in rural Thailand", *Erdkunde*, Vol. 63/2, pp. 141-160, www.jstor.org/stable/25648199.

Mansuri, G. and V. Rao (2004), "Community-based and-driven development: A critical review", *The World Bank Research Observer*, Vol. 19/1, pp. 1-39.

Marta, S. (2013), "Innovative regional development theories and policies for food and nutrition security", *Quaderni del Dipartimento di Scienze Economiche e Sociali (DISCE)*, No. 1 392.

Mazoyer, M. and L. Roudart (2006), *A History of World Agriculture: From the Neolithic Age to the Current Crisis*, Earthscan, London.

McCann, P. (2008), "Globalization and economic geography: The world is curved, not flat", *Cambridge Journal of Regions, Economy and Society*, Vol. 1/3, pp. 351-370, http://dx.doi.org/10.1093/cjres/rsn002.

McCann, P. and A. Rodríguez-Pose (2011), "Why and when development policy should be place-based", *OECD Regional Outlook 2011: Building Resilient Regions for Stronger Economies*, OECD Publishing, Paris, http://dx.doi.org/10.1787/9789264120983-16-en.

McGuire, J.W. (2011), "Social policies in Latin America: Causes, characteristics, and consequences", *ACSPL Working Paper Series*, Vol. 1, Article 1, pp. 1-53, http://wesscholar.wesleyan.edu/wps/vol1/iss1/1.

Meso, P. et al. (2006), "Information infrastructure, governance, and socio-economic development in developing countries", *European Journal of Information Systems*, Vol. 18/1, pp. 52-65, http://dx.Doi.org/10.1057/ejis.2008.56.

Misselhorn, A. et al. (2012), "A vision for attaining food security", *Current Opinion in Environmental Sustainability*, Vol. 4/1, pp. 7-17, http://dx.doi.org/10.1016/j.cosust.2012.01.008.

Myrdal (1957), *Rich Lands and Poor*, monograph.

Nel, E. (2004), "Local development initiatives: A new development paradigm for urban areas an assessment with reference to Stutterheim", *Development Southern Africa*, Vol. 11/3, pp. 363-378.

North, D.C. (1990), *Institutions, Institutional Change and Economic Performance*, Cambridge University Press, United Kingdom.

OECD (forthcoming *a*), *Better Policies for Development*, OECD Publishing, Paris.

OECD (forthcoming *b*), *OECD Regional Outlook 2016*, OECD Publishing, Paris.

OECD (forthcoming *c*), *OECD Territorial Review of Peru 2016*, OECD Publishing, Paris.

OECD (2016), *A New Rural Development Paradigm for the 21st Century: A Toolkit for Developing Countries*, Development Centre Studies, OECD Publishing, Paris, http://dx.doi.org/10.1787/9789264252271-en.

OECD (2015), *The Metropolitan Century: Understanding Urbanisation and its Consequences*, OECD Publishing, Paris, http://dx.doi.org/10.1787/9789264228733-en.

OECD (2014), *OECD Territorial Reviews: Colombia 2014*, OECD Publishing, Paris, http://dx.doi.org/10.1787/9789264224551-en.

OECD (2013a), *Rural-Urban Partnerships An Integrated Approach to Economic Development*, OECD Publishing, Paris, http://dx.doi.org/10.1787/9789264204812-en.

OECD (2013b), *Global Food Security: Challenges for the Food and Agricultural System*, OECD Publishing, Paris, http://dx.doi.org/10.1787/9789264195363-en.

OECD (2011), *Water Governance in OECD Countries: A Multi-level Approach*, OECD Studies on Water, OECD Publishing, Paris, http://dx.doi.org/10.1787/9789264119284-en.

OECD (2010), "Agricultural policies and rural development: A synthesis of recent OECD work", OECD, Paris, available at: www.oecd.org/agriculture/44561502.pdf.

OECD (2009a), *How Regions Grow: Trends and Analysis*, OECD Publishing, Paris, http://dx.doi.org/10.1787/9789264039469-en.

OECD (2009b), *OECD Economic Outlook*, OECD Publishing, Paris, http://dx.doi.org/10.1787/eco_outlook-v2008-sup2-en.

OECD (2006), *The New Rural Paradigm: Policies and Governance*, OECD Publishing, Paris, http://dx.doi.org/10.1787/9789264023918-en.

OECD and FAO (2010), *OECD-FAO Agricultural Outlook* 2010-2019, OECD Publishing, Paris, http://dx.doi.org/10.1787/agr_outlook-2010-en.

Gráda, C.Ó. (2011), "Famines past, famine's future", *Development and Change*, Vol. 42/1, pp. 49-69.

Olinto, P. et al. (2013), "The state of the poor: Where are the poor, where is extreme poverty harder to end, and what is the current profile of the world's poor?, *Economic Premise*, No. 125, World Bank, Washington, DC, available at: http://siteresources.worldbank.org/EXTPREMNET/Resources/EP125.pdf.

Osmani, S.R. (2005), "The impact of globalization on poverty in Bangladesh", *Policy Integration Department Working Paper*, No. 65, International Labour Organization, Geneva, available at: www.ilo.int/wcmsp5/groups/public/---dgreports/---integration/documents/publication/wcms_079177.pdf.

Ostry, J.D., A. Berg and C.G. Tsangarides (2014), "Redistribution, inequality, and growth", *IMF Staff Discussion Notes*, International Monetary Fund, Washington, DC, available at: www.imf.org/external/pubs/ft/sdn/2014/sdn1402.pdf.

Parkinson, M. et al. (2012), "Second-tier cities in Europe: In an age of austerity, why invest beyond the capitals?", Liverpool John Moores University, Liverpool, United Kingdom.

Partridge, M.D. and D.S. Rickman (2008), "Place-based policy and rural poverty: Insights from the urban spatial mismatch literature", *Cambridge Journal of Regions, Economy and Society*, Vol. 1/1, pp. 131-156, http://dx.doi.org/10.1093/cjres/rsm005.

Peck, J. and E. Sheppard (2010), "Worlds apart? Engaging with the World Development Report 2009: Reshaping economic geography", *Economic Geography*, Vol. 86/4, pp. 331-340, http://dx.doi.org/10.1111/j.1944-8287.2010.01093.x.

Piketty, T. (2014), *Capital in the Twenty-First Century*, Harvard University Press, Cambridge, Massachusetts.

Pingali, P., K. Stamoulis and R. Stringer (2006), "Eradicating extreme poverty and hunger: Towards a coherent policy agenda", *ESA Working Paper*, No. 06-01, Food and Agriculture Organization, Rome.

Pinstrup-Andersen, P. (2009), "Food security: Definition and measurement", *Food Security*, Vol. 1/1, pp. 5-7, http://dx.doi.org/10.1007/s12571-008-0002-y.

Pisani, E. and G. Franceschelli (2011), "Territorial approaches for rural development in Latin America: A case study in Chile", *Revista de la Facultad de Ciencias Agrarias, Universidad Nacional de Cuyo*, Vol. 43/1, pp. 201-218, http://revista.fca.uncu.edu.ar/images/stories/pdfs/2011-01/T43_14_Pisani.pdf.

Porter, M.E. (2000), "Location, competition, and economic development: Local clusters in a global economy", *Economic Development Quarterly*, Vol. 14/1, pp. 15-34, http://dx.doi.org/10.1177/089124240001400105.

Pretty, J. (2008), "Agricultural sustainability: Concepts, principles and evidence", *Philosophical Transactions of the Royal Society B*, Vol. 363/1 491, pp. 447-465, http://dx.doi.org/10.1098/rstb.2007.2163.

Ravallion, M., S. Chen and P. Sangraula (2007), "New evidence on the urbanization of global poverty", *Population and Development Review*, Vol. 33/4, pp. 667-702, http://dx.doi.org/10.1111/j.1728-4457.2007.00193.x.

Reardon, T. and C.P. Timmer (2007), "Transformation of markets for agricultural output in developing countries since 1950: How has thinking changed?", Chapter 55 in: *Handbook of Agricultural Economics: Agricultural Development: Farmers, Farm Production and Farm Markets*, Vol. 3, pp. 2 807-2 855, http://dx.doi.org/10.1016/S1574-0072(06)03055-6.

Reardon, T., K. Stamoulis and P. Pingali (2007), "Rural nonfarm employment in developing countries in an era of globalization", *Agricultural Economics*, Vol. 37, Supplement s1, pp. 173-184, http://dx.doi.org/10.1111/j.1574-0862.2007.00243.x.

Reddy, D.N. et al. (2013), "Rural non-farm employment and rural transformation in India", International Crops Research Institute for the Semi-Arid Tropics, *Working Paper Series No. 57*, Telangana, India.

Reimer, B. and S. Markey (2008), "Place-based policy: A rural perspective", Human Resources and Social Development Canada, Ottawa, Ontario.

Rigg, J. (2006), "Land, farming, livelihoods, and poverty: Rethinking the links in the rural south", *World Development*, Vol. 34/1, pp. 180-202, http://dx.doi.org/10.1016/j.worlddev.2005.07.015.

Riley, L. and A. Legwegoh (2014), "Comparative urban food geographies in Blantyre and Gaborone", *African Geographical Review*, Vol. 33/1, pp. 52-66, http://dx.doi.org/10.1080/19376812.2013.805148.

Rodríguez-Pose, A. (2013), "Do institutions matter for regional development?", *Regional Studies*, Vol. 47/7, Special Issue: Theme Issue: Regions as Knowledge and Innovative Hubs, pp. 1 034-1 047, http://dx.doi.org/10.1080/00343404.2012.748978.

Rodríguez-Pose, A. (2012), "Trade and regional inequality", *Economic Geography*, Vol. 88/2, pp. 109-136, http://dx.doi.org/10.1111/j.1944-8287.2012.01147.x.

Rodríguez-Pose, A. (2010), "Economic geographers and the limelight: The reaction to the World Development Report 2009", *Economic Geography*, Vol. 86/4, pp. 361-370, http://dx.doi.org/10.1111/j.1944-8287.2010.01094.x.

Rodríguez-Pose, A. and D. Hardy (2015), "Addressing poverty and inequality in the rural economy from a global perspective", *Applied Geography*, Vol. 61, pp. 11-23, http://dx.doi.org/10.1016/j.apgeog.2015.02.005.

Rodríguez-Pose, A. and S.A.R. Tijmstra (2007), "Local economic development in sub-Saharan Africa", *Environment and Planning C: Government and Policy*, Vol. 25/4, pp. 516-536, http://dx.doi.org/10.1068/c5p.

Rodrik, D., A. Subramanian and F. Trebbi (2004), "Institutions rule: The primacy of institutions over geography and integration in economic development", *Journal of Economic Growth*, Vol. 9/2, pp. 131-165, http://dx.doi.org/10.1023/B:JOEG.0000031425.72248.85.

Rojas-Caldelas, R. et al. (2010), "Approaches to analysing the rural-urban interface: Comprehensive development views from town and countryside", in: *The Sustainable City VI: Urban Regeneration and Sustainability*, WIT Press, United Kingdom, pp. 359-370.

Sankhe, S. et al. (2010), *India's Urban Awakening: Building Inclusive Cities, Sustaining Economic Growth*, McKinsey Global Institute, Delhi, available at: www.mckinsey.com/global-themes/urbanization/urban-awakening-in-india.

Saxena, N.C. (2003), "The rural non-farm economy in India: Some policy issues", Rural Non-Farm Economy and Livelihood Enhancement, DFID-World Bank Collaborative Research Project, *National Resource Institute Report No. 2 752*, Natural Resources Institute, available at: http://projects.nri.org/rnfe/pub/papers/2752.pdf.

Schejtman, A. and J. Berdegué (2008), "Towards a territorial approach for rural development", *IPPG Discussion Paper Series*, No. 17, available at: www.ippg.org.uk/papers/dp17.pdf.

Scoones, I. (2009), "Livelihoods perspectives and rural development", *The Journal of Peasant Studies*, Vol. 36/1, pp. 171-196, http://dx.doi.org/10.1080/03066150902820503.

Scott, A.J. (2002), "Regional push: Towards a geography of development and growth in low- and middle-income countries", *Third World Quarterly*, Vol. 23/1, pp. 137-161, http://dx.doi.org/10.1080/01436590220108216.

Sen, A. (1999), "Democracy as a universal value", *Journal of Democracy*, Vol. 10/3, pp. 3-17.

Shi, X, N. Heerink and F. Qu (2007), "Choices between different off-farm employment sub-categories: An empirical analysis for Jiangxi Province, China", *China Economic Review*, Vol. 18/4, pp. 438-455, http://dx.doi.org/10.1016/j.chieco.2006.08.001.

Singh, I. (1990), *The Great Ascent: The Rural Poor in South Asia*, Johns Hopkins University Press, Baltimore, Maryland.

Storper, M. and A.J. Venables (2004), "Buzz: Face-to-face contact and the urban economy", *Journal of Economic Geography*, Vol. 4/4, pp. 351-370, http://dx.doi.org/10.1093/jnlecg/lbh027.

Tabellini, G. (2010), "Culture and institutions: Economic development in the regions of Europe", *Journal of the European Economic Association*, Vol. 8/4, pp. 677-716, http://dx.doi.org/10.1111/j.1542-4774.2010.tb00537.x.

Thirtle, C., L. Lin and J. Piesse (2003), "The impact of research-led agricultural productivity growth on poverty reduction in Africa, Asia, and Latin America", *World Development*, Vol. 31/12, pp. 1 959-1 975, http://dx.doi.org/10.1016/j.worlddev.2003.07.001.

Tilman, D. et al. (2011), "Global food demand and the sustainable intensification of agriculture", *Proceedings of the National Academy of Sciences*, Vol. 108/50, pp. 20 260-20 264, http://dx.doi.org/10.1073/pnas.1116437108.

Tomaney, J., A. Pike and A. Rodríguez-Pose (2010), "Local and regional development in times of crisis", *Environment and Planning A*, Vol. 42/4, pp. 771-779, http://dx.doi.org/10.1068/a43101.

UCFA (2010), "Updated comprehensive framework for action", United Nations High Level Task Force on the Global Food Security Crisis September, available at: www.fao.org/fileadmin/user_upload/ISFP/UCFA_Final.pdf.

UN (2013), "Millennium Development Goals fast sheet", United Nations, available at: www.un.org/millenniumgoals.

UNCTAD (2015), *The Least Developed Countries Report 2015: Transforming Rural Economies*, United Nations Conference on Trade and Development, http://unctad.org/en/pages/PublicationWebflyer.aspx?publicationid=1393.

UNDP (2015), *2014 Human Development Report: Sustaining Human Progress: Reducing Vulnerabilities and Building Resilience*, Human Development Report, United Nations Development Programme, New York, available at:www.undp.org/content/dam/undp/library/corporate/HDR/2014HDR/HDR-2014-English.pdf.

Valdés, A. and W. Foster (2010), "Reflections on the role of agriculture in pro-poor growth", *World Development*, Vol. 38/10, pp. 1 362-1 374.

Valdés, A., W. Foster and K. Wye (2005), "Reflections on the role of agriculture in pro-poor growth", paper prepared for the research workshop: The future of small farms, Wye College, Kent.

van der Ploeg, J.D. et al. (2000), "Rural development: From practices and policies towards theory", *Sociologia Ruralis*, Vol. 40/4, pp. 391-408, http://dx.doi.org/10.1111/1467-9523.00156.

World Bank (2009), *World Development Report 2009: Reshaping Economic Geography*, The World Bank, Washington, DC, available at: https://openknowledge.worldbank.org/handle/10986/5991.

World Bank (2007), *World Development Report 2008: Agriculture for Development*, The World Bank, Washington, DC, available at: https://openknowledge.worldbank.org/handle/10986/5990.

Chapter 2.

A territorial approach to food security and nutrition policy: The case of Cambodia

The Royal Government of Cambodia is committed to improve the food security and nutrition (FSN) situation in the country, and has put various policy mechanisms in place to deal with its multidimensional nature. Implementation has presented some challenges, most notably in ensuring that all regions and provinces benefit equally from the progress achieved to date. As things currently stand, FSN outcomes vary across regions and provinces, and the capacity to deal with territorial disparities is constrained by co-ordination failures and disconnects between various tiers of government, as well as between the many development organisations and non-governmental organisations operating in the country. Adopting a territorial approach would help to ensure that policies are delivered effectively to where they are most needed, and that policies and programmes are linked up to prevent fragmentation and duplication of efforts.

Key findings

The adoption of a territorial approach is likely to be a viable avenue for promoting a more even geographic distribution of the benefits of food security and nutrition (FSN) initiatives in Cambodia. Cambodia experienced considerable economic growth between the mid-1990s and 2007. Nevertheless, levels of poverty remain high, especially in rural areas. Moreover, there is considerable territorial variation in the prevalence of issues related to FSN.

The Royal Government of Cambodia has prioritised FSN, for example, making it the focus of a Cambodian Millennium Development Goal. The establishment of the Council for Agriculture and Rural Development and the Technical Working Group for Social Protection and Food Security and Nutrition as well as the formulation of the National Strategy for Food Security and Nutrition 2014-2018 reflect the government's commitment to eradicate issues of FSN.

The implementation of FSN strategies is, in practice, constrained by several factors. Among them are capacity constraints, co-ordination failures and disconnects between various tiers of government. A territorial approach would: ensure that FSN interventions are delivered at the sub-national level and reflect local conditions; promote the design of holistic and integrated approaches; improve inter-actor co-ordination and encourage synergies between FSN initiatives and other development interventions.

The issue of food security and nutrition in Cambodia

The overall food security and nutrition situation in Cambodia is improving

The Royal Government of Cambodia employs a multidimensional definition of FSN that is based on four core pillars: availability, access, use/utilisation and stability. The National Strategy for Food Security and Nutrition 2014-2018 has been developed in accordance with this approach, and states clearly that "by 2018, Cambodians will have substantially improved physical, social and economic access to sufficient, safe and nutritious food to meet their dietary needs and food preferences and optimise the utilisation of this food to keep a healthy and productive life". The strategy relies on in-depth analysis to contextualise and justify its FSN policies.

According to a recent assessment by the Ministry of Agriculture, Forest and Fisheries, Cambodia has achieved national food security at least in terms of availability and has produced quantities of rice that have matched or exceeded domestic demand (i.e. consumption) since 1995. Cambodia produces large surpluses of rice each year and is now one of the world's most prominent rice exporters: its rice surplus increased from 2.5 million tonnes in 2010 to around 3 million tonnes in 2013 and 2014 (Ministry of Agriculture, Forestry and Fisheries, 2015). At the sub-national level, the majority of Cambodia's 25 provinces and their capital cities achieved positive levels of rice production in 2012, 2013 and 2014. The only provinces that failed to do so were three of the country's less agriculturally oriented provinces: Phnom Penh, Koh Kong and Preah Sihanouk. In spite of this success, the benefits from rice production are not distributed evenly at the sub-national level. Inequality is acute in rural areas, where the majority of the individuals are smallholder farmers with limited land for production.

Cambodia is active in other types of agricultural production as well. It has the potential to produce fruit and vegetables, but in practice, its capacity to do so has been constrained by, among other things, inadequate infrastructure and the consequent inability to manage perishable produce. The implications of this are two-fold: 1) Cambodia imports large quantities (70% of supply) of fruits and vegetables (CARD, 2014a); and 2) Cambodians consume insufficient quantities of fruit and vegetables.[1] Cambodia's livestock sector, on the other hand, is better developed. The commercial poultry and pork production sectors have fared especially well in recent years. The livestock sector has benefited tremendously from both technical extension services and the provision of training and knowledge dissemination to farmers. Fishing and the collection of non-timber forest products also contribute to Cambodia's agricultural production.

The production of subsidiary and industrial crops by small-, medium- and large-scale farms has increased in recent years as well. Between 2009 and 2014, the number of hectares cultivated for the production of subsidiary and industrial crops increased from 669 990 to 953 597.

Per capita income in Cambodia increased from USD 248 to USD 1 117 between 1994 and 2015. This sizeable increase in gross domestic product (GDP) per capita has increased the average Cambodian's net purchasing power and has improved Cambodian households' access to food. Cambodia's economic growth is most immediately attributable to the recovery of its construction and tourism sectors, increases in the export of agricultural products and clothing exports. Not surprisingly, the country was adversely affected by the global financial crisis. The economy has, however, recovered and the pre-crisis economic growth trajectory has been restored. Economic growth has been accompanied by a sizeable reduction in poverty. In 2013, 18.8% of the population was living below the national poverty line. That said, close to 3 million Cambodians still live in poverty, 90% of them in the countryside (World Bank, 2015). A further 8.1 million people remain classified as "near poor" (i.e. living just above the poverty line) and are therefore at risk of falling back into poverty. While considerable progress has been made in the reduction of poverty, much work remains to be done.

Food prices have fluctuated considerably in recent years. The international food price crisis came to a head in 2008. Food and rice prices then decreased in 2009 before increasing again in 2011. They have declined gradually in the years since. Local consumer prices and food price indices in Cambodia are, however, on an upward trajectory.[2] Moreover, the ratio of food to non-food prices – an indicator of the food purchasing power of households – increased 22% in the period between the food price crisis and 2011 (CARD, 2014a). This decline in purchasing power constitutes an especially pronounced barrier for rural households. Most rural households are net food buyers and, as a consequence, spend the main part of their household income on food. A rapid assessment of the impact of rising food prices on the poor and vulnerable conducted by the Cambodia Development Resource Institute in June 2012 indicated, for example, that households in the poorest quintile (in terms of wealth) spent more than two-thirds of their budget on food (CDRI, 2012). Rural households are therefore particularly vulnerable to volatility in food prices.

The impact of the 2008 food price crisis is manifested in child anthropometrics. Between 2000 and 2005, acceptable progress was made in the nutritional intake of children aged 5 and under. This progress stagnated between 2005 and 2010. Progress resumed as the Cambodian economy recovered. That said, in 2014, 23.9% of children aged 5 and under were classified as underweight and 32.4% suffered from stunted growth, leaving considerable room for further progress.

Much room for improvement also remains in terms of female nourishment. Little progress was made towards addressing the low body mass index scores of women between 2000 and 2010. In 2010, one out of five Cambodian women was undernourished and 6% of women were shorter than 145 centimetres, indicating that they had suffered from malnourishment as children. Malnourishment among women is correlated with higher levels of maternal mortality, increased incidence of premature births, lower birth weights and malnutrition among children. The number of overweight women (BMI >25) has also increased significantly. In 2000, 6% of women were classified as overweight. By 2010, this figure had risen to 11%.[3] Moreover, urban, middle-class obesity is likely to emerge as a significant concern as processes of urbanisation intensify and value chains and dietary patterns evolve.

Food security and nutrition progress varies across provinces and social groups

Poverty and issues of FSN are closely correlated. An examination of spatial patterns of poverty offers insight into the territorial dimension of FSN. Poverty rates vary dramatically across Cambodian regions. The poverty incidence rate, for example, is as low as 6.5% in some territories and as high as 50.9% in others. In 2013, the National Institute of Statistics and the United Nations World Food Programme prepared a study for the Royal Government of Cambodia to support the geographical targeting of health and poverty interventions. Motivated by the necessity of accurate statistical information for efficient and effective policy design,[4] the study provides estimates of poverty and malnutrition rates at the district level. The analysis revealed relatively low levels of poverty in Phnom Penh and slightly higher levels in the plains, river valleys and the shores around the Tonlé Sap Lake. The highest levels of poverty were found in the northeast uplands.[5]

Food security trend analyses based on food expenditure data from the 2004 and 2009 Cambodia Socio-Economic Surveys (CSES) suggest that overall food consumption in Cambodia has improved. The percentage of the population that consumed less than the minimum daily energy requirement fell from 37% in 2004 to 33% in 2009. There is, however, interpersonal and territorial variation in undernourishment. Undernourishment was, for example, higher in the lowest wealth quintile (59%). Similarly, while undernourishment decreased in Kompong Thom, the North, Northeast, Phnom Penh, Takeo and West and Centre, it increased in Siem Reap, Northwest and South Coastal (Figure 2.1).[6]

There is a pronounced urban-rural gap in terms of youth nourishment. In 2010, 42.2% of rural children were chronically malnourished and 30% were classified as underweight. In urban areas, on the other hand, 27.5% of children aged 5 and under were malnourished and 18.4% were underweight. The malnourishment gap between urban and rural areas did decrease between 2010 and 2014, but it remains sizeable.[7]

Certain territories are also more afflicted by childhood malnutrition. The incidence of childhood malnutrition is, for example, exceptionally high in poorer locations and settlements around Phnom Penh.

Childhood malnutrition is also more frequently observed among impoverished segments of society. In 2014, for example, 41.9% of children aged 5 and under in the poorest wealth quintile suffered from stunted growth. The figure was 18% for children in the highest wealth quintile.[8]

Some key challenges to sustained food security and nutrition progress

Food availability and access in Cambodia are constrained by several factors.

Figure 2.1. **Prevalence of undernourishment by region, 2004 and 2009**

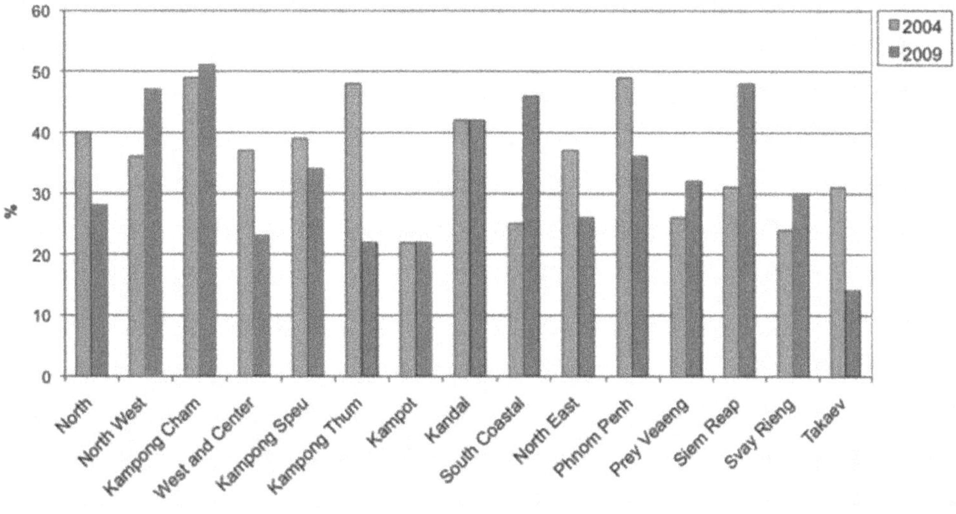

Source: NIS (2011), "Food security trend analysis: Cambodia Socio-Economics Survey 2004-2009".

Policies targeting FSN have tended to adopt a sectoral orientation and, more specifically, a singular focus on rice-based farming. Rice-based farming is characterised by low productivity and is especially vulnerable to climatic variation. The prioritisation of a single sector gives rise to an insufficiently sectorally diversified rural economy that offers few non-agriculturally related employment opportunities to the rural population. The absence of employment opportunities forces rural residents to seek employment primarily in urban centres. Interestingly, economic assessment (UNCDF, 2010) has indicated that the eco-tourism and renewable energy sectors are potential sources of economic growth and development for Cambodia's rural areas. Actualising this potential, however, is fraught with obstacles. For rural areas to reap the economic benefits of tourism, for example, concerted efforts will have to be made to ensure that rural communities develop the capacity to manage local cultural and ecological sites, many of which are protected. Similarly, rural areas will require assistance to access carbon financing mechanisms and develop small-scale renewable energy options (UNCDF, 2010). The expansion of the renewable energy sector in rural areas will have the added benefit of reducing Cambodia's reliance on coal and wood charcoal, with positive implications for processes of deforestation in rural regions. Opportunities for poverty reduction may also exist in the expansion of pre-existing rubber, pepper and silk clusters (UNDCF, 2010: 15).

Insufficiently developed transport and market infrastructure systems are notable barriers to the expansion of the agricultural sector and the rural economy more broadly. Poor farmers are hampered by inadequate irrigation systems and poor market integration and, as a result, often struggle to improve their food security and nutrition status.

The most prominent challenges relating to food use and utilisation include: a higher incidence of malnutrition in rural areas, issues related to the upscaling of nutritional interventions in the health sector, inadequate provision of nutritional education, poor access to sanitation in rural areas, poor hygiene in rural areas and limited access to nutrition services among poorer households.

Table 2.1. **Nutritional status of children under the age of 5**

Background characteristic	Height-for-age		Weight-for-height				Weight-for-age			
	% below -3 SD	% below -2 SD	% below -3 SD	% below -2 SD	% below +2 SD	Mean Z-score (SD)	% below -3 SD	% below -2 SD[2]	% above +2 SD	Mean Z-score (SD)
Resident										
Urban	5.9	23.7	2	7.5	3.1	-0.4	2.6	14.8	1.9	-0.9
Rural	9.4	33.8	2.4	9.9	1.8	-0.7	5	25.4	0.4	-1.3
Province										
Banteay Meanchey	6.9	28.6	0.7	7.8	0.7	-0.5	5.3	17	0	-1.1
Kampong Cham	8.6	33.5	1.5	8.1	2.2	-0.7	4.2	25.7	0.8	-1.3
Kampong Chhnang	13.5	42.8	3.1	11.2	2.2	-0.9	5.1	35.6	0	-1.5
Kampong Speu	10	40.5	2.5	11.5	1.3	-0.8	6.9	29.4	0	-1.5
Kampong Thom	10.7	36.4	3.1	13	3.4	-0.8	7.1	27.7	1.9	-1.3
Kandal	3.5	28.1	3.2	9.2	0.2	-0.8	4.7	26.2	0	-1.3
Kratie	10.5	38.4	2.7	6.5	0.5	-0.7	4.4	25.1	0	-1.4
Phnom Penh	4.9	17.9	1	8.4	3.7	-0.4	2.2	12.9	3.4	-0.8
Prey Veng	8.7	32.7	2.9	8.6	1.8	-0.6	3.4	22.2	0.3	-1.3
Pursat	18.4	38.8	5.7	12.3	4.7	-0.6	7.9	31.6	0.4	-1.4
Siem Reap	11.3	35.9	2.3	9.5	1	-0.7	6.9	26.2	0.4	-1.3
Svay Rieng	8.2	32.8	2.7	7.6	3.6	-0.6	3.6	20.8	0.5	-1.2
Takeo	6.4	30.7	5	14.6	1.5	-0.8	4.4	22.7	0	-1.3
Otdar Meanchey	14	36.3	7.2	15.1	5.3	-0.7	5.2	26.4	0	-1.3
Battambang/Palin	5	24.9	0.3	7.9	0.7	-0.6	1.8	18.2	0.5	-1.1
Kampot/Kep	8.3	25.2	0.9	8.2	1.9	-0.7	3.5	21.1	0.7	-1.3
Preah Sihanouk/Kaoh Kong	10.4	33.4	3.1	10.5	1.8	-0.6	6.5	22	0	-1.2
Preah Vihear/Steung Treng	14	44.3	1.3	13.8	2.3	-0.7	5.9	30.7	0.1	-1.5
Mondol Kiri/Ratanak Kiri	14.6	39.8	1.4	8.2	1.2	-0.6	0.6	26.2	0.3	-1.4

Source: NIS (2015), "Cambodia Demographic and Health Survey 2014: Key indicators report", available at: http://countryoffice.unfpa.org/cambodia/drive/2014CDHSKIR_2-20-2015.pdf.

Cambodia is especially vulnerable to economic and natural crises, both of which inevitably influence food supply and nutritional outcomes. The food crisis of 2008 exemplifies this. During the crisis, the price of food, and rice in particular, increased dramatically, reducing the purchasing power of poor households. The resulting changes in food consumption patterns adversely affected the nutrition and health of Cambodia's population. Similarly, increases in food price inflation since 2007 and the global financial crisis in the latter part of the decade have increased poverty and vulnerability.

Flood and drought exercise the greatest influence on annual rice production in Cambodia. In 2014, for example, rice production was affected by a prolonged drought in the early and mid-stages of the wet season. These factors have a direct impact on the well-being and welfare of the population. Flooding in 12 provinces in 2014, for example, resulted in 49 deaths. Similarly, mass flooding in 2011 affected 1.5 million people, displaced 214 000 and resulted in the death of 247 (FAO and WFP, 2012).

Recognising Cambodia's vulnerability to economic and natural crises, the government developed and implemented the National Social Protection Strategy (2010-15). This involves measures designed both to address emergencies and short-term disruptions as well as to reduce poverty and promote development. Many of the plan's food security-related interventions have not, however, been adequately scaled up to address the needs of the population.

In practice, Cambodia's capacity to prevent, prepare for and respond to such crises is limited. Food security-related social protection measures are often project-based, *ad hoc* and have yet to be scaled up. Moreover, programmes that directly target food-insecure households and other vulnerable groups are inadequate. Consequently, economic and natural crises often have massive adverse implications on malnutrition and chronic food security.

Policies and programmes

Addressing FSN has been made a priority by the Cambodian government and deemed instrumental in achieving the Cambodian Millennium Development Goals. FSN features in one form or another in: the government's overarching agenda as articulated in the Rectangular Strategy for Growth, Employment, Equity and Efficiency Phase III (2014-18); the National Strategic Development Plan (2014-18); the National Strategy for Food Security and Nutrition 2014-2018; and in other more narrowly defined policies and strategies (Table 2.2). The Rectangular Strategy for Growth, Employment, Equity and Efficiency Phase III outlines the broad policy directions for the improvement of FSN and identifies priorities for enhancing the availability of, access to, utilisation of and stability of food. The National Strategic Development Plan addresses the implementation of the Rectangular Strategy for Growth, Employment, Equity and Efficiency Phase III and is thus supplemental to it.

The National Strategy for Food Security and Nutrition is a logical extension of the government's overarching agenda (RS III). The Rectangular Strategy for Growth, Employment, Equity and Efficiency Phase III is broadly concerned with: agricultural intensification and diversification, land reform, sustainable natural resource management, the enhancement of health and nutrition, and the establishment of social safety nets. Accordingly, the National Strategic Development Plan includes policy actions targeting the availability of, access to, utilisation of and stability of the food supply.[9]

The National Strategy for Food Security and Nutrition has identified the following FSN-related objectives:

1. Objective 1: Increase availability and access of food through more productive and diversified agriculture and livestock production, sustainable fisheries and forestry, and from non-agricultural employment and income opportunities.
2. Objective 2: Improve the use and utilisation of food in Cambodian households, to reduce child and maternal malnutrition and enhance human and economic development.
3. Objective 3: Improve food security-related social protection and enhance poor and vulnerable households' ability to cope with risks and shocks to increase the stability of their food supply.

Action under the National Strategy for Food Security and Nutrition is conducted at three levels, macro, meso and micro, and takes the form of individual programmes or projects. FSN-related programmes and projects are generally implemented by sector-specific ministries (the Ministry of Agriculture, Forest and Fisheries; the Ministry of Water Resources and Meteorology; the Ministry of Rural Development; the Ministry of Health, etc.) with support from non-governmental organisations (NGOs), international organisations and United Nations agencies. These programmes and projects are sectoral in nature and aim to address issues including: livelihood enhancement, natural resources, community health, nutrition, social safety nets and rural health. In other words, they do not address FSN as a cross-cutting issue.

The roles of the key ministries addressed in Table 2.2 are described below.

The Ministry of Agriculture, Forest and Fisheries (MAFF), which is responsible for agricultural production and, by extension, FSN, has developed the Agricultural Sector Strategy Development Plan (ASDP 2014-2018). The plan is composed of five programmes: 1) productivity, diversification and commercialisation; 2) livestock production; 3) sustainable fisheries management; 4) sustainable forestry management; 5) strengthening institutions and human resources. The programmes are subdivided into 60 sub-programmes, including approximately 600 activities. The progress of each programme is measured against pre-established targets and indicators.[10] Funding for the plan comes from both the government and external partners (the African Development Bank, International Fund for Agricultural Development and the European Union).

The Ministry of Agriculture, Forest and Fisheries also promotes the creation of new producer organisations. As of 2014, Cambodia had 516 community fisheries (477 inland and 39 marine), 370 of which were registered with the ministry. The ministry has also recently issued a declaration (*prakas*) for the establishment of community forestry management committees, and 19 have so far been created.

The Ministry for Economy and Finance (MEF) is involved in FSN policy through the Emergency Food Assistance programme, which is active in 7 provinces and 200 communities and offers subsidised seeds and fertiliser to poor farming households.

The Ministry for Economy and Finance also promotes education by providing scholarships in two of the provinces in which it is active, and through in-school nutrition programmes executed in partnership with the World Food Programme. It also invests in infrastructure development. The aim of infrastructure development is two-fold: first, it creates employment and income-generating opportunities for individuals in rural areas. Second, it improves the production capacity of rural farmers. Finally, the Ministry for

Economy and Finance provides extension services, including training and education to farmers.[11]

Table 2.2. **List of key programmes and policies that explicitly target food insecurity**

Dimension of food security and nutrition	Strategies and plans	Lead ministry	Time frame
1. Food availability and access	Agricultural Sector Strategic Development Plan; Strategy on Agriculture and Water (SAW); related Programme Design Document	MAFF MAFF/MOWRAM	2009-13 2006-10 2010-13
	Policy Paper on the Promotion of Paddy Production and Rice Export (Rice Policy)	MEF, MAFF	2010-15
	Strategic Planning Framework for Livestock	MAFF	2011-20
	Animal Health Medium-Term Priority Plan	MAFF	2011-15
	Strategic Planning Framework for Fisheries	MAFF	2010-19
	National Forest Programme	MAFF	2010-29
	Agriculture Sector Strategic Development Plan	MAFF	2014-18
	Agricultural Extension Policy in Cambodia	MAFF	Long-term
2. Food utilisation	Health Sector Strategic Plan (HSSP II)	MoH	2008-15
	National Nutrition Strategy (NNS)	MoH/NNP	2009-15
	Fast-Track Road Map for Improving Nutrition	MoH/NNP	2014-20
	National Strategy for Rural Water Supply, Sanitation and Hygiene	MRD	2014-25
	National Policy on Feeding of Infants and Young Children	MoH	2002 (revised 2008)
	National and Policy Guidelines for Micronutrient Supplementation to Prevent and Control Deficiencies in Cambodia	MoH/NNP	November 2011
3. Food stability	National Social Protection Strategy (NSPS)	CARD	2009-13
	Disaster Management Law	NCDM	
	National Action Plan (SNAP) for Disaster Risk Reduction	NCDM	2008-13
	Sub-Decree on the Establishment of Cambodian Food Reserve System	NCDM	June 2012
	National Adaptation Programme of Action to Climate Change (NAPA)	MoE	Long-term
	Response Strategy to the Impact of Climate Change	MAFF	2014-18
	Cambodian Climate Change Strategic Plan (CCCSP)	MoE	
	Action Plan for Disaster Risk Reduction in Agriculture	MAFF	2014-18
	Law on Agricultural Co-operative	MAFF	Long-term

Notes: MAFF: Ministry of Agriculture, Forest and Fisheries; MOWRAM: Ministry of Water Resources and Meteorology; MEF: Ministry of Economy and Finance; MoH: Ministry of Health; NNP: National Nutrition Programme; MRD: Ministry of Rural Development; CARD: Council for Agriculture and Rural Development; NCDM: National Committee for Disaster Management; MoE: Ministry of Environment.

The Ministry of Rural Development (MRD) has developed two main FSN-oriented programmes. One is focused on food security; the other is oriented towards nutrition.

The food security programme is currently active in three provinces and provides cash and/or rice to poor households. These transfers are supplemented by the provision of agricultural support and money to purchase seeds, livestock, etc. by the Department of Community Development. The department also trains farmers in the use of fertilisers for various types of agriculture.

The National Nutrition Programme (NNP), on the other hand, centres on the provision of food and non-food related (i.e. AIDS, malaria, etc.) education and training. Training efforts are co-ordinated with those of NGOs and international organisations. Additionally, the Ministry of Rural Development has some oversight over water and sanitation infrastructure development.

The Ministry of Health (MoH) is responsible for the National Nutrition Strategy. This adopts a multisectoral approach to food insecurity and is primarily focused on maternal and childhood malnutrition. The present focus of the Ministry of Health is implementing measures outlined in the National Strategy for Food Security and Nutrition.

Institutional framework and governance of food security and nutrition in Cambodia

Horizontal co-ordination

At least 12 ministries and government agencies are active in promoting FSN. These include: the Ministry of Agriculture, Forestry and Fisheries; the Ministry of Health; the Ministry of Rural Development (MRD); the Ministry of Education, Youth and Sport (MOEYS); the Ministry of Water Resources and Meteorology (MOWRAM); the Ministry of Planning (MOP); the Ministry for Economy and Finance; the Ministry of Land Management, Urban Planning and Construction (MLMUPC); the Ministry of Environment (MOE); Tonlé Sap Authority (TSA); the National Committee for Disaster Management (NCDM); and the Council for Agriculture and Rural Development (CARD) (Figure 2.2). Each ministry has its own annual budget, which is subject to review by the Ministry of Economy and Finance and requires approval by the council minister, National Assembly and Senate. The annual budget is proposed based on sectoral priorities aligned with those of the National Strategic Development Plan 2014-18.

The institution responsible for co-ordinating FSN-related policies, strategies, action plans, programmes and projects among the relevant ministries and departments at the national level is the Council for Agriculture and Rural Development. One of the most important co-ordination structures employed by the Council for Agriculture and Rural Development is the Technical Working Group on Social Protection and Food Security and Nutrition (TWG-SP&FSN),[12] which is mandated to provide FSN-related technical inputs for all action plans and national strategies. A second co-ordination structure is the Food Security Forum (2003). This is open to all ministries and relevant stakeholders (including civil society) and aims to share experiences and identify the priorities for FSN. The Technical Working Group on Social Protection and Food Security meets twice a year and reports directly to the prime minister. It addresses budgetary concerns, sets indicators/targets and approves the priorities identified by the Food Security Forum.

Vertical co-ordination

There is no provincial equivalent to the Council for Agriculture and Rural Development, which co-ordinates FSN policies at the national level. The Council for Agriculture and Rural Development has, however, made efforts to train provincial authorities.

The case of Takeo is a useful exemplification of the challenges faced in the vertical co-ordination of FSN policy in the Cambodian context. Efforts to address FSN in Takeo are highly fragmented, as a result of the absence of a co-ordination mechanism to align the agendas, programmes and priorities of different actors. Overlap between departments is not uncommon. For example, both the Department of Health (DoH) and the Department of Human Affairs (DoHA) provide training in cooking and household sanitation for women, in particular young mothers, and the Department for Rural Development (DoRD) also deals with sanitation education. Similarly, both the DoHA and DoRD promote on- and off-farm income-generating activities, albeit for different target populations: the DoHA focuses on women's trades while the DoRD provides vocational training in, for example, machine repairs.

Figure 2.2. **Institutional arrangements for horizontal co-ordination of food security and nutrition in Cambodia**

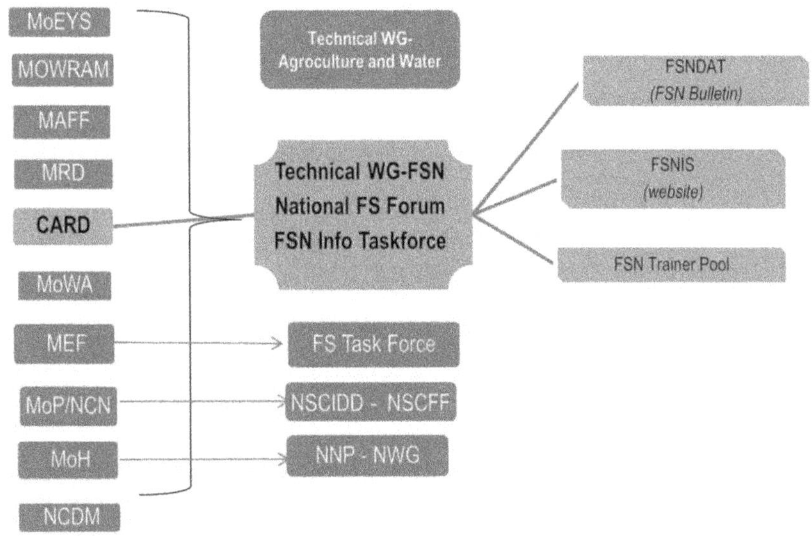

Source: CARD (2014a).

Challenges for effective food security and nutrition policies and governance

Cambodia's national FSN policy framework would seem to be quite advanced, and a comprehensive national strategy for FSN has been set up. FSN is, however, still not perceived by authorities as a "cross-cutting issue" (CARD, 2014b: 40-41) but rather as a sectoral issue closely linked to agricultural productivity. A number of more specific challenges remain for FSN policy as well. Many of these relate to policy implementation and programme delivery.

Efforts to implement FSN policies and actions are constrained by a lack of capacity and resources among ministries and government institutions. FSN interventions therefore often rely on external support, especially at the sub-national level. Sub-national authorities in particular lack the necessary mechanisms or structures for co-ordination with and between government agencies and development partners. FSN has thus been addressed largely on an unsustainable project-based approach. Holistic and integrated programme-based approaches for FSN that operate across sectors do not yet exist at the regional level.

FSN policies at the sub-national level have tended to be small in scale and narrow in geographic scope. Co-ordination between those responsible is spotty (given a dearth of co-ordination structures), leading to duplication and overlap between sub-national initiatives. Other challenges include high transaction costs that have deterred investment; an inability to develop sustained capacity in sub-national departments and councils; and an overreliance on external funding. Not surprisingly, the effectiveness of programmes has suffered as a result.

FSN policy also suffers from top-down policy making and severe disconnects between the national level and sub-national authorities. National development plans are devised at the national level with little sub-national involvement, input or consultation. Sub-national development plans are developed in accordance with national plans and their objectives, targets and priorities. Sub-national policies are therefore designed and budgets are set without sufficient consideration of local conditions and opportunities, which ultimately limits their efficiency and effectiveness.

Recent intervention to boost FSN

The government has, however, taken steps to address the above challenges:

- The Council for Agriculture and Rural Development was established in 2004 to promote co-ordination and collaboration between and among government bodies and development partners at the national level.
- A National Trainer Pool was established in 2008 to increase capacity to address FSN challenges. Numerous national and sub-national level government officials have participated in and benefited from FSN capacity building. Training is based on an integrated and holistic understanding of FSN.
- A specific inter-ministerial task force for FSN information management was established in 2009 under the Technical Working Group on Social Protection and Food Security, to support the development of an FSN-related information network. The ultimate aim was to enhance co-ordination of various initiatives and take advantage of potential synergies and complementarities. A small, cross-sectoral Food Security and Nutrition Data Analysis Team (FSNDAT) was also established in 2010.

Despite these promising steps, sub-national authorities are still not fully involved in FSN policy formulation and implementation, and co-ordination failures among sub-national authorities and between national and sub-national authorities are omnipresent.

Concluding remarks

The adoption of a territorial approach to FSN could address many of the shortcomings that have plagued Cambodia's efforts to address issues of FSN.

A territorial approach to FSN would feature the integration of local stakeholders in the development of national and sub-national level strategic plans to address FSN. This would permit the tailoring of FSN initiatives to local needs, priorities and specificities. "One-size-fits-all" policies developed by national authorities would no longer be relied upon as heavily to address issues of FSN in Cambodia's heterogeneous sub-national territories.

A territorial approach would promote the implementation of a holistic and integrated approach to FSN and rural development. Such an approach would aim to diversify rural economies rather than increase their dependence on a single sector. It would, for example, exploit opportunities in tourism, renewable energy and other sectors. Diversification would have the effect of creating employment and income-generating opportunities in non-agricultural sectors, which would, among other things, decrease rural outmigration and increase rural economies' resilience to macroeconomic and natural shocks. In short, sector-based policies would be abandoned in favour of cross-cutting approaches.

Territorial approaches could also help resolve co-ordination challenges that have plagued FSN efforts in Cambodia. This could conceivably enhance co-ordination not only between sub-national and national authorities, but with external actors as well. This would facilitate the development of sustained and holistic approaches and decrease reliance on short-term, *ad hoc*, sectoral, project-based interventions.

Finally, a territorial approach would encourage coherence and reveal synergies between FSN-oriented interventions and those targeting other aspects of economic development.

Notes

1. Between 1992 and 2009, the average Cambodian's fruit and vegetable consumption was less than the recommended dietary intake.
2. They experienced a small decline in 2009.
3. Female over-nutrition is higher in urban environments than in rural ones (16% versus 5%). Similarly, it is higher for the wealthiest quintile than for the lowest wealth quintile (17% versus 5%) (CDHS, 2010).
4. The foreword of the publication states: "by knowing where the poor and malnourished are, we believe the Royal Government of Cambodia and development partners can more effectively and efficiently meet their specific needs through poverty reduction and development projects, public health nutrition interventions, and increasingly, through social protection measures to reach the poorest and most vulnerable Cambodians".
5. It should be noted that relative estimates may be skewed by the confluence of high levels of poverty and malnutrition and lower population in remote areas (Haslett, Jones and Sefton, 2013).
6. Geographical classification based on the sample included in National Institute of Statistics (2011: 2): "At the end of the 12 months, reliable estimates were produced for 10 individual provinces: Kampong Cham, Kampong Speu, Kampong Thom, Kampot, Kandal, Phnom Penh, Prey Veng, Siem Rieng and Takeo. The other 14 provinces were grouped according to zones (North, Northwest, Northeast, South Coastal, and West and Centre)."
7. In 2014, 23.7% of urban children were chronically malnourished compared to 33.8% of rural children. Similarly, 25.4% of children in rural areas were underweight compared to 14.8% in urban ones.
8. Acute malnutrition in general is correlated with relative poverty (Table 2.1).
9. The policy actions outlined in the NSDP as well as those included in the NSFSN are linked to and will facilitate the achievement of Cambodia's Millennium Development Goals.
10. No explicit food security indicators are included, only production-related ones.

11. Examples of Ministry of Economy and Finance interventions include support for efforts to rehabilitate canals and the distribution of seeds to restore crops the mass flooding in 2011 and 2013.

12. Technical working groups are government/donor co-ordination for sectors or cross-cutting issues established to enhance alignment and harmonisation of development support. The TWG-SP&FSN chaired by CARD is one of the 19 such groups in Cambodia.

References

CARD (2014a), "National Strategy for Food Security and Nutrition (NSFSN 2014-18)", Council for Agricultural and Rural Development in consultation with the Technical Working Group for Social Protection and Food Security and Nutrition (TWG-SP&FSN), Phnom Penh, Cambodia, available at: www.cdc-crdb.gov.kh/cdc/documents/Sector_Strategy/5_Social_Protection_Food_Security_Nutrition/National_Strategy_for_FSN_2014_2018_Eng.pdf.

CARD (2014b), "National progress report on food security and nutrition", Council for Agricultural and Rural Development, Phnom Penh, Cambodia.

National Institute of Statistics (2010), *Cambodia Demographic and Health Survey* (CDHS), Ministry of Planning and Directorate General for Health, Phnom Penh, Cambodia.

CDRI (2012), "Rapid assessment of the impact of rising food prices on the poor and vulnerable and policy response in Cambodia", Cambodia Development Research Institute in partnership with NGO Forum on Cambodia, Phnom Penh, available at: www.cdri.org.kh/webdata/download/conpap/foodpriceincreases.pdf.

FAO and WFP (2012), "FAO/WFP crop and food security update mission to Cambodia – Report", Food and Agriculture Organization and World Food Programme, Rome, available at: www.fao.org/3/a-al988e.pdf.

Haslett, S., G. Jones and A. Sefton (2013), *Small-Area Estimation of Poverty and Malnutrition in Cambodia*, National Institute of Statistics, Ministry of Planning, Royal Government of Cambodia and the United Nations World Food Programme, Phnom Penh, Cambodia, www.wfp.org/content/cambodia-small-area-estimation-poverty-and-malnutrition-april-2013.

Ministry of Agriculture, Forestry and Fisheries (2015), *Annual Report 2014-2015*, Ministry of Agriculture, Forestry and Fisheries, Phnom Penh, Cambodia.

Ministry of Planning (2013), "Annual progress report: Achieving the Millennium Development Goals – Report prepared on the status in 2013", Ministry of Planning, Royal Government of Cambodia, December, Phnom Penh, Cambodia.

National Institute of Statistics (NIS) (2015), "Cambodia Demographic and Health Survey 2014: Key indicators report", Ministry of Health, Phnom Penh, available at: http://countryoffice.unfpa.org/cambodia/drive/2014CDHSKIR_2-20-2015.pdf.

National Institute of Statistics (NIS) (2011), "Food security trend analysis: Cambodia Socio-Economics Survey 2004-2009", Ministry of Planning, Royal Government of Cambodia, Phnom Penh, Cambodia.

NCDD (2013), "Overview", www.ncdd.gov.kh/en/about-ncdd/overview.

UNCDF (2010), *Local Development Outlook Cambodia*, United Nations Capital Development Fund, New York, New York, www.uncdf.org/en/node/2305.

World Bank (2015), "Cambodia: Overview", www.worldbank.org/en/country/cambodia/overview.

Chapter 3.

A territorial approach to food security and nutrition policy: The case of Colombia

The government of Colombia aims to provide an integrated response to food security and nutrition (FSN) challenges, tackling economic, social and health dimensions through a cross-sectoral approach involving several key ministries. The country struggles with geographic disparities, and FSN issues are more severe in poor and remote rural areas, where the institutional capacity to deal with those further tends to be low. In addition, the armed conflict has put many people's livelihoods and security at risk. It also further complicates the gathering of territorial information to support policy making to reach the food insecure (e.g. size of local communities, displaced populations, etc.). Despite these challenges, however, promising examples exist, as in the department of Antioquia, where the successful implementation of a multidimensional FSN policy inspired both national policy makers and international development organisations. This example shows the viability of territorial approaches to tackle place-specific FSN issues through local institutions.

Key findings

The case of Colombia provides an instructive illustration of the need for territorial approaches to food security and nutrition (FSN) policy. In Colombia, issues of FSN are especially prevalent in poor rural communities. Issues of FSN are attributable to several factors, including: extreme poverty, high levels of informality, scarce regional accessibility, and of course, the armed conflict. Recognising this, the national government has developed a multidimensional FSN strategy that aims to increase communities' structural resilience to food insecurity and malnutrition. The implementation of the strategy has proved challenging, and issues related to FSN have persisted. The multidimensional approach that characterises the national strategy, for example, has been lost sight of in the implementation of the policy. Policies have largely been spatially blind and mostly based on the direct provision of foodstuffs and cash transfers. Moreover, policies, programmes and investment have clustered in urban areas and more accessible regions, despite the concentration of FSN challenges in rural areas.

Features of food insecurity and malnutrition in Colombia

Food security and nutrition challenges are more intense in poor and/or rural communities

In Colombia, 40.8% of the population is affected by issues related to FSN (ENSIN, 2010). There is, however, considerable cross-territorial variation in the prevalence of these issues that reflects the disparities in income per capita that exist across Colombia's territorial communities (OECD, 2012). Colombia is composed of 32 departments, plus the district of Bogotá, which are in turn subdivided into 1 102 municipalities. Granular territorial data are unfortunately not available for all 32 departments. The analysis that follows is therefore based only on a selection of departments for which suitable statistical information is available.

Sixteen of Colombia's 32 departments display levels of food insecurity and malnutrition at the household level that exceed the national average (40.8%). Perhaps not surprisingly, extreme poverty is also pervasive in the departments where issues of FSN are especially pronounced. Of these 16 departments, the highest levels of extreme poverty are found in La Guajira (38%) (DANE, 2010), a department situated on the Venezuelan border in the north of the country that is also home to a large aboriginal community (Table 3.1).[1]

There is also cross-territorial variation in the average dietary energy consumption (DEC). Average DEC reflects the number of calories consumed per person per day. In order to assess the regional disparities in calorie consumption, the FAO divided Colombia into six regions (*Norte, Atlantica, Oriental, Central, Pacifica* and Bogotá) and measured DEC in each of them. Atlantica's average DEC of 1 881 kcal/person/day was the lowest of the regions considered. The highest levels of average DEC, by contrast, were found in Bogotá, where DEC was approximately 1 000 kcal/person/day greater than in the *Atlantica* region. Average DEC in the four other regions considered ranged from 2 353 kcal/person/day in the Eastern region to 2 002 kcal/person/day in the Archipelago region.

Food insecurity and malnutrition are more severe in rural Colombia (ENSIN, 2010). The number of rural households affected by food insecurity is 57.5% and 17% of children in rural areas display growth delays as a result. In urban areas, only 38.4% of urban households are affected by food insecurity and 11.6% of children suffer from growth delays.[2] There is also evidence to suggest that this urban-rural food insecurity divide is manifested in average DEC as well. That said, rural-urban variation in DEC is less severe than it is for other measures of food insecurity and malnutrition.

Table 3.1. **Food insecurity and extreme poverty in Colombian departments**

	Departments with a concentration of households exposed to food insecurity above the national average	Percentage of households living in extreme poverty at the department level
Nariño	67.7%	18.6%
Choco	64.2%	33.5%
Sucre	62.9%	28.6%
Bolívar	61.7%	14.9%
Magdalena	61.4%	23.5%
Cordoba	60.2%	25.6%
La Guajira	59.1%	37.6%
Cauca	57.6%	35.9%
Caquetá	54.4%	9.9%
Atlántico	54.4%	9.4%
Cesar	53.9%	18.6%
Norte de Santander	47.3%	11.0%
Huila	43.8%	25.9%
Boyacá	43.6%	19.2%
Antioquia	43.5%	10.5%

Note: Data on extreme poverty are not available for all departments in Colombia.

Source: DANE (2010), DPS, OECD (2012); ENSIN (2010), National Survey of Food Security and Nutrition.

Income inequality tends to be greater in rural areas. Several rural departments have levels of income inequality that exceed the national average. Colombia's income inequalities are reflected in, among other things, patterns of land ownership. Fieldwork has revealed that access to land is one of the main determinants of poverty in rural communities. The Gini index measuring concentration of land ownership confirms that a relatively small number of individuals own a disproportionately large percentage of land in Colombia. Colombia's relatively high Gini coefficient of 0.86[3] (UNDP, 2009) is consistent with those of other Latin American countries, in particular Brazil and Argentina (World Bank, 2004). Rural dwellers who do not own land – of which there are many – are left with little choice but to work as informal labourers in agriculture. They are, as a result, exposed to greater income fluctuation, at greater risk of falling into poverty, and are more likely to face issues of food insecurity.

Remote areas are vulnerable to food insecurity and malnutrition

Remote rural regions are frequently subject to food insecurity and malnutrition, given the difficulty of supplying food to isolated locations and of establishing physical markets there. Colombia has a polycentric urban structure, and in 2014, 47 of its cities had a population larger than 100 000. However, its stock of transport infrastructure is grossly underdeveloped relative to its Latin American counterparts and also to numerous Asian and OECD countries (OECD, 2014). Transport costs are thus relatively high.[4] The roads mostly connect rural areas with urban centres, rather than with other rural areas. This is also true for adjacent communities even within the same department: roads link the communities to cities but not to each other. The immediate consequence of the functional isolation of rural regions is that the bulk of agricultural output is absorbed by city markets, which is also where the price of products is set.

Table 3.2. **Average dietary energy consumption**

	Average dietary energy consumption (DEC; kcal/person/day)	Share of DEC from protein (%)	Share of DEC from fat (%)	Share of DEC from total carbohydrates and alcohol (%)
Total	2 238	11.00	28.91	59.27
Area				
Urban	2 273	11.50	30.33	57.17
Rural	2 126	9.26	23.98	66.55
Region				
Atlántica	1 881	10.33	28.67	60.05
Oriental	2 353	11.12	28.52	59.63
Central	2 088	11.00	28.41	59.79
Pacifica	2 197	10.07	27.46	61.40
Bogotá	2 843	12.20	31.21	55.99
Archipelago	2 002	12.46	33.04	52.94

Source: FAO elaboration based on household survey data (2007).

The inaccessibility of many rural areas has a paradoxical effect. Because rural areas are so cut off, farmers must ship their production to cities. The cities then redistribute food, among other places, to rural areas. This not only renders rural environments dependent on urban ones, but rural dwellers may face prohibitive prices for the food they consume because of high interregional transport costs.

The armed conflict is a systemic cause of food security and nutrition challenges

Armed conflicts go hand in hand with food insecurity. In Colombia, sustained low-intensity conflict has caused structural distortions in regional economies and societies that contribute to food insecurity and malnutrition. The implications of the conflict are numerous. Among them are the erosion of institutions and the rule of law in conflict-stricken territories and the outmigration of population. The International Displacement Monitoring Centre estimates that 5.7 million people (*desplazados*) have been forced to leave their communities (iDMC, 2014) and have lost (or are not in possession of) a formal property title for their holdings. As a result, most are suffering from severe food insecurity and extreme poverty. Developing and implementing policies to resolve the challenges faced by these displaced individuals – issues of FSN included – is hampered by the lack of data on their numbers and whereabouts.

The armed conflict, which has persisted in some territories since the 1950s, has contributed to the reinforcement of the urban-rural divide (OECD, 2012). In urban areas, security is not a major issue. Rural areas, on the other hand, suffer from social unrest and the lack of basic public institutions. The persistent conflict has created a highly fragmented territorial system, which in turn has limited the country's capacity to capitalise on its relatively high level of urbanisation. Armed conflict and illegal activities have also contributed to the wide variations in sub-national governments' capacities.

The governance system of the food security and nutrition policy

There are a number of entities responsible for the governance of FSN policies in Colombia. That issues of food insecurity and malnutrition are managed by not one, but several entities, is a reflection of Colombia's recognition of the multidimensionality of FSN. The national definition of food security and nutrition is based on five dimensions: 1) the availability of food; 2) food accessibility; 3) consumption; 4) biological value; and

5) food safety and quality. Based on these factors, the government has engineered a broad policy framework that incorporates economic and socio-economic dimensions and cuts across different policy sectors, with the ultimate aim of providing an integrated response to FSN challenges. The policy framework prescribes roles for a variety of institutional actors, including several that may not be directly linked to FSN policy.

Colombia's National Department for Welfare and the Family Welfare Institute

The National Department for Welfare (Prosperidad Social) is one of the pillars of Colombia's FSN policy. It was created in 2011, with a mandate to co-ordinate and implement national interventions promoting peace, social inclusion and FSN. It is composed of the following subentities:

- Unit for the Care and Reparation of Victims (*Unidad de Atención y Reparación Integral a las Víctimas*)
- The Colombian Family Welfare Institute (*Instituto Colombiano de Bienestar Familiar*)
- The Centre of Historical Memory (*Centro de Memoria Histórica*).

The National Department for Welfare and the agencies associated with it are responsible for the delivery of some of Colombia's most important social policies – many of which address issues of FSN either directly or indirectly. These include: *Mas Familias en Acción* and *De Cero a Siempre*. Both these initiatives are designed to promote social inclusion – one of the key priorities of the Colombian government in its National Development Plan 2014-2018 (OECD, 2014).

Mas Familias en Acción aimed to provide 3 million households with conditional cash transfers in 2015. The overarching objective of the programme is to break the cycle of poverty via the provision of economic opportunity and key public services. Cash is transferred to poor citizens on condition that they fulfil a series of obligations, including: enrolling their children in public schools and ensuring their children are vaccinated and attend regular medical check-ups. *Mas Familias en Acción* is perhaps the policy with the greatest potential for reducing food insecurity in Colombia's poor communities. Its 2015 budget was USD 340 million.[5]

De Cero a Siempre is Colombia's strategy for the provision of integral early childhood care. It is managed by the Colombian Family Welfare Institute in co-ordination with several other administrative bodies, including international organisations, donor agencies and Colombia's civil society. The programme's primary aim is to provide support to early childhood development providers in vulnerable communities – i.e. Afro-Colombians and indigenous groups – through access to health, nutrition, education and other services for the most vulnerable communities. The programme has a network of more than 200 local offices across the country. It aimed to provide support to 1.4 million children in 2015, with the objective of reaching 1.7 million in 2018.

The National Department for Welfare is also responsible for the implementation of more granular policies to improve FSN across Colombia. It is, for example, piloting an initiative to reconnect citizens with food production. The policy is based on three phases. The first phase involves the provision of both a small agricultural holding and agricultural training to food-insecure households. The second phase focuses on agricultural productivity, aiming to help households generate a surplus from their holdings. The third phase consists of measures designed to help households convert their surplus production into a stable source of income.

The Ministry of Health and Social Protection

The Ministry of Health and Social Protection is a second key actor in Colombia's efforts to address issues of FSN, in large part due to its responsibility for the 10-year National Plan for Health (2012-2022). Sub-national governments are formally obliged to produce their own health plans as well. These plans, however, must reflect the priorities and the overall approach of the national plan, and sub-national governments are provided expert assistance to ensure they are capable of doing so. This, in theory, promotes coherence between sub-national- and national-level health policies.

A Vice-Ministry for Health, set up in 2013, is responsible for issues related to FSN. and works closely with the *Observatorio de Seguridad Alimentaria y Nutricional*. The *Observatorio* is in charge of monitoring FSN trends in connection with key variables such as age, health conditions and gender. Insights and data it produces inform the design of evidence-based policies. Information it collects is disseminated via a dedicated Internet site.[6] The Ministry of Health operates a network of 31 observatories and is working with the *Observatorio* to improve integration of FSN-related information across sectors.

The Ministry of Agriculture and Rural Development

Annual budget allocations indicate that agricultural policy is one of Colombia's foremost priorities, not least because of its implications for FSN.[7] Colombia's Ministry of Agriculture and Rural Development is responsible for several important FSN policies.

The ministry co-ordinates the work of several agencies; many of which explicitly address FSN. The two most relevant are the Colombian Institute for Rural Development and the Vice-Ministry for Rural Development. The institute helps to reconnect displaced rural citizens with their landholdings, and also provides agricultural inputs and capacity building to farmers to improve their productivity and allow them to generate income from their agricultural activities. Since 2013, the Colombian Institute for Rural Development has worked closely with the Vice-Ministry for Rural Development, which has three branches. The first is concerned with the land property rights of displaced citizens. The second focuses on increasing agricultural productivity. The third works to improve access to services in rural communities. Efforts to improve access to services have relied on a territorial approach to rural development, a significant development in Colombia's FSN policy framework (OECD, 2014). The *Programa de Desarrollo Rural Integral con Enfoque Territorial* is perhaps the most tangible outcome of the recently adopted territorial approach to development. It is a quasi-experimental policy implemented in partnership with local governments in eight regions, with the aim of improving rural households' accessibility to public services.

The National Department for Planning

National investment in Colombia is guided by four-year national development plans drawn up by the National Department for Planning. FSN is a priority of the current (2014-18) national development plan. Sub-national levels in Colombia are required to produce their own development plans – with technical assistance from the National Department for Planning – in accordance with nationally identified aims and priorities. The importance of addressing FSN is thus reflected in both the national and sub-national development plans.

The National Department for Planning's role in the national FSN policy framework has been formalised by the National Council for Economic and Social Policy. This council is chaired by Colombia's president and is the highest authority in the country. In 2008, the National Council for Economic and Social Policy restructured and reoriented Colombia's FSN policy. Several bodies were created as part of this renewal, each of which is addressed in subsequent sections.

Sub-national entities and international FSN stakeholders: Antioquia's experience

Colombia's regions exhibit considerable variation in both economic performance and institutional capacity (OECD, 2014). Institutional and economic challenges often go hand in hand, especially in poor territories. Municipalities and departments that suffer from economic and institutional deficiencies are often less capable of delivering policies that support FSN. Where regional economic conditions are more favourable, however, there is evidence to suggest that sub-national governments can, and do, work synergistically with other entities to pioneer new policy solutions to address FSN.

In 2002, the department of Antioquia implemented a multidimensional FSN policy, the *Mejoramiento Alimentario y Nutricional de Antioquia* (MANA). The policy has achieved international visibility and attracted the FAO, World Food Programme and other donor agencies to Antioquia. The policy's success has influenced Colombia's national FSN policy and been replicated to some degree in other policies.

Antioquia is one of the wealthiest departments of Colombia (OECD, 2014). Its regional capital, Medellín, recently devised and implemented a local economic development strategy that contributed to the successful revitalisation of the city and its business community. The city benefits from reasonably well-functioning institutions, as indicated by the availability of administrative information on citizens facing food insecurity and malnutrition. Despite its wealth, however, the percentage of its households suffering from some form of food insecurity is above the national average.[8] In the early 2000s, the regional government thus decided to implement an evidence-based, multidimensional policy to promote food security.

The department allocated USD 360 million over four years (2010-2014) to the *Mejoramiento Alimentario y Nutricional de Antioquia* policy. It is composed of a series of sub-initiatives. The most relevant are:

- **A supplementary feeding programme for young children.** *Mejoramiento Alimentario y Nutricional de Antioquia* provides children aged 6 and under with food enriched with vitamins and nutrients. Its scope is narrower than that of the *De Cero a Siempre* policy. Efforts have been made to co-ordinate the programmes and avoid inefficient duplications and overlap.
- **A school feeding programme.** *Mejoramiento Alimentario y Nutricional de Antioquia* provides children aged 6-14 with access to food and nutrition. The window of age eligibility is greater in rural areas.
- **Initiatives to increase citizen awareness of FSN principles and to improve access to basic services, including health care.** Citizens are heavily involved in these actions. Citizen engagement is expected to facilitate the dissemination of good practices and increase awareness of challenges related to malnutrition, especially within vulnerable populations. *Mejoramiento Alimentario y Nutricional*

de Antioquia thus encourages the generation of social capital that, in turn, facilitates the delivery of public policies more generally.

- **Direct support to households that engage in small-scale farming.** The *Huertas Familiares* initiative provides selected households with access to small holdings, inputs and capacity building to improve their food and nutrition security. It also helps households generate a surplus that can be sold in local markets and serve as a stable source of income. This programme is delivered with the direct support of the FAO.

Local stakeholders attribute the success of the *Mejoramiento Alimentario y Nutricional de Antioquia* policy, at least in part, to its continuity and relative budgetary stability in the past decade. This has allowed it to transition from the status of a "programme" to that of a full-fledged "policy". The policy is also mainstreamed through departments and regional policies to ensure that other policies are coherent and foster FSN objectives.

Co-ordination mechanisms

Co-ordinating the actions of the many bodies involved in Colombia's FSN policy is essential to ensure that interventions are executed efficiently and effectively. Colombia has relied on two main tools to promote co-ordination since the creation of the National Council for Economic and Social Policy and the restructuring of FSN policy. The first is the intersectoral commission for FSN, the *Comisión Intersectorial de Seguridad Alimentaria y Nutricional* (CISAN). This functions as a mechanism for various stakeholders to keep each other informed of policy decisions, so they can articulate their concerns and offer opportunities for co-operation and co-ordination. The second key tool is the eight-year National Plan for FSN 2012-2019 (*Plan Nacional de Seguridad Alimentaria y Nutricional – PNSAN 2012-2019*). This collects information on the policy initiatives from the various actors associated with the *Comisión Intersectorial de Seguridad Alimentaria y Nutricional* and synthesises it in a common national strategy.

Challenges for effective food security and nutrition policy

Colombia exemplifies the need for the adoption of a territorial approach to FSN. Empirical evidence suggests, first, that the impact of the country's efforts to address food insecurity and malnutrition has been limited, and, second, that any reduction in the number of households and individuals exposed to FSN may in fact be a product of Colombia's economic development – manifested in, among other things, rising household incomes – rather than of concerted FSN policies.

National stakeholders and international experts have identified the shortcomings and challenges facing Colombia's FSN policy. These are discussed in subsequent sections.

Food security and nutrition policy is space-blind, due to the lack of regional data

Colombia is making a concerted effort to improve the availability of sub-national statistics (OECD, 2014). The design and implementation of policies, however, including those oriented towards FSN, are hampered by a lack of data and consequently tend to assume a space-blind character. Public authorities lack basic information on the size of most local communities – especially in rural areas; the number of displaced citizens (*desplazados*) and property rights. They are thus unable to tailor interventions to the needs of heterogeneous territorial communities and are left with little choice but to implement "one-size-fits-all" policies. FSN issues, however, are best addressed in evidence-based policy frameworks tailored to territorially unique features, opportunities and challenges.

Conditional cash transfers, for example, are delivered to poor households without taking into account the conditions and characteristics of the areas where they live. One consequence is that rural inhabitants may encounter more difficulty than their urban counterparts in satisfying the sometimes stringent conditions on which transfers are based, due to their limited access to schools and hospitals.

The food security and nutrition policy governance system lacks coherence and co-ordination

The governance of FSN policy in Colombia faces several challenges. One is the adoption of different narratives and definitions of FSN by the various Colombian authorities and institutional stakeholders that manage FSN policy. The definition used by the Ministry of Health, for example, differs from that used by the National Department for Welfare. Certain institutions emphasise subsistence – the mere availability of food – while others stress access to food, which, in turn, involves multiple dimensions, including income. These variations detract from FSN policy coherence and reduce the likelihood of developing a policy that uses all available financial and human resources to make territorial communities more resilient to food insecurity and malnutrition.

On paper, the Colombian approach to FSN is multidimensional. In practice, however, governance of the policy is fragmented and lacks leadership and vision. Colombia has pursued several programmes and policies to promote FSN. International organisations and donor agencies and the initiatives they implement add an additional layer of complexity. The various co-ordination tools relied upon by the Colombian government have proved insufficient. The *Comisión Intersectorial de Seguridad Alimentaria y Nutricional*, for example, does not actually require its stakeholders to co-ordinate with each other. Stakeholders are only obligated to inform counterparts about their policies. This has the effect of undermining the premise on which the commission was founded.

Implementing FSN policy at the sub-national level has proved particularly challenging. The incoherency of policy frameworks constitutes a profound challenge at the local level. There is an urgent need to encourage co-ordination across the FSN policy interventions and the programmes of various departments and municipalities. Most departments and municipalities lack the capacity, funds and political will to implement their own FSN actions. Interterritorial co-operation would seem to be one avenue for mitigating these constraints and perhaps even revealing synergies and complementarities. Instead, department and municipalities remain dependent on the aid provided by central-level bodies as the Colombian Family Welfare Institute.

Food security and nutrition policy is not linked to the policy agenda for competitiveness

Food insecurity and malnutrition are more pronounced in poor communities. Social programmes like conditional cash transfers[9] have been implemented in some of these communities. The current FSN policy framework does not, however, prioritise the mobilisation of local non-agricultural assets and investment opportunities to promote the economic development and competitiveness that are inevitably linked to issues of FSN.

The classification of FSN policy as a social policy and its association with agriculture – small-scale and subsistence agriculture in particular – prevents regional agents who are working to implement the FSN policy from capitalising on their knowledge of local conditions and development opportunities (OECD, 2014). Because FSN measures are generated within the framework of agricultural policy, policy makers the instruments and flexibility to attend to competitiveness in sectors beyond agriculture. OECD data (2014), however, show that the richest departments are those in which both agriculture and manufacturing represent a large share of the local economies, suggesting that sectorial diversification is essential.

Food security and nutrition policy has an urban bias, and is not adapted to the specific needs of ethnic groups or women

Even though food insecurity and malnutrition are more severe in rural areas, most programmes and investment are channelled to densely populated, accessible and relatively rich territories. This urban bias of FSN policy reflects the ease with which policies of national agencies, international organisations and donor agencies can be delivered in more favourable socio-economic and institutional environments. The only programmes implemented in rural regions tend to either be direct responses to emergencies or based on direct cash transfers. This is compounded by the fact that welfare programmes in Colombia are designed primarily for urban workers who are not involved in farming activities. As a consequence, most rural workers struggle to access basic rights such as land ownership and welfare.

The FSN policy framework does not adequately meet the needs of aboriginal and ethnic communities in the north (La Guajira) and along the Pacific coast. These communities are among the poorest in the country and are especially exposed to food insecurity and malnutrition. The contextual rigidity of the policy framework inhibits its capacity to deliver in distinctly different social and cultural contexts.

Greater effort could also be made to empower women in the framework of FSN policy. Recent initiatives show that women can, and do, play a key role in addressing FSN. *Fundación NU3* – a non-profit organisation in Barranquilla – for example, focuses on the empowerment of women in efforts to eradicate poverty and hunger. *Fundación NU3*'s interventions operate across three main axes: 1) nutrition and food safety; 2) nutritional recovery; and 3) education. The foundation also operates an education and awareness-oriented pregnancy prevention programme for young people aged 12-19. Policy initiatives like these that could be mainstreamed and scaled up in all departments.

Concluding remarks: What would a territorial approach look like in Colombia?

A territorial approach to FSN is a viable avenue for developing and implementing a broad, resilient policy framework in which state institutions, non-governmental organisations (NGOs), citizens and businesses can co-ordinate their actions to ensure that all citizens have access to adequately developed regional networks of public goods and services. Instituting a territorial approach to food security means addressing three main sets of challenges.

Evidence-based policy making

The collection of granular, sub-national statistics is the first step in putting into practice a territorial approach. Colombia is actively upgrading its national information systems (OECD, 2013b). Increased availability of sub-national data will undoubtedly benefit FSN initiatives. It would, for example, help public authorities actively monitor regional situations and quickly intervene in places that need special attention – i.e. conflict-stricken territories or areas with high numbers of *desplazados*. The availability of updated and granular regional statistics would also permit the more accurate and precise identification of populations at risk of food insecurity and malnutrition, which can facilitate long-term planning. Evidence-based policy making has the added benefit of clarifying the rationale for policies for the general public, enhancing government accountability.

Multi-level governance and co-ordination of policies

Efforts to improve the governance of FSN policies have thus far focused on the central level. However necessary, they have overlooked the importance of integrating sub-national governments into policy planning and delivery. Involving sub-national authorities can inform policy making and help tailor policy delivery to communities' specific needs and conditions. Regions are heterogeneous entities, and the coastal Atlantic region, for example, requires treatment distinctly different from the mountainous Andean region. Uniform implementation of a single policy is not the most efficient way to solve a problem that manifests itself in very different ways in heterogeneous territories. The engagement of sub-national authorities is essential for diagnosing and addressing regional differences.

Empirical evidence suggests that aligning policy agendas across levels of government and adapting national policy frameworks to sub-national characteristics and conditions would improve policy efficiency and effectiveness, using "knowledge pooling". This means aggregating information collected from various levels of government and relevant stakeholders about the needs of and opportunities in a given territory. Multi-level governance systems encourage participation and citizen engagement, thus facilitating processes of knowledge pooling. Moreover, multi-level governance helps assess the effect of policies, generating information that feeds into subsequent knowledge pooling and policy design.

Identifying complementarities and managing trade-offs among different strands of policy are essential for ensuring that scarce resources are deployed as efficiently as possible. The boundaries of sectoral policies are well defined at the national level. Most FSN policies are delivered by national authorities as a social policy (welfare), with only two exceptions: some interventions are delivered through the national health care system; and to a lesser extent, part of the policy is the responsibility of the Ministry of Agriculture. National-level co-ordination mechanisms minimise overlap and duplication in the provision of policies by these independent bodies. No such co-ordination mechanisms exist at the sub-national level or between the national and sub-national levels. This prevents synergies within and between levels of governments.

Co-ordination across policy sectors is also critical for developing a holistic approach to competitiveness in the context of FSN policy. Farming is presumed to be the only business opportunity available for people exposed to food insecurity and malnutrition. Policies to provide poor households with opportunities for generating new income have therefore been based in the agricultural sector. Meanwhile, armed conflict has deprived many rural residents of their land, starting large-scale rural-to-urban migration. Policy makers must acknowledge that income-generating opportunities for the poor exist outside agriculture. Policies supporting self-employment and entrepreneurship, as well as employment in the manufacturing and service sectors, for example, could help address household poverty and the associated FSN issues it often generates. Simply stated, the importance of the non-farm rural economy should not be underestimated, or the role of entrepreneurship and job creation in offering opportunities to new arrivals in the cities.

Notes

1. Extreme poverty data are not available for the department of Putumayo. It should be noted, however, that levels of household food insecurity in Putumayo (57.2%) exceed the national average. Similarly, food insecurity and extreme poverty data are not available for Amazonas.
2. Exact figures for food insecurity and malnutrition are to some degree dependent on the definition of rurality used. Using an alternative definition of urban/rural based on population density and proximity to urban centres could conceivably yield lower estimates for food insecurity and malnutrition (cf. OECD, 2014).
3. As a benchmark, the lowest value for the Gini Index of land distribution is that of Japan, with 0.382 (World Bank, 2004).
4. For a discussion of the factors that led to a rural-urban divide in Colombia, see OECD (2014).
5. *Familias en Acción* alone represents 0.5% of Colombia's total consolidated budget in 2015, USD 68 billion.
6. www.sispro.gov.co.
7. Approximately USD 2.2 billion was allocated to agricultural policy in 2015. The current budget compares with USD 250 million allocated to the sector in 2004. Also, budget allocation to agriculture has become more stable in recent years, facilitating policy design and delivery.
8. It is important to note, however, that the magnitude of this figure is probably forced upward by: *i)* the completeness of FSN data, thanks to the use of a better monitoring system and the implementation of a specific policy to monitor FSN; and *ii)* the potentially positive correlation of a programme supporting FSN and the percentage of citizens that self-identify with the challenge.
9. Monetary transfers to poor families, while necessary to eradicate poverty, may also create dependency. Recipients have little incentive to improve their conditions, because they risk losing the benefit. The large number of citizens who depend on social policy also affects the sustainability of the policy. This translates into a high variability of transfers – which, in turn, depend on the budget allocated to welfare at the national level. Thus, poor citizens are also exposed to unpredictably large variations in their income. This negatively affects not only resilience but public trust in the capacity of the public sector to reduce extreme poverty, food insecurity and malnutrition.

References

DANE (2010), Departamento Administrativo Nacional de Estadística, Colombia. http://www.dane.gov.co/

iDMC (2014), "Global estimates 2014: People displaced by disasters", Internal Displacement Monitoring Centre, Norwegian Refugee Council, Geneva, www.internal-displacement.org/publications/2014/global-estimates-2014-people-displaced-by-disasters.

OECD (2014), *OECD Territorial Reviews: Colombia 2014*, OECD Publishing, Paris, http://dx.doi.org/10.1787/9789264224551-en.

OECD (2013), *Rural-Urban Partnerships An Integrated Approach to Economic Development*, OECD Publishing, Paris, http://dx.doi.org/10.1787/9789264204812-en.

UNDP (2009), *Human Development Report, Overcoming Barriers: Human Mobility and Development*, United Nations Development Programme, New York, available at: http://hdr.undp.org/sites/default/files/reports/269/hdr_2009_en_complete.pdf.

World Bank (2004), *World Development Report 2004: Making Services Work for Poor People*, The World Bank, Washington, DC, available at: https://openknowledge.worldbank.org/bitstream/handle/10986/5986/WDR%202004%20-%20English.pdf?sequence=1.

Website

ENSIN (2010), Encuesta Nacional de la Situacion Nutricional en Colombia 2010 (ENSIN), http://ghdx.healthdata.org/record/colombia-national-survey-nutritional-situation-2010, (accessed June 2015).

Chapter 4.

A territorial approach to food security and nutrition: The case of the Côte d'Ivoire

The Côte d'Ivoire's approach to rural development has long been oriented towards agricultural development. Since the civil conflict, the government has relied upon a sectoral approach to food security and nutrition (FSN) and rural development. Current policies focus on the organisation, management and "institutionalisation" of a number of value chains within the agricultural sector. Food insecurity in the Côte d'Ivoire is spatially concentrated. Chronic malnutrition is highest in northern parts of the country and in the regions of Nord (39.3%), Nord Est (39.3%), Ouest (34.2%) and Nord Ouest (31.8%) in particular. The lowest levels of chronic malnutrition are found in the capital region of Abidjan (17.9%). Households that are afflicted by chronic malnutrition tend to be those reliant on subsistence farming or on the production of handicrafts, and those headed by individuals with lower levels of education. Innovative policy tools will be required to address rural development and food security in the coming decades. These tools should account for regional differences and be capable of co-ordinating actions in different sectors, focusing not only on agricultural intensity and diversification but prioritising non-farm activities.

Key findings[1]

Food security and rural development are intimately related. Issues of food insecurity and malnutrition in the Côte d'Ivoire are concentrated in rural areas, many of which have higher levels of poverty. Diversifying economic activities, creating non-farm employment opportunities and providing better access to basic services to rural populations will contribute to food security and enhance standards of living in the country.

The Côte d'Ivoire's approach to rural development has long been oriented towards agricultural development. Public and private investment channelled into export crops in the 1960s led to rapid development and urbanisation along the southern coast. This created North-South disparities that the five-year plan of 1971-75 sought to address through the extension of education services to rural areas, the creation of nucleus villages with improved public services and by establishing regional development funds. While disparities persisted, this represented a concerted effort to promote more territorially equitable development. A global collapse in commodity prices and local drought caused an economic downturn in the 1980s that bred social unrest. A series of liberalisation measures were implemented as part of broader structural adjustment programmes in 1994 in an effort to place the Côte d'Ivoire back on an upward development trajectory. Civil conflict between 2002 and 2011 halted many government functions that the new government is working to put back into action.

Since the civil conflict, the government has relied upon a sectoral approach to food security and nutrition (FSN) and rural development. Current policies focus on the organisation, management and "institutionalisation" of a number of value chains (*filières*) in the agricultural sector.

Rural areas in the Côte d'Ivoire have undergone a significant transformation in recent decades. The fertility rate is high (4.9 children per woman), and the rural population has continued to increase in absolute terms (from 2.9 million in 1960 to 9.5 million in 2013). In relative terms, however, the rural population has decreased. In 2013, the rural population only accounted for 47% of the total population. The prevalence of agriculture in national economic output has also decreased – agriculture only accounted for 22% of the Côte d'Ivoire's gross domestic product (GDP) in 2013. In spite of this, unemployment remains high and the road network, once one of the more developed in the sub-region, has suffered from underinvestment.

Food insecurity in the Côte d'Ivoire is spatially concentrated. Chronic malnutrition is highest in northern parts of the country and in the regions of Nord (39.3%), Nord Est (39.3%), Ouest (34.2%) and Nord Ouest (31.8%) in particular. The lowest levels of chronic malnutrition are found in the capital region of Abidjan (17.9%) (MICS, 2006). Households afflicted by chronic malnutrition tend to rely on subsistence farming or the production of handicrafts and those headed by individuals with lower educational levels.

The shortcomings of sectoral approaches to rural development are exemplified by the Ivorian experience. The existing value chain-oriented approaches to rural development tend only to benefit those directly involved in the chain. A lack of cross-sector co-ordination has also had a negative impact on natural resources and environmental services.

Any future efforts to address rural development and food security must consider the rapidly growing youth population. Annual entry into the workforce is expected to double, from 400 000 people to 800 000, by 2050. Such efforts to promote rural development must also prioritise non-farm activities, rather than focusing solely on agricultural intensity and diversification, as is now the case.

Introduction

Food insecurity and malnutrition tend to be more acute in rural areas and among low-income groups. This is very much the case in the Côte d'Ivoire, where poverty, food insecurity and malnutrition are concentrated in a few regions that have lower population densities and poor accessibility. A lack of non-farm employment opportunities, low agricultural productivity and political instability, as well as ongoing conflict, are the main challenges authorities face in promoting rural development and FSN in the Côte d'Ivoire. These domestic challenges have been compounded by a variety of negative international macroeconomic shocks that have weakened the Ivoirian economy and adversely affected the purchasing power of the population.

Ivorian authorities have employed a wide variety of strategic approaches in their efforts to mitigate these challenges, address issues of FSN and increase rural development. The diversity of the strategies employed is a product of the heterogeneity of domestically and internationally imposed challenges the Côte d'Ivoire has encountered in recent decades. Its approach to rural development thus far has been fragmented and overly reliant on agricultural activities. The uni-dimensionality of rural development approaches and their failure to account for the multitude of factors that impinge upon rural livelihoods has only exacerbated problems of poverty and, in turn, malnutrition in rural areas.

The objective of this case study is twofold: First, it describes the evolution of the Côte d'Ivoire's rural development and food security strategies. Second, it provides guidance for improving future policy actions that aim to increase living standards in rural areas and reduce food insecurity and malnutrition.

The remainder of the case study will proceed as follows. The first section provides an overview of the Côte d'Ivoire's development trajectory from 1960 to present. The second section disaggregates this development trajectory into its key phases and explores the rural development and food security policies associated with each phase. The third section contemplates the effectiveness of the strategies outlined in the second section. Finally, the case study provides a series of concluding remarks.

The Cote d'Ivoire's development path, poverty and food security

The Côte d'Ivoire's development trajectory may be distinguished into four distinct periods. The first includes the 20 years after independence in 1960. In this period, the country was considered the "West African miracle". The expansion of the agricultural sector and development of the manufacturing and service sectors in Abidjan led to annual increases in GDP that, in some years, exceeded 10%. The start of the second phase was marked by the collapse of the international prices of cocoa and coffee in 1979. The sharp declines in commodity prices, coupled with increasing debt, triggered a deep recession in 1980, followed by a 15-year period of economic stagnation. This economic crisis forced the country to pursue difficult structural reforms (Figure 4.1). Political tensions led to a military coup in 1999 that marked the beginning of the country's third developmental phase. The ten years that followed the political crisis brought further economic turmoil, recession and armed conflicts. The present phase of development began in 2011. GDP has grown at a rate of 8-10% since the start of this fourth phase, and the Côte d'Ivoire recently established the objective of becoming an "emerging nation" by 2020. The perceived feasibility of this objective is a product of robust internal and external demand, major public and private infrastructure investment for reconstruction, strong donor backing and positive international prospects.

Figure 4.1. **Evolution of GDP in the Côte d'Ivoire, 1960-2013**

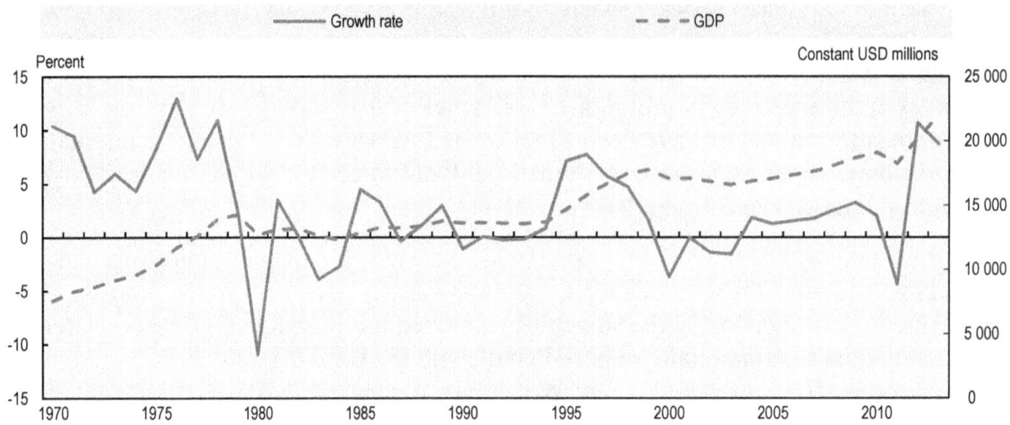

Source: World Development Indicators, http://data.worldbank.org/data-catalog/world-development-indicators.

Agriculture remains the engine of the Ivorian economy. There is, however, evidence of some economic diversification. The share of GDP attributable to agricultural activity, for example, fell from 50% in 1960 to approximately 27 % today (Figure 4.2). Similarly, employment in agriculture as a percentage of total employment fell from 82% in 1960 to 38% in 2010 (FAOSTAT). The Côte d'Ivoire's changing economic profile is a reflection, among other things, of urbanisation in a context where the rural population remains dependent on agricultural activities. Industrial activities and extractive industries (oil, gas and gold), by way of comparison, account for 15% and 7% of GDP respectively. The service sector in the Côte d'Ivoire has also come to account for an increasingly large share (48%) of GDP.[2] The growth of the sector is attributable, most immediately, to the increasing importance of the trade and transport of agricultural production and increasing urbanisation.

The Côte d'Ivoire's demographic transition is more advanced than many of its counterparts in sub-Saharan Africa. That said, job creation to accommodate an increasingly large working-age population is likely to present a challenge in coming decades.

The Côte d'Ivoire's population has increased more than six-fold in the last 20 years – from 3 million in 1960 to 20 million in 2013 – and is only expected to increase. The population growth rate in 2012 was 2.3%, and projections indicate that the population will double, to 44 million, in the next 35 years (UN medium scenario).

Moreover, the Côte d'Ivoire's younger population is exceptionally large. In 2015, individuals of 15 and under accounted for an estimated 41% of the total population. Individuals of age 25 or less made up 61% of the population. The youthfulness of the population means that the number of young people entering the labour market will increase from 430 000 today to 800 000 by 2050. In the next ten years, the country will have to provide jobs to 7 million young people. Moreover, nearly half of new workers will live in rural areas. There is evidence, however, to suggest that a demographic transition is under way. The fertility rate has decreased from approximately 8 births per woman in the early 1970s to less than 5 today (Figure 4.3).[3] This has had the effect of increasing the activity ratio to levels that exceed the Social Security Administration average (1.15). The Côte d'Ivoire's activity ratio stands at 1.23 active persons for each inactive person and is anticipated to reach 1.65 by 2050.

Figure 4.2. **Evolution of sector contribution to GDP in the Côte d'Ivoire, 1960-2013**

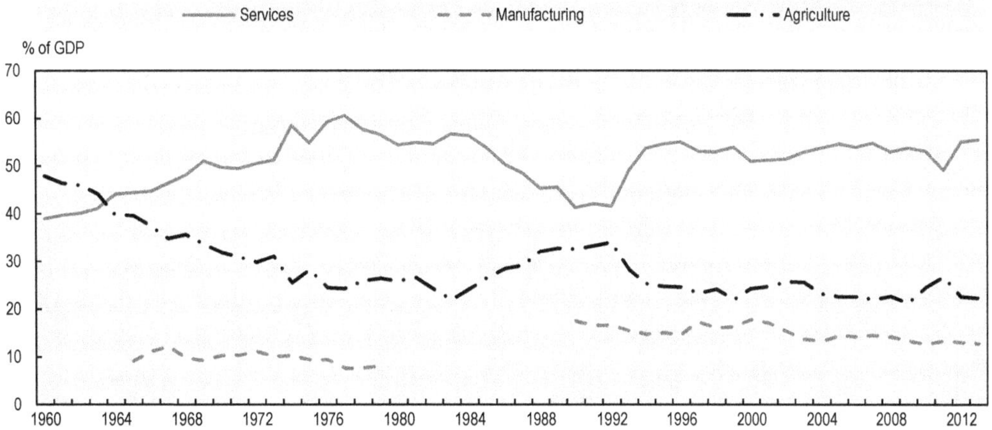

Source: World Development Indicators, http://data.worldbank.org/data-catalog/world-development-indicators.

Figure 4.3. **Evolution of population growth and fertility rates in the Côte d'Ivoire**

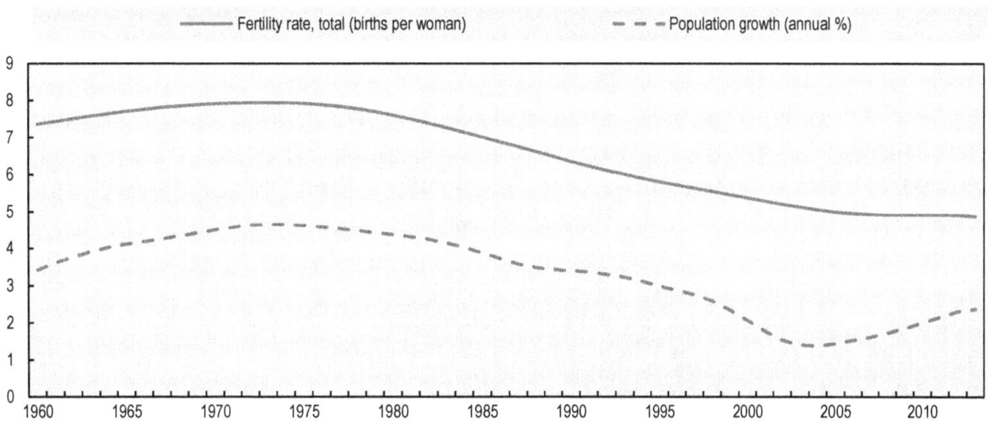

Source: World Development Indicators, http://data.worldbank.org/data-catalog/world-development-indicators.

The Côte d'Ivoire also has one of the highest immigration ratios in the world, fuelled by a steady flow of immigrants over the last 50 years. Before the political crisis in the later 20th century, individuals of foreign origin accounted for an estimated 25-30 % of the total population. Immigration has, however, tapered off.

At 55%, the Côte d'Ivoire's urbanisation rate is high by SSA standards. The country urbanised rapidly during the first phase of development (7-10% per year). The pace of urbanisation has since declined (3-4%), in large part due to the economic woes that plagued the country during the 1990s and 2000s. The Côte d'Ivoire's urban structure is best described as asymmetrical – its primacy index is 6.3. Abidjan, the main economic hub and harbour, is its only large city, home to 4.5 million-5 million inhabitants.

Poverty in the Côte d'Ivoire has increased in recent decades and has become increasingly concentrated in rural areas. Conflict and political crisis have contributed to an almost 40% increase in the poverty rate.[4] In 1985, the poverty rate was 10%. By 2008, it had risen to 49%. Perhaps even more worrying is that the poverty rate has increased faster in rural areas. The rural poverty rate reached 62% in 2008 (DSRP, 2009). Moreover, certain regions are more impoverished than others. Poverty rates are highest in northern and western regions of the country. In 2008, the Nord region had a poverty rate close to 80%. Poverty rates in the Ouest and Centre-Ouest regions were close to 63% in the same year (Figure 4.4).

Figure 4.4. **Territorial distribution of poverty in the Côte d'Ivoire**

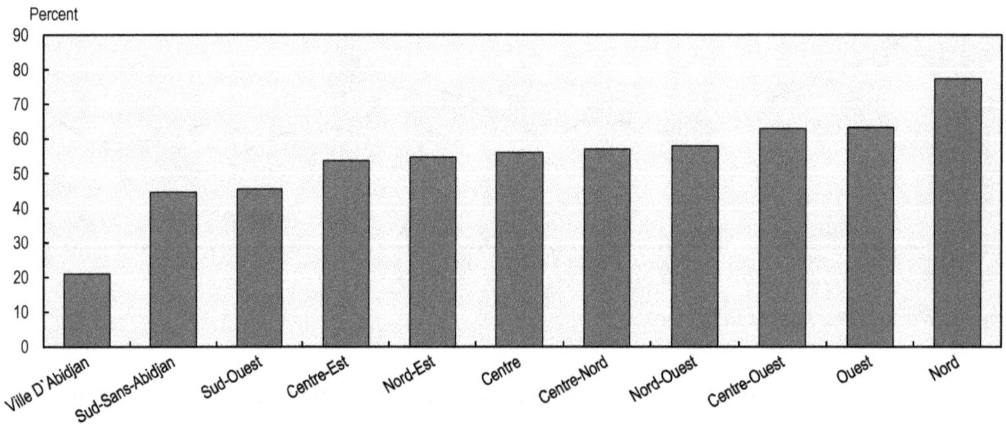

Source: DSRP (2009), "Stratégie de Relance du Dévéloppement et de Réduction de la Pauvreté".

Issues of FSN are especially pronounced in rural areas. In 2012, 35% of children aged 5 and under in the Côte d'Ivoire's rural areas suffered from chronic malnutrition, compared to 21% in urban areas. Chronic malnourishment among children was the highest in the Nord (39%) and Nord-Est (34%) regions (Figure 4.5). Chronic malnutrition is further concentrated in the most marginalised segments of society. In 2012, for example, 38% of children aged 5 and under from the poorest segment of the population suffered from stunted growth. Only 16% of children from the richest segment suffered from stunted growth (Table 4.1 and Annex 4.A1). Patterns similar to those highlighted above may be observed in statistics concerning the share of underweight children. The regions with the highest percentages of underweight children were Nord (20%) and Nord-Est (24%). The share of underweight children also tended to be higher in the poorest population group (21%) relative to the richest group (10%) (Table 4.1 and Annex 4.A1).

Evolution of strategies for rural development and food security

With the exception of a few isolated, short-lived programmes, the Côte d'Ivoire has yet to implement a policy oriented explicitly towards promoting rural development. After independence, the government prioritised agricultural development to increase economic development. It was anticipated that by prioritising agricultural production, efforts to increase farmers' incomes, and increased public investment funded by tax revenues, would naturally and inevitably yield rural development. Efforts were therefore made to modernise and increase the intensity and productivity of agricultural activities. A *laissez-faire* approach was adopted towards the production of coffee and cocoa, though peasant farmers were provided with minimal technical support, to encourage productivity. State intervention was employed to encourage diversification and in the promotion of exports. The evolution of this system can be split into four periods.

Figure 4.5. **Territorial distribution of chronic malnutrition in the Côte d'Ivoire (children less than 5 years old)**

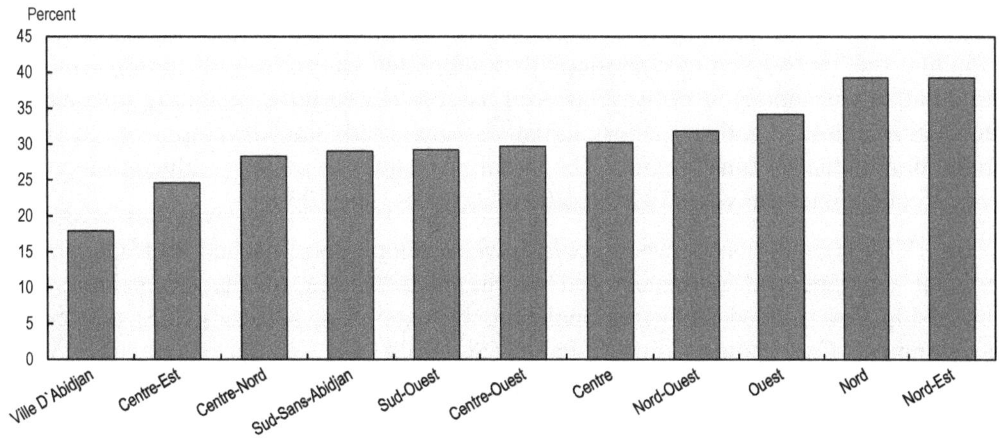

Source: EDS (2012), *Enquête Démographique et de Santé et à Indicateurs Multiples.*

The filière approach (1960 to mid-1970s)

The government established a number of *ad hoc* organisations dedicated to the development of specific areas of production in an effort to promote agricultural diversification.[5] These public enterprises and joint ventures had their own board, CEO and personnel and were managed like private companies. Each was linked with research institutions that provided higher quality seeds and technical assistance to support the production of profitable and exportable productions. The production of staple food crops, on the other hand, did not benefit from any dedicated body. Farmers did, however, elect to cultivate staple crops alongside coffee, cocoa and other products prioritised by newly formed organisations. This ensured that sufficient quantities of staple crops were produced to meet the growing demand of an increasingly urban population.

The marketing of coffee and cocoa – the two main export crops – was traditionally managed by the private sphere. This legacy of minimal state involvement was retained in the new system. The role of the state was limited to: 1) setting the rules in agreement with private operators; 2) defining a yearly unique farm gate price and regulating downstream costs; and 3) controlling exports through the marketing board – the Caisse de Stabilisation – which taxed and approved them based on a price target. Under the *filière* approach, annual increases in the guaranteed price, the president's personal political support to "planters" and the facilitation of access to land resources for any producer – including foreigners – created an effective set of incentives that resulted in booming production of non-staple products.

Under the *filière* approach, agricultural growth and increasing farmers' incomes were the pillars of rural development. A National Agency for Rural Development existed briefly in the early 1970s. Policies aimed at improving education, health, living conditions and transport infrastructures were place-neutral and did not specifically target rural areas. In this period, FSN was addressed indirectly via policies targeting agricultural productivity and growth.

From the mid-1970s to 1989

In the mid-1970s, the Côte d'Ivoire attempted to adopt a regional approach to rural development to tackle growing regional asymmetries between the southern part of the country, which was benefiting from the cocoa boom, and the lagging north. Major infrastructure projects, like the construction of a hydroelectric dam on the Bandama River and the development of a new harbour in San Pedro were put into operation in the central region. Efforts were also made to promote the development of the Southwest region, including the "railway cities operation" that supported enterprises in small towns along the Abidjan-Ouagadougou railway, as well as accelerated urban planning operations in secondary cities. Another major initiative supported the development of cotton production, in the savannah region. The initiative resulted in cotton production increasing from 35 000 tonnes per year (1970) to 400 000 tonnes (late 1990s).

In 1977, competition between *sociétés de développement* caused inefficiencies and regional overlaps and ultimately led to the restructuring of the extension system. Leadership was divided along regional (and by extension, sectoral) lines between the Development Corporation of Oil Palm (SODEPALM) in the south; the *Société d'Assistance pour la Modernisation de l'Agricultur*e (SATMACI) in the middle region; and the *Compagnie Ivorienne de Développement de Textiles* (CIDT) in the north.[4] Several agro-industrial estates and regional development programmes associated with the previous approach were, however, maintained. This bred institutional complexity that contributed to the economic crisis of the late 1980s. Returns from the efforts to promote regional development were minimal over this period, and rural development remained a by-product of agricultural and sectoral growth.[6]

Standardisation and privatisation (1989-2011)

The extension system was profoundly reshaped with the structural reforms in the early 1990s. In 1989, the World Bank launched the "National support project to extension services" to restructure the extension systems. *Sociétés de développement* were absorbed into a public-private partnership called the National Agency for Rural Development. The agency, which sought to enhance agricultural production and improve farmers' access to inputs, was privatised in 1998.

Easy access to land, coupled with migration flows, created social tensions that were exacerbated by a deep economic crisis. A new law was enacted that formally limited the ownership of land property to the state, local governments and Ivorian nationals. The situation of immigrants deteriorated as a result of the law.

International donors pressured the government to liberalise the coffee and cocoa sectors. Fixed producer prices were progressively removed, and the Caisse de Stabilisation implemented a more transparent system for sales management. In 1999, the country experienced a military coup. During the 2000s, private governance prevailed in the coffee and cocoa sectors. New administrative bodies were created with representatives from exporters, carriers, grinders, banks, producers' organisations and the state, including the *Bourse du café et du cacao* (a regulation fund) and the *Autorité de régulation du café et du cacao*. The pre-existing taxation system based on exports remained. The *Comité de gestion de la filière café-cacao* (CGFCC) was set up in 2008, providing a new regulatory system. Under the CGFCC, taxes were no longer linked to the exported volume, and instead were applied to the value added and limited to 22 % of the CAF price.

Issues of food security and nutrition were mainly addressed in the National Health Development Plans that covered the periods between 1996-2005 and 2009-13. A variety of other smaller policies and projects targeting malnutrition were also implemented through national initiatives or in partnership with international donors. According to the *Programme National de Nutrition* (PNN, 2010), some of the most relevant policy actions in the early 1990s included: the *Initiative Hôpitaux Amis des Bébés*, a project funded by the United Nations Children's Fund (UNICEF) to fight micronutrient deficiencies; campaigns against iodine deficiency; and inter-ministerial actions authorising and promoting salt iodisation for human and animal consumption. In the late 1990s, the National Action Plan for Nutrition set up the National Nutrition Programme within the Ministry of Health and Public Hygiene. This was one of the most effective actions for tackling FSN-related problems. In the late 2000s, free health care was granted to malnourished children in areas where issues of FSN were prevalent, and the Ivorian Agency of Food Safety was set up (PNN, 2010). The Poverty Reduction Strategy launched in 2009 (DSRP, 2009) incorporated food security as one of its main pillars. In 2010, discussions for the review of the National Nutrition Plan started and a new protocol for managing malnutrition was adopted in 2009 and later revised in 2013.

Renewal of the filière approach (2011-present)

The top priority of the new regime is to restart the Côte d'Ivoire's economic engine. To this end, the *Plan National de Développement* allocated 25% of its resources to infrastructure and transport development, 15% to the energy and mining sectors, and 8.5% to the agricultural sector. Investment objectives were based on the *Programme National d'Investissement Agricole*, and later the *Programme d'Investissement Détaillé*. The *Plan National de Développement* does not explicitly address rural development. It is, however, reflected in its thematic actions, related to education, health and living conditions. New regulating bodies, including the *Conseil du Café-Cacao* and the *Conseil du Coton et de l'Anacarde* were also established in 2012. These are jointly managed with the private sector.

The adoption of an integrated approach to agricultural development is another priority of the new regime. The approach is based on "multi-stakeholder platforms" (*interprofessions*),[7] whose responsibilities include: the definition of an overarching strategic vision, the identification of objectives and actions, the dissemination of research and knowledge, the provision of training and education, and the promotion of agro-industrial development. The prioritisation of an integrated approach to agricultural development is founded in the perception that such an approach will yield a more equitable distribution of the benefits from growth and development. *Filières* are once again the focus of the new strategic approach. Rural development is not, however, explicitly prioritised in the new approach.

The *Programme National d'Investissement Agricole* has been one of the main tools for addressing FSN. The estimated amount of money to be dedicated to the implementation of this plan is CFA 71 632 million in West African francs (PNN, 2010). The programme is guided by the objective of achieving national food security by 2015. In addition to promoting family farming, the *Programme National d'Investissement Agricole* targets FSN via efforts to revitalise the animal, fishery, aquaculture and vegetable sectors. The initiatives employed in the pursuit of the programme's objectives include: projects promoting the rice sector, investment in maize and soy production for animal nutrition, projects encouraging animal and fish food production, projects supporting the production of vegetable crops, and projects to rehabilitate and equip breeding stations.

Overall assessment

The Côte d'Ivoire has built a strong commercial agricultural sector through pro-active policies. Cocoa and coffee are the country's main exports. Agricultural diversity has, however, increased significantly in recent years. Natural rubber, cashew and palm oil are now important exports (FAOSTAT). Moreover, the share of food in total merchandise imports has fallen in the last decade to 10%, in large part due to a combination of improvements in staple production (notably rice in recent years) and an increased reliance on locally produced food as a result of the economic crisis.

Economic successes have not led to human development in rural areas. Levels of human development are low in the Côte d'Ivoire. In 2013, it ranked 171st out of 187 in terms of human development. It was plagued by political and economic crises. They are not, however, the only factors to which the failure to translate strong agricultural production to human development may be attributed.[8]

The consequences of the inability to transform agricultural performance into human development are especially pronounced for rural areas. The government has never explicitly targeted rural areas. It has proceeded to gradually equip the administrative centres of each *département* with health facilities, electric power and schools, but infrastructure in rural areas remains underdeveloped.[9] North-South disparities persist alongside the pronounced urban-rural divide. Abidjan's primacy has contributed to the pro-South polarisation of the territorial organisation of the country, and the coffee- and cocoa-producing regions in the south have benefited from a dense transport network and early connection to the power grid.

Malnutrition and rural poverty have increased in recent decades, despite government efforts. Economic turmoil and conflict have contributed to an increase in the incidence of malnutrition – the number of undernourished individuals doubled between 1992 and 2014. Aware of this issue, the government is attempting to implement universal health care. A pilot project was scheduled for 2015.

Figure 4.6. **Evolution of undernourishment in the Côte d'Ivoire**

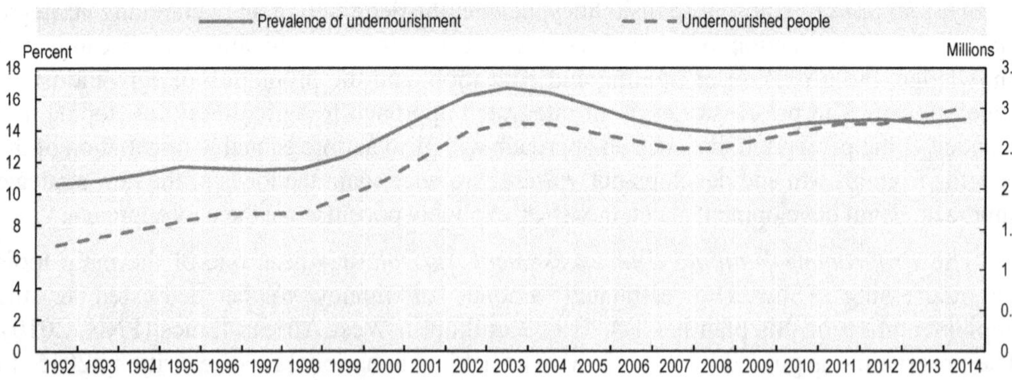

Source: World Development Indicators, http://data.worldbank.org/data-catalog/world-development-indicators.

In the 1980s, only 10% of the population was living below the national poverty line (WDI). In the 1990s, however, the situation worsened. Extreme poverty increased from 8% in 1985 to 30% in 1998. Over the same period, the percentage of the population living below the USD 2 poverty line increased from 21% to 57% (WDI). The situation grew more dire during the 2000s: by the end of the decade, 60% of the population was living under the USD 2 poverty line. GDP per capita also fell back to levels seen in the early 1960s. Rural areas have always been more deeply affected by poverty – poverty ratios in rural areas are twice those in urban areas. The urban-rural gap has persisted: in 2008, 54% of rural dwellers were living under the national poverty line (Figure 4.7). Sharp regional differences have persisted as well. Until 1985, rural poverty was higher in the northern savannah areas. The drop in cocoa and coffee producers' prices in 1989, however, led to a dramatic change: poverty spread to the forest zone, especially in the Western region. Abidjan was somewhat sheltered from the collapse until 1993. The geographic proliferation of poverty led to a decrease in income inequality in the early 1990s (WDI), but institutional and governance challenges led to an increase in the Gini coefficient, from 32 in 1990 to 42 in 2010.

In the 1980s, 31% of the Ivorian budget was allocated to education and the development of pro-active education policies.[10] During structural adjustment, however, this dropped to 22% (1990-93) and then to 19% in the late 1990s. Gross enrolment levels in primary school also declined in the 1990s (WDI). Today, the average Ivorian has 2.8 years of schooling (WDI). The situation is even worse in Northwest regions – more than half of children in the Northwest do not attend school. The literacy rate (40%) has been almost stagnant for 20 years (WDI). The Côte d'Ivoire also suffers from low levels of enrolment in secondary and tertiary education.

Access to infrastructure in the Côte d'Ivoire is relatively good by regional standards despite the minimal progress made in recent years. Progress is most noticeable in access to water. Nearly 70% of the population in rural areas now has access to water (WDI). Sanitation infrastructure, on the other hand, is grossly underdeveloped. Only 10% of rural dwellers have access to adequate sanitation. The Côte d'Ivoire is an exporter of electricity to its neighbouring countries. Less than 40% of rural areas, however, are connected to the power grid, and in several *départements* in the north, fewer than 15% of the population has access to electricity. The road network is relatively well developed by Social Security Administration (SSA) standards, with paved roads connecting main urban centres. This is not the case, however, in the Northwest region, where infrastructure deteriorated during the 2000s. Its rehabilitation is now a public investment priority. The secondary road network is poorly developed both in the north and across the country more generally.

Figure 4.7. **Evolution of poverty in the Côte d'Ivoire**

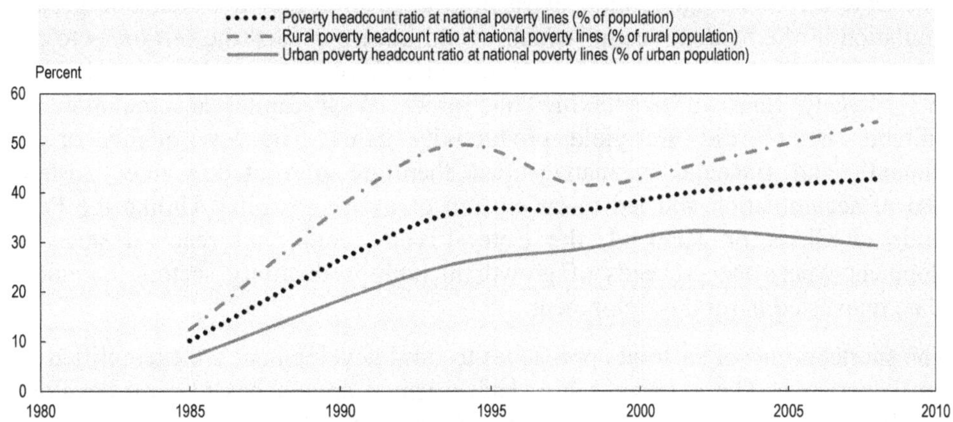

Source: World Development Indicators, http://data.worldbank.org/data-catalog/world-development-indicators.

Concluding remarks

The Côte d'Ivoire's early economic achievements are attributable to the establishment of a clear strategic vision that built trust and reduced risk for farmers. The development of a powerful agro-industrial sector was a product of pro-active public policies and the promotion of public-private partnerships. The integrated commodity chain (*filière)* approach provided knowledge and information as well as extension services through dedicated agencies. The broader strategic framework relied on economic openness; easy access to land and migrant labour; a stable price environment; guaranteed commercialisation based on public-private agreements; and strong political support to farmers. This framework bred trust amongst agents, reduced risk and ultimately led to increased investment and diversification.

This model proved too inflexible to adapt to evolving conditions. The economic "miracle" ended abruptly in the early 1980s as a consequence of an overspecialisation in exports; falling commodity prices; an unfavourable US dollar to CFA franc parity; a lack of anticipation of the need to improve productivity and investment in human capital; deteriorating governance and the mismanagement and successive postponement of reforms. The Côte d'Ivoire's agricultural boom had relied on the extensive exploitation of natural resources and labour. This resulted in considerable increases in agricultural output, without comparable increases in productivity or economic diversification. Reliance on natural resources and labour was sustainable so long as factor inputs were easily accessible and widely available. The system was, however, unable to cope with increased pressure on and demand for natural resources. As the agricultural sector suffered, a lack of employment opportunities in other sectors led to tensions between local and immigrant populations, both of which were competing for relatively few jobs.

Conflict also had systemic and profound adverse effects. The political and social tensions led to a political crisis and, in turn, a civil war. This only served to weaken the overall economy[11] and exacerbate poverty.

The Côte d'Ivoire's agriculturally oriented approach left important rural challenges unaddressed. Agricultural production and diversification were prioritised and rural development *per se* was never an overt priority of public policy – it was anticipated the agricultural expansion would give rise to rural development. What minimal public investment was made in rural infrastructure and services yielded limited results.

The Côte d'Ivoire's agricultural expansion failed to trigger a sustainable process of accumulation in the modern sector, which would have provided the resources to plough investment back into rural areas on a large scale. Capital accumulation in the modern sector – largely financed by "taxing" the proceeds of capital accumulation in the agricultural sector – did not yield productivity gains. The low quality of public investment[12] and financial mismanagement therefore prevented a new, sustainable process of accumulation and led to an erosion of existing capital. Unlike the People's Republic of China or Thailand, the Côte d'Ivoire could not reach a stage in its development where the proceeds of growth in high-productivity sectors, e.g. industry, could be reinvested in rural development.

The shortcomings of sectoral approaches to rural development are exemplified by the Ivorian experience. The existing value chain-oriented approaches to rural development tend only to benefit those directly involved in the chain. A lack of cross-sector co-ordination has also had a negative impact on natural resources and environmental services.

Future efforts to address rural development and food security must consider the rapidly growing younger population. Annual entry into the workforce is expected to double, from 400 000 people to 800 000 by 2050. Future efforts to promote rural development must also prioritise non-farm activities and not focus solely on agricultural intensity and diversification, as is now the case.

Notes

1. The information on rural development policies in this report was collected through a consultancy carried out by CIRAD under the supervision of the OECD Development Centre.
2. This figure does not reflect the frequent provision of services in the informal sector.
3. The ratio was estimated at 4.6 in the 2000s (WPP, 2010) and is estimated at 4.9 now.
4. The national poverty line was established in 2008 as 661 CFA francs per day, which is approximately USD 2.35 PPP (2005).
5. Several *sociétés de développement* or SODE were set up: the *Société d'assistance technique pour la modernisation de l'agriculture en Côte d'Ivoire* (SATMACI), initially created in 1958, focused on coffee and cocoa; SODEPALM on palm and coconut, associated with PALMINDUSTRIE for oil production; SODEFOR on timber; SODEFEL on fruits and vegetables; SODEPRA on animal production; SODESUCRE on sugar; CIDT for cotton, etc. They were "flagships of progress in rural areas" (Sawadogo, 1977). For *filières* where private firms were in place – rubber, banana and pineapple – the state would delegate the role of supporting farmers.
6. Technical ministries continued to develop their own programmes with the objective of improving ratios of population coverage.
7. The *Fonds interprofessionnel pour la recherche et le conseil agricoles*, for example, finances research, extension, training and support to farmers' organisations. It receives support from the government and donors. Actions are implemented through the National Centre for Agricultural Research and the National Agency for Rural Development, which depend on these product-targeted funds for developing their activities. As a consequence, in spite of its name, the National Agency for Rural Development only provides occasional support to local governments engaging in territorial rural development planning.
8. The "big push" of the 1960s and 1970s, for example, did not translate into significant improvements in living standards. During the 1980s, the Côte d'Ivoire was not performing better in terms of human development than other sub-Saharan African countries with lower GDPs and lower growth rates.
9. One limited exception were the *Fonds régionaux d'aménagement rural* (FRAR) created in 1974, which co-funded schools, water access, roads, health centres, etc. with villagers contributing 40-60% of the investment (more in the richer south, less in the north).

10. Including an innovative system of educational TV (*télévision scolaire*) targeting rural areas in the 1970s.

11. GDP per capita moved back to levels last seen in 1960s.

12. This was exemplified by the poor performance of public companies such as Sodesucre, or the building of "cathedrals in the desert", such the world's largest basilica in Yamoussoukro.

References

DSRP (2009), Stratégie de Relance du Dévéloppement et de Réduction de la Pauvreté.

EDS (2012), *Enquête Démographique et de Santé et à Indicateurs Multiples*.

MICS (2006), *Enquête par Grappe à Indicateurs Multiples*.

PNN (2010), "Rapport du landscape analysis pour la Cote d'Ivoire", Ministère de la Santé et de l'Hygiène Publique.

United Nations, Department of Economic and Social Affairs, Population Division (2011), "*World Population Prospects: The 2010 Revision*", Vol. I: Comprehensive Tables. ST/ESA/SER.A/313

Websites

ANADER (n.d.), www.anader.ci (accessed September 2015).

Barro-Lee, Educational Attainment dataset, www.barrolee.com (accessed August 2015).

Conseil du Café-Cacao (n.d.), www.conseilcafecacao.ci (accessed September 2015).

FIRCA (n.d.), www.firca.ci (accessed July 2015).

FAOSTAT (n.d.), Food and Agriculture Organization of the United Nations, Statistics Division, http://faostat3.fao.org/home (accessed August 2015).

UNCTAD (n.d.), United Nations Conference on Trade and Development, http://unctad.org/en/Pages/Statistics.aspx (accessed July 2015).

World Development Indicators –WDI (n.d.), http://data.worldbank.org/data-catalog/world-development-indicators (accessed August 2015).

World Population Prospect –WPP (n.d.), http://esa.un.org/wpp (accessed September 2015).

World Urbanization Prospect –WUP (n.d.), http://esa.un.org/unpd/wup (accessed August 2015).

Annex 4.A1.
Nutritional status of children under 5

Table 4.A1.1. **Nutritional status of children under 5 years old, 2012**

Height-for-age Centred mean score				Weight-for-height				Weight-for-age			
	% below 3 SD	% below 2 SD		% below 3 SD	% below 2 SD	% above 2 SD	Centred mean score	% below 3 SD	% below 2 SD	% above 2 SD	Centred mean score
Centre	15.1	30.2	(1.3)	1.1	9.3	0.9	(0.4)	6.1	17.3	0.4	(1.0)
Centre-Est	6.7	24.6	(1.1)	0.7	7.4	3.2	(0.3)	2.3	13.4	1.7	(0.8)
Centre-Nord	13.9	28.3	(1.3)	0.6	4.0	4.1	(0.0)	3.1	9.6	1.5	(0.8)
Centre-Ouest	13.1	29.7	(1.3)	3.3	8.1	4.5	(0.1)	2.8	14.8	1.2	(0.8)
Nord	17.6	39.3	(1.5)	0.7	5.8	2.4	(0.3)	4.7	20.1	0.0	(1.1)
Nord-Est	16.4	39.3	(1.6)	3.3	11.1	2.0	(0.5)	6.9	24.2	0.0	(1.3)
Nord-Ouest	12.8	31.8	(1.3)	1.7	6.3	2.3	(0.1)	4.1	14.6	1.2	(0.9)
Ouest	14.9	34.2	(1.4)	0.7	6.2	2.6	0.0	2.5	16.2	1.1	(0.8)
Sud	11.7	29.0	(1.1)	1.3	9.3	2.7	(0.2)	3.1	15.6	1.9	(0.8)
Sud-Ouest	7.0	29.2	(1.0)	2.4	7.5	2.9	(0.1)	2.8	12.9	0.7	(0.7)
Ville d'Abidjan	5.2	17.9	(0.8)	2.0	8.3	3.4	(0.2)	2.4	10.6	0.7	(0.6)
Mother's educational attainment											
No education	13.8	31.8	(1.3)	1.7	8.0	2.8	(0.2)	4.2	16.1	0.7	(0.9)
Primary	9.5	28.7	(1.1)	2.3	8.9	3.3	(0.2)	2.0	13.8	1.4	(0.8)
At least secondary	3.7	16.2	(0.7)	0.7	4.1	2.5	(0.2)	1.1	8.3	0.7	(0.5)
Quintiles of well-being index											
Poorest	19.4	38.4	(1.6)	1.6	10.0	2.4	(0.2)	6.0	20.7	0.4	(1.1)
Poor	13.1	35.5	(1.4)	2.0	5.9	3.6	(0.1)	2.6	16.0	1.6	(0.9)
Middle	10.9	27.7	(1.2)	1.5	6.9	2.9	(0.2)	3.0	12.8	0.8	(0.8)
Rich	8.1	24.2	(1.0)	1.6	7.4	2.3	(0.2)	3.0	11.7	0.9	(0.7)
Richest	4.9	15.5	(0.7)	1.8	6.9	4.2	(0.2)	1.0	10.0	1.3	(0.5)
Total	12.2	29.8	(1.2)	1.7	7.5	3.0	(0.2)	3.4	14.9	1.0	(0.8)

Source: EDS (2012), *Enquête Démographique et de Santé et à Indicateurs Multiples.*

Chapter 5.

A territorial approach to food security and nutrition policy: The case of Morocco

Morocco is making a concerted effort to reduce its internal regional inequalities, and has gone some way towards "territorialising" both sectoral policies and democratic decision-making processes. Interventions aimed to improve the food security and nutrition (FSN) situation in marginalised areas range from human development to rural infrastructure provision and the promotion of endogenous development potential in local areas. The country's political decentralisation agenda has further helped to bring decision making closer to the people, and has facilitated the formulation of policies tailored to context-specific needs and opportunities. Nevertheless, challenges remain, including weak horizontal co-ordination mechanisms across sectors, which risk leading to duplication of effort and a lack of scaled interventions. Fragmented territorial information systems further complicate implementation of the government's continuing commitment to adopt territorial approaches. Moving forward, increased capacity at the local level, as well as the involvement of sub-national authorities in policy-making processes at all levels, will be critical.

Key findings

Morocco has achieved considerable economic progress in recent decades. Sustained economic growth between 2001 and 2011 resulted in a significant increase in average income per capita and led to a reduction in the incidence of poverty from 15% to 6%. The gains from economic growth have not, however, been distributed evenly, and regional disparities have increased. Between 1985 and 2011, for example, relative poverty decreased by 90% in the regions of the south, but only by 50% in Doukkala-Abda and Gharb-Chrarda-Béni Hssen. Similarly, 67% of the country's poor and 59% of the country's vulnerable populations live in rural and remote areas.

In May 2005, the king of Morocco called for increased efforts to reduce marginalisation and lift vulnerable people and regions out of poverty and announced the establishment of the National Human Development Initiative (*Initiative Nationale pour le Développement Humain*). In 2014, the king acknowledged the considerable progress made towards these objectives but noted that poverty, vulnerability and acute social inequality remained prevalent.

Recognising the need for further progress, the king commissioned the Economic, Social and Environmental Council, the Moroccan Central Bank and relevant national and international institutions to conduct a study of Morocco's total wealth between 1999 and 2013. The Ministry of the Interior was also instructed to conduct an assessment of local infrastructure and service needs in Morocco's rural areas. This revealed that 29 000 *douars*[1] spread across 1 272 municipalities suffered from serious infrastructural deficiencies and under-provision of basic social services. In July 2015, the king launched an initiative to promote development in 2 500 rural villages (home to 12 million people) via infrastructural upgrading and better provision of basic services (roads, schools, health care centres, drinkable water, etc.).

In 2008, the government of Morocco launched the Green Morocco Plan (*Plan Maroc Vert* or PMV), whose objective is to mobilise the diverse development potential of Morocco's regions. It features a two-pronged strategy designed to: 1) promote the expansion of larger-scale and commercial farms; and 2) support smallholder family farms and encourage the transformation of family farms into family enterprises. The main focus of the Green Morocco Plan is undoubtedly agricultural expansion. That said, the strategy also includes measures to promote local development via the mobilisation of local assets and opportunities.

The Nutrition Strategy 2011-2019 is contributing to the achievement of the aims of the National Human Development Initiative and to food security more generally. The second strategic pillar of the strategy is focused on increasing the country's supply of safe food by increasing the agricultural capacity of smallholders. As of 2014, 56% of income-generating projects outlined in the National Human Development Initiative had been implemented in rural areas.

The Halieutis Plan, the primary focus of which is the competitiveness and conservation of marine ecosystems, also addresses issues of food security and nutrition (FSN) via the promotion of the diversification the national diet, and includes an increased target for fish consumption of 16 kilogrammes per capita per year by 2020.

All these strategies feature a strong territorial dimension. The National Human Development Initiative, for example, stresses the importance of adopting a territorial approach that uses strategic planning processes to ensure consistency and coherence across sectoral programmes and the actions of local authorities. Similarly, the Green

Morocco Plan is based on a thorough analysis and mapping of the country's territorial assets. Likewise, the Mountain Strategy is based on the principle of "positive discrimination". The country's lagging areas have also been prioritised since the rural infrastructure development efforts implemented in the 1990s. The new Constitution of 2011 reflects a territorial focus as well. It explicitly states that "the territorial organisation of the Kingdom is decentralised, founded on an advanced regionalisation" (Article 1), and enshrines the principle of the free administration of local authorities and the subsidiarity of the central authority.

Various instruments have been employed to promote the development of lagging areas, including regional development agencies, regional agricultural plans, regional funds, rural development funds, communal plans, plan contracts (*contrats de plan*), and targeted and untargeted safety nets. A detailed poverty and vulnerability mapping exercise conducted at the regional, provincial and commune level was completed in 2007 (Haut-Commissariat au Plan, 2009).

These strategies and the Constitution of 2011 reflect a commitment to the employment of territorial approaches for the eradication of poverty and food insecurity. Authorities have faced challenges in implementing territorial approaches. These include: weak horizontal co-ordination and the regressive effects of geographic targeting systems and financing due to, for example, weak and fragmented territorial information systems; capacity constraints at the decentralised level; and the prevailing top-down innovation process.

In sum, the main challenge faced by Moroccan authorities is putting into practice its robust commitment to territorial approaches to address poverty and food insecurity. The inclusion of local institutions and stakeholders in the policy-making process, the introduction of effective horizontal governance mechanisms, and the development of multisectoral and multi-actor approaches that reflect the multidimensional nature of FSN and poverty are the keys to overcoming these challenges. Two recently approved organic laws concerned with the implementation of a stronger decentralisation process at the prefecture, province and municipality level (No. 112.14 and No. 113.14) are steps in the right direction.

Food security and poverty: Two nested problems

Morocco is extremely vulnerable to global price volatility, in large part due to its dependence on food imports.[2] This alone does not make the country food insecure. That said, rising food prices constitute a prominent threat to the health and well-being of Moroccan households – and poor ones in particular – who spend up to 70% of their incomes on food. Moreover, given the number of Moroccans who live marginally above the poverty line (approximately 12% of the population), even small fluctuations in food prices can have dramatic impacts on national poverty rates. The groups most exposed to price volatility are the rural landless, the marginal farmers and the urban poor. The middle class is also not immune to price volatility. Middle-class households spend approximately 40% of their incomes on food (Harrigan 2012; Ghanem, 2015). Suffice it to say, household food security is a salient issue in Morocco. It also has major political implications, as shown by its contribution to the social unrest in 2011.

Morocco has made impressive progress towards addressing undernutrition over the course of the last decade (Table 5.1). However, levels of obesity in Morocco (17% of the population is categorised as obese) now exceed the world average (11.7%). Suffice it to say, aspects of FSN remain unaddressed (Ministère de la Santé, 2011).

Table 5.1. **Undernutrition in Morocco**

	2004	2011
Stunted children (under 5)	18.10%	15%
Wasted	9.30%	2.30%
Underweight	10.20%	3.10%

Source: Ministère de la Santé (2011), "La stratégie nationale de la nutrition 2011-2019", available at: www.unicef.org/morocco/french/Strategie_Nationale_de_Nutrition_.pdf.

Food insecurity and poverty are closely correlated in Morocco, in part because of the share of income (approximately 70%) poor households spend on food. Approximately 4 million people live below the national poverty line, 3 million of them in rural areas. The incidence of poverty is especially high in rural areas (10% in 2011) relative to urban ones (3.5%). Rural households are often dependent, either directly or indirectly, on agriculture. Many of them, however, only have access to a limited amount of non-irrigated arable land, with minimal agricultural potential. Moreover, many famers do not have a formal title to their land and as a consequence face difficulties obtaining credit, which limits their opportunity to engage in new economic activities and diversify their incomes.

Urban-rural disparities in food security and poverty are compounded by inter-regional ones. Climactic and geographic conditions vary substantially across the country. Structural aridity affects 80% of the land surface, and water scarcity has become more pronounced as demand for water has increased (AfDB, OECD and UNDP, 2014). The spatial distribution of poverty is, at least in part, attributable to cross-territorial variation in geographic conditions. Arable coastal areas are, for example, less afflicted by poverty. Mountainous areas, by contrast, are generally arid and, as a result, the home of most of the poorest Moroccans. There are also high concentrations of poverty in the country's fishing communities, scattered along the coast (IFAD, 2009; Adidi, 2011).

Simply stated, issues of food insecurity and poverty are concentrated in areas characterised by adverse geographic conditions, low population density, and limited access to basic physical and social infrastructure. These conditions generally coincide with those of rural and remote areas.

Poverty and food insecurity are attributable to several factors. Chief among them are factors that hinder agricultural development, including low diversification of agricultural activities; land tenure factors; climactic variation and volatility; poor soil conditions; insufficient water resources; degradation of natural resources; poor access to credit; farmers' lack of organisation; and insufficient access to financial services, basic social services and infrastructure. These are compounded by the weakness of social capital, including community organisations that lack the necessary training and support to take charge of their own development (IFAD, 2009).

The prevalence of spatial disparities in poverty and food insecurity has led to an ambitious initiative whose objective is to promote development in 2 500 rural villages that are home to 12 million people (approximately 30% of the population).

Reliance on agriculture for food security is not enough to reduce territorial differences

The development of the agricultural sector is essential for increasing rural standards of living in Morocco. It should thus feature prominently in any strategy to promote inclusive growth, and reduce inequality and territorial disparities. This can decrease dependence on food imports and minimise the country's vulnerability to volatility in global food prices.

Economic growth in Morocco is closely linked to the performance of the agricultural sector. In 2013, Morocco's economy grew by 4.7%, aided by a 17.9% increase in value added in the agricultural sector (AfDB, OECD and UNDP, 2014).[3] Similarly, annual economic growth slowed in 2015, in large part because of a 1.8% decrease in value added in agriculture (AfDB, OECD and UNDP, 2014).

The expansion of family farming has been identified as one avenue for improving Morocco's food security and food sovereignty.[4] The Green Morocco Plan, for example, prioritises family farm development. Family farming employs approximately 10% of the population and accounts for 70% of land holdings. Family farms, however, face numerous constraints in the pursuit of productivity and profitability, including ambiguous land titles, poor transport and communication infrastructure, and lack of access to credit and market information (Ghanem, 2015).

Agricultural expansion is not, however, sufficient to make rural areas "attractive, competitive and preserved" (Ministère de l'Agriculture et de la Pêche Maritime, 2010). Efforts to diversify the economy need to reflect the development potential and capital endowments of the territories where they are implemented. Developing social services and infrastructure are also essential. The implementation of the Rural Development Strategy 2020 and the National Human Development Initiative, and the establishment of the Rural Development State Secretary and the assessment of intangible capital commissioned by the king in 2014 all work toward that end. They also represent an awareness of the need for integrated approaches to identify and capitalise on regional development potential.

Results from territorial approaches for food security are encouraging

Promotion of inclusive growth and equity has been a priority on Morocco's development agenda. "Territorialisation" is also prioritised in many of Morocco's development strategies and policies. The earliest attempts to address geographic disparities date back to the 1990s (Box 5.1).

Infrastructure-oriented reforms have since been complemented by a series of socially oriented integrated projects and programmes.[5] The National Human Development Initiative, for example, focuses on the provision of social services to address issues of poverty, regional inequality and exclusion. It also reflects an awareness of the limitations of fragmented, sectoral approaches, as well as of the necessity for more integrated and effective approaches. The initiative's primary objective is to strengthen co-ordination between sectoral interventions implemented at the local level. The following five operational programmes have been in operation since the launch of the second phase of the National Human Development Initiative and the expansion of its budget in 2011:

1. Rural Poverty Programme
2. Urban Social Exclusion Programme

3. Vulnerable Populations Programme
4. transversal programme committed to non-targeted communes and areas
5. programme focusing on the implementation of the National Human Development Initiative in local areas (*mise à niveau territoriale*).

Box 5.1. **Main steps undertaken to strengthen territorial approaches**

1. 1999: Launch of the Rural Development Strategy 2020 and establishment of an interministerial permanent committee in charge of rural development
2. 2003: Establishment of the High Commission on Water and Forests and the Fight against Desertification (Haut Commissariat aux eaux et forêts et la lutte contre la désertification)
3. 2003: Preparation of a legal framework to strengthen the role of associations in development
4. 2004: Appointment of the state secretary in charge of Rural Development (Secrétariat d'État chargé du développement rural)
5. 2004: Preparation of the National Framework and the National Territorial Development Map (*Schéma national et la Charte nationale de l'aménagement du territoire*)
6. 2008: Preparation of the Agricultural Atlas of Morocco (*Atlas de l'agriculture marocaine*)
7. 2011: Adoption of the new Constitution
8. 2014: Organic laws for the implementation of the decentralisation process in Morocco (Nos. 112.14 and 113.14)
9. September 2015: First direct elections of the regional and municipal councils

Source: FAO, Ministry of Agriculture and the World Bank (2006), "État des lieux de la mise en œuvre de la Stratégie 2020", available at: www.fao.org/3/contents/4ad27601-5cc5-59f9-b82e-5518b78f0711/k1461f00.pdf and other sources.

The National Human Development Initiative employs a multi-level governance structure, composed of a central strategic inter-ministerial committee and regional, provincial and local committees. Provincial and local social action divisions provide further support for the implementation of the initiative. These social divisions function as intermediaries between local HDI committees and citizens.[6]

Food security-oriented policies in Morocco also adopt a marked territorial dimension.[7] The Green Morocco Plan, the Halieutis Plan and the National Nutrition Strategy all emphasise the spatial disparities in agricultural development potential and issues of FSN.

The Green Morocco Plan, launched in 2008 by the Ministry of Agriculture, identifies agriculture as a key driver of economic growth. Its overarching objective is to enhance the country's food security and increase food production and, in turn, revenue, especially for small-scale and family farmers. The territorial orientation of the Green Morocco Plan is evident (Box 5.3). The plan features two pillars. Pillar I addresses large-scale, industrial agriculture. At present, Pillar I is experimenting with a private-public partnership model to upgrade key value chains (cereal, legumes, citrus fruit, olives and vines). The value-chain approach is based on the contracts that involve all upstream and downstream actors.

An annual meeting of all actors that compose the value chains is held to evaluate achievement and progress. Pillar II supports smallholders and poor farmers living in remote areas. It covers 75% of Morocco's farmers (Economic Commission for Africa, 2012). It is oriented towards the diversification of sources of income in rural areas through, for example, the promotion of olive oil as a substitute for cereals in marginal and difficult areas, or the development of new sectors, including eco-tourism and aquaculture (AfDB, OECD and UNDP, 2014). The Green Morocco Plan has benefited from and is dependent on important decentralisation reforms, including the establishment of regional directorates of agriculture, regional chambers of agriculture and the National Agency for Agriculture extension.

Box 5.2. Achievements of the National Human Development Initiative in rural areas

As of 2014, the National Human Development Initiative had implemented 38 341 projects and 8 294 development actions, most of which targeted rural areas. Of those development actions, 7 432 targeted income-generation activities. These initiatives have benefited 9.7 million people. The resources allocated to initiatives between 2005 and 2014 exceeded MAD 29 billion. Investments have been spread across several sectors (Table 5.2).

Table 5.2. **Share of total projects by sector**

Sectors	Number of projects
Education	22%
Agriculture	20%
Youth and sports	14%
Drinkable water	11%
Infrastructure (roads)	10%
Health	8%

In the agricultural sector, 7 435 projects were implemented:

- 3 063 projects in the livestock sector, 45 945 beneficiaries
- 300 projects at the promotion of local products, 7 407 beneficiaries
- 288 projects in the fisheries sector, 4 320 beneficiaries
- 122 projects in the tourism sector, 1 845 beneficiaries
- more than 723 actions targeting smallholder farmers, 10 845 beneficiaries.

Source: INDH (2014)

One of the main operational instruments employed by the Green Morocco Plan are the regional agricultural plans. Regional agricultural plans are formulated with the involvement of local and regional actors. They are validated by the Ministry of Agriculture prior to their implementation. Partnerships between relevant stakeholders and territorial institutions are also employed (*collectivités locales*). These partnerships have led to the creation of value-chain programme contracts (*contrats programmes filières*) between the state and private sector and interprofessional organisations. Partnerships between the state and local banks are also promoted and strengthened to provide more liquidity to family farms.

Figure 5.1. **Central and territorial governing bodies of the National Human Development Initiative**

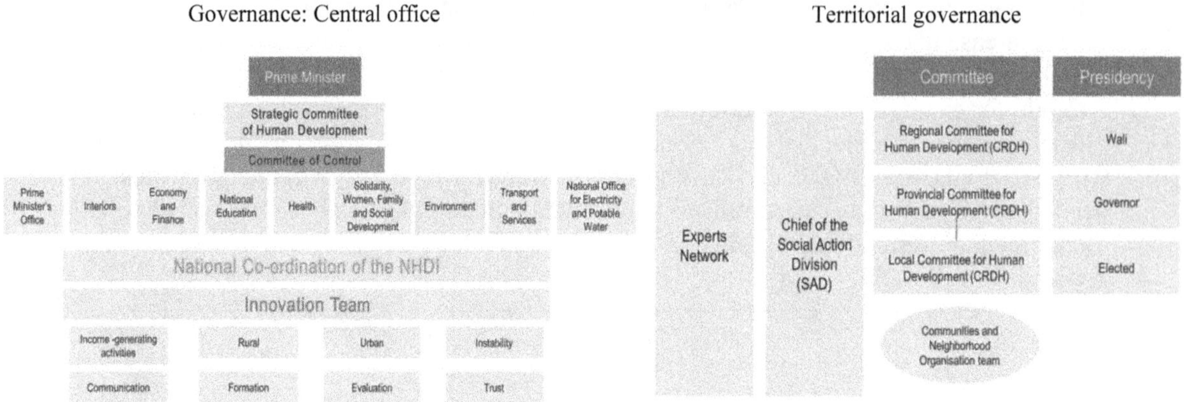

Source: INDH (2014), "Organisational chart", www.indh.gov.ma/index.php/en/gouvernance-et-financement/organes-d-appui.

Box 5.3. The territorial perspective of the Green Morocco Plan

The territorial approach is evident in:

1. The plan's recognition that the agro-ecological systems and the opportunities they offer differ across regions.
2. The use of a tool designed to develop regional competitiveness enables agriculture producers to meet the demands of external and domestic markets.
3. The recognition of the importance of agriculture's interactions with all components of the natural environment, as a requirement for sustainable development and preservation of environmental heritage.
4. The recognition that the relationships between farms and the territories they use vary across space and in accordance with farmers' functions in production systems and territorial specific land-allocation procedures.
5. The commitment to decentralisation, as demonstrated by the support it provides to local leaders, to the stimulation of contractual partnerships at the regional and local level, and to encouraging new forms of territorial governance.

The contractual agriculture system (*aggrégation*) is an especially innovative tool incorporated in the Green Morocco Plan. The contractual agriculture system encourages co-operation among farms and downstream packaging and processing co-operatives to enhance farmers' access to inputs, credit, technology and markets (Box 5.5).

The mid-term evaluation of the Green Morocco Plan conducted in 2015 indicated that the plan has provided support to 771 535 smallholders. Pillar II of the plan has contributed to: an increase in the average agricultural GDP per capital of approximately 48% in rural areas; improvements in rural livelihoods; reductions in malnutrition (now at approximately 4.9%); and the eradication of hunger in rural areas (now at approximately 0.5%). The success earned Morocco the FAO prize for the realisation of the Millennium Development Goals two years in a row (2014 and 2015). Morocco also serves as an exemplar for other developing countries, with which Morocco is currently developing South-South co-operation agreements. The success has also inspired the government to step up its effort to consolidate the results of the first phase and further reduce rural poverty, through a stronger emphasis on the promotion of "solidarity agriculture" (*agriculture solidaire*) and an increased focus on marginal areas.

The Halieutis Plan was launched in 2009. It is guided by two objectives: 1) to promote the conservation of fishery resources and marine ecosystems; and 2) to boost productivity and quality in the fishery sector to enhance its competitiveness in the global economy. The plan is most immediately focused on increasing the fishery sector's contribution to GDP and exports. FSN does, however, factor into the plan. More specifically, the plan aims to increase the domestic consumption of fish from 10 kilogrammes per capita per year to 16 kilogrammes per capita per year. As of 2015, the plan contained 16 main projects to improve the fishery value chain. It also aims to create three processing poles – in Tangier, Agadir and Laâyoune-Dakhla – for a total of MAD 9 billion (Ministère de l'Agriculture et de la Pêche Maritime, 2014).

The aims of Morocco's National Nutrition Strategy are twofold: 1) to improve the availability of and financial access to alimentary products; and 2) to ensure sanitary quality and safety of alimentary products. Actions to achieve these objectives include the employment of reinforced price regulation mechanisms, initiatives targeting the productivity of small-scale farmers and the effort to capitalise on local agricultural products. The nutrition strategy is interdisciplinary in nature. Its decision-making body, the Comité intersectoriel de nutrition, is composed of representatives from the public and private sectors, local communities and civil society. In addition, nine ministries were involved in the design and implementation of the strategy. The strategy's approach is, however, wholly centralised and has no regional or local dimension (Ministère de la Santé, 2011).

Box 5.4. **Nutrition in Morocco**

- 15% of infants are born with a low birth weight
- about 70% of children are not exclusively breastfed until the recommended age of six months
- 23% of children under the age of 5 are stunted, 9% are underweight and 10% are wasted.

Moreover, Morocco has seen a recent increase in obesity, including:

- 16% of children under the age of 5
- 43% of those aged 15 and above
- over 50% of women either overweight or obese.

Source: Ministère de la Santé (2011), "La stratégie nationale de la nutrition 2011-2019", available at: www.unicef.org/morocco/french/Strategie_Nationale_de_Nutrition_.pdf.

Territorial approaches are supported by the new Constitution adopted in 2011, which boosted the country's democratisation process through the enhancement of regionalisation (Commission consultative de la régionalisation, 2010). In January 2015, new organic laws regulating the organisation of the various levels of government were passed by the parliament, including: 1) regions, reduced from 16 to 12; 2) prefectures, 16; 3) provinces, 74; and 4) municipalities (*communes*), 1 503. Elections to all local councils will now be held through direct suffrage. The executive powers previously held by the regional *walis*, have been transferred to the president of the Regional Council, while the *walis* support the implementation of the regional development programmes (Bureau of the Committee of the Regions, 2012).

Box 5.5. *Aggrégation* in the Green Morocco Plan

Aggrégation is one of the key pillars of the Green Morocco Plan (PMV). Its main purpose is to reorganise and encourage co-ordination between agricultural actors, with the goal of tapping unrealised agricultural potential.

Aggrégation is based on the principle of an equitable distribution of the profits and revenues among the participating actors. Processes involve two types of contractual partnerships: 1) public-private partnerships between the government and a private entrepreneur that is responsible for the aggregation of other actors; and 2) private partnerships between the "aggregator" and the actors it is to aggregate (*agrégés*).

There are two main types of aggregations: 1) business-oriented *aggrégations*; and 2) service-oriented *aggrégations* in which the role of the aggregator is simply provide assistance and support to *agrégés*.

The demonstrated advantages of the aggregation system are that:

- It is viable in contexts of land fragmentation, inadequate supplies of primary products and poorly defined land property rights.
- It permits the integration of smallholders and family farmers into the market economy.
- It provides improved technologies and capacities to smallholders.
- It allows family farmers to benefit from financial markets.
- It facilitates risk sharing.

Table 5.3 provides some examples of aggregation models:

Table 5.3. **Aggregation models in Morocco**

Aggregation models	Objective
Nonprofit farmers' associations	Share and disseminate improved agricultural practices, promotion of the supply chain and seeking market opportunities.
Production-oriented co-operatives	Joint enterprises for farmers engaging in the production of goods, supplying services and inputs, investments and market promotion, operated by its members for their mutual benefit.
Marketing-oriented co-operatives	Profit-based co-operatives, whose main objective is the collection, storage and marketing of agricultural products.
Commercial contracts	Based on individual contracts between suppliers and processors or distributors.
Contract farming	Commercial agreements between a buyer and farmers that establish conditions for the production and marketing of a farm product or products. Typically, the farmer agrees to provide agreed quantities of a specific agricultural product. These should meet the quality standards of the purchaser and be supplied at the time determined by the purchaser. In turn, the buyer commits to purchase the product and, in some cases, to support production through, for example, the supply of farm inputs, land preparation and the provision of technical advice.
Integrated facilitation project (*Projet d'animation intégré*)	Public or private organisation appointed by the government to support the promotion of good agricultural practices and market development.

The reform also includes provisions to reduce regional disparities (IMF, 2013). The most notable of these are a plan to upgrade human capital in lagging areas and the establishment of two new funds – one for capacity building, one for developing regional solidarity – to promote equalisation. The capacity-building fund is funded by the central government, with the aim of addressing shortcomings in infrastructure, human development and basic social services. The regional solidarity fund, on the other hand, funded by regions themselves, aims to smooth out regional disparities. The reform also proposes increasing transfers to the regional council to help achieve development objectives. More specifically, the reform proposes: 1) higher regional taxes; 2) increased borrowing capacity for regions; 3) an increase (from 1% to 5%) in the shares of proceeds from corporate and income taxes allocated to regions; 4) an equal division between the central government and the regions of registration fees and special taxes on motor vehicles; and 5) making regions eligible for VAT receipts with respect to investment. One of the important operational instruments associated with the new governance system are the municipality development plans (*plans communaux de développement*). Communes are now responsible for the preparation and implementation of development plans. The central government (Ministry of the Interior) provides the necessary support to communes via the Direction of the Local Communities (*collectivités locales*), the Social Development Agency (*Agence de développement social*) and the Regional Agency for the Implementation of Projects (*Agence régionale d'exécution des projets*).

Despite encouraging results, challenges remain

Morocco's socio-economic achievements are acknowledged in the Finance Act and Budget of 2015. The report notes that Morocco has met almost all of the Millennium Development Goals. Its most significant accomplishments are the fulfilment of the goals related to poverty reduction and food security. The latter was completed two years ahead of schedule (Ministère de l'Économie et des Finances, 2014).

Gross income per capita increased from MAD 15 798 to MAD 27 980 between 2001 and 2013.[8] This corresponds to an annual increase of 5%. Poverty and vulnerability have decreased as a result of this robust economic growth. In 2001, 15.3% of the population was living in poverty and 22.8% were classified as vulnerable. By 2011, both of these figures had fallen, to 6.2% and 13.3% respectively. The expansion of the economy was also correlated with increased employment – 2 million new jobs were created and unemployment fell to 9.2% in 2013. Hunger (0.5% of the population) has also been almost completely eradicated in Morocco.

Considerable socio-economic progress has been made in rural areas in particular. The percentage of the rural population living in poverty decreased from 25.1% to 10% between 2001 and 2013. Similarly, the percentage of the population classified as vulnerable declined by 7%. Agricultural GDP per capita increased 48% (from MAD 5 400 to MAD 8 000) between 2008 and 2014 as well. That said, 67% of Morocco's impoverished population and 58.8% of its vulnerable population still live in rural areas, suggesting that considerable work remains to be done to address Morocco's urban-rural divide.[9]

Interpersonal income inequality in Morocco has increased in recent years. Morocco's Gini coefficient was greater in 2011 (0.408) than it was in both 2001 (0.406) and 1991 (0.393). Inequality and poverty are intimately related. The Haut Commissariat au Plan estimated that a 1% increase in inequality resulted in a 2.6% increase in poverty in Morocco in 1985, a 4.1% increase in 2001 and a 5.9% increase in 2007. It also estimated that in 2007, 31.3% of inequalities in consumption expenditure were attributable to the education level of the head of the family; 18.7% were linked with the sector in which the head of the family was active; and 11.6% were the result of household location.

An analysis conducted by the Ministry of Economy and Finance indicated that geographic disparities may be decreasing. Morocco's lagging areas achieved GDP growth rates that exceeded the national average (6%) between 2001 and 2013: Laâyoune-Boujdour-Sakia El Hamra's growth rate was 12.5%; Oued Ed-Dahab-Lagouira's growth rate was 11.1%; Chaouia-Ouardigha's growth rate was 8%; Marrakech-Tensift-Al Haouz's growth rate was 6.9%; and Meknès-Tafilalet's growth rate was 6.2%. The only lagging region that did not achieve a growth rate above the national average was Gharb-Chrarda-Béni Hssen (4.1%). These lagging regions have also achieved gradual economic diversification and have begun to specialise in certain economic activities.

There is inter-regional variation, however, in terms of poverty reduction. Between 1985 and 2011, for example, relative poverty declined by 90% in southern regions. In the poorest regions, including Doukkala-Abda and Gharb-Chrarda-Béni Hssen, on the other hand, relative poverty only decreased by 50%. It is therefore inferred that while Morocco's economic growth may have contributed to some measure of inter-regional convergence, it has not been overly pro-poor and its benefits have not been realised by all members of society (Ministère de l'Économie et des Finances, 2014).

It is clear that Morocco has achieved meaningful socio-economic progress. That said, the implementation of the territorial approach appears to have been constrained by factors relating to:

- **Financing and targeting issues:** The funds allocated by the National Human Development Initiative do not always reach the poorest and most vulnerable people. According to the Ministry of Economy and Finance, fund disbursement, as of 2013, was greater in provinces with poverty rates of 10% than in provinces with poverty rates of 20%. It would seem that the funds have a regressive effect. This may partly explain why socio-economic infrastructural investment in lagging (often rural) areas has failed to yield the anticipated benefits. In short, it would seem that many issues related to the geographic targeting of funds remain unresolved.
- **Territorial information:** Morocco has yet to develop information aggregation systems to facilitate integrated planning. Territorial management frameworks (*schémas d'aménagement des territoires*); the National Territorial Development Map (*Charte nationale de l'aménagement du territoire*) prepared by the Ministry of Urbanisation and Territorial Management; the Agricultural Atlas prepared by the Ministry of Agriculture, and the territorial indicators under preparation at the Ministry of Economy and Finance all represent efforts in this direction. However, institutional arrangements for their implementation and application to integrated planning at the national and sub-national level have yet to be proposed.
- **Governance and institutions:** Decentralised governments in Morocco are often under-capacitated. Lazarev (2013) and Mansour and Castel (2014), for example, observe, that: 1) processes of regionalisation in Morocco will encounter challenges relating to institutional capacity and the availability of human resources with the appropriate skills at the local level; and 2) the participatory mechanisms of the communal development plans are weak, due to a lack of experience among relevant actors. It has also been suggested that synergies between social and sectoral programmes have not been fully realised due to a lack of co-ordination between programmes. Moreover, while Morocco has shifted from a sectoral to a convergence approach, a truly integrated approach to

development has yet to be adopted. Finally, while the law on regionalisation has been passed by the parliament, an implementation plan has not yet been drawn up.

- **Innovation:** Morocco has tested, piloted and scaled up innovative territorial approaches. These good practices, including the aggregation system (Box 5.5) are worthy of sharing with other countries. That said, processes of innovation tend to be centrally led and need to be supplemented by local-level innovation.

Box 5.6. **Enhanced regionalisation**

Enhanced regionalisation is the Moroccan model of decentralisation. It is based on direct elections of decentralised administrations, a strong accountability system and mechanisms to strengthen the participation of local populations in policy- and decision-making processes. Regional councils are composed of elected members with formal voting power, as well as locally elected members of the parliament, presidents of professional chambers and representatives of trade unions, all of whom assume a consultative role.

The reform also provides for a greater role for women, allowing for equal access for women and men to government responsibilities.

Regions are encouraged to set up consultation processes to facilitate the participation of civil society and the private sector in the development of regional development plans.

Major responsibilities and competences, such as water, energy and public transport, are to be transferred to the regions and other lower-level decentralised administrations on the basis of the subsidiarity principle. The assignment of these responsibilities is accompanied by transfers of the resources, financial and otherwise, necessary to fulfil them. Decentralised administrations will also have their own resources to promote local initiatives.

A special fund ranging from MAD 128 billion-215 billion has been established to close the gap between the regional education, health and road infrastructure levels with national and international standards. A second fund has also been created to promote regional solidarity and the reduction of territorial disparities.

The first steps towards regionalisation were taken in 1971. It was only in 1997, however, that regions became legally recognised entities. In January 2010, a robust decentralisation plan was enacted alongside the creation of the Consultative Committee on Regionalisation (CCR). Political parties, trade unions, professional associations and government agencies were engaged in a two-year consultation process conducted by the CCR for the constitutional reform of 2011.

Enhanced regionalisation began in 2014, with the reduction of the number of regions from 16 to 12. In early 2015, the parliament passed three organic laws regarding the regions (Organic Law 111-14), the prefectures and provinces (Organic Law 112-14) and the communes (Organic Law 113-14) that formalise the detailed roles and responsibilities of the new decentralised administrations. In September 2015, the first municipal and regional elections were held.

Conclusions

FSN in Morocco is influenced by international supplies and prices of food. Morocco will face challenges increasing domestic agricultural capacity and production, in large part due to limited supplies of water, population growth, urbanisation and changing consumption patterns. Morocco's poorest citizens are and will increasingly be vulnerable to volatility in food prices as a result of their relative expenditure on food.

Expanding the agricultural sector is a necessary step for improving the livelihoods of the rural population, reducing poverty and addressing geographic disparities in socio-economic well-being and development. It is not, however, a sufficient one. Agriculturally oriented interventions should be complemented by efforts to promote economic diversification and social protection.

The development of the Green Morocco Plan, the Halieutis Plan, the National Forestry Plan, the National Nutrition Strategy, the National Human Development Initiative and the National Safety Net Programme are all evidence of Morocco's commitment, financial and otherwise, to socio-economic development and progress.

These interventions have been complemented with governance reforms, with the constitutional reform of 2011 and enhanced regionalisation, which devolves competences, resources and programmatic autonomy to regional, prefectural and municipal councils.

Morocco has taken meaningful steps towards establishing a stronger and more inclusive governance system. Nevertheless, the implementation of interventions and initiatives are frequently constrained by several related challenges. Multidimensional, multisectoral and multi-actor issues, including food security, nutrition and poverty, are therefore often addressed by uncoordinated sectoral approaches.

A lack of horizontal co-ordination and a relative absence of harmonised guidelines often lead to overlaps and duplication of interventions. Integration of decentralised institutions, both of deconcentrated government bodies and stakeholders, in policy and planning processes is generally weak.[10] It also tends to be focused on the implementation of the policies and programmes designed at the national level. Moreover, the contribution of these actors to policy design and monitoring is not systematic. As a result, the ownership of policies and programmes at the decentralised level is generally very weak. This is further exacerbated by the lack of capacities of decentralised institutions. From an institutional and governance perspective, another possible area of tension is the co-existence of the modern institutional systems associated with the reform and traditional governance system in many rural areas. While the roles and responsibilities of traditional and modern institutions are codified in laws and regulations, integrating the two systems has proved difficult in practice.

Issues related to the delivery of funds to the targeted population have also yet to be addressed. The National Human Development Initiative contains provisions to address this. But a concerted effort will need to be made to improve the effectiveness of social expenditure and ensure that it does not have regressive effects (Breisinger et al., 2012). Moreover, the disbursement and effectiveness of social investments and expenditure are constrained by procedural and operational obstacles, and obstacles related to monitoring.

Another factor hampering efforts to promote growth and development in remote and marginal areas is the absence of information aggregation systems to facilitate integrated planning. Integrated territorial innovation systems function not only as a means to collect and synthesise "technical data" on territorial assets, but also as a means to empower local communities and promote innovative processes for economic, human and social capital development at the local level.

Notes

1. A small rural village or settlement grouping between 50 and 400 households and generally distant from one another. It constitutes the basic entity of the rural municipality but it is not included in the national geographic nomenclature and its name can change form one administrative service to another.

2. The country's cereal dependence ratio is 54% (world average: 16%) and 20% of Morocco's export revenues are spent on food imports (Ghanem, 2015).

3. In 2013, 14% of GDP was attributable to the agriculture sector.

4. Family farming is defined as a "type of agricultural production system managed by one or more members of a family and primarily reliant on non-wage labour" (Ghanem, 2015). Harrigan (2012: 2) notes that "the concept of 'food sovereignty' is gaining currency in the region, whereby nation states secure greater control and power over their sources of food, and adopt strategies that are not just dictated by international market forces".

5. They include: the *Projet de développement rural des zones montagneuses de la Province d'Al Haouz*, the *Projet de développement rural intégré centré sur la petite et moyenne hydraulique* (DRI-PMH), the *Projet de développement rural intégré de mise en valeur des zones bour* (DRI-MVB), the *Projet d'aménagement du bassin versant de l'Oued Lakhdar*, the *Projet Al Haouz*, DRI-PMH, DRI-MVB, the *Plan d'électrification rurale globale* (PERG), the *Programme d'approvisionnement groupé en eau potable des populations rurales* (PAGER), *the Programme national de construction des routes rurales* (PNRR).

6. www.indh.gov.ma.

7. It should be emphasised that Morocco does not have a specific food security strategy, despite the vulnerability of the country and population to all dimensions of food security (availability, access, stability and nutrition).

8. 1 dirham (MAD) = USD 0.103 in 2015.

9. It should be noted, however, that social disparities have not increased since 2001 (Ministère de l'Économie et des Finances, 2014).

10. Exceptions include the Green Morocco Plan, which is based on a strong vertical integration of interventions.

References

Adidi, A. (2011), “De l’aménagement du territoire au développement territorial: Quelle transition et quelle articulation? ”, Archive ouverte en Sciences de l’Homme et de la Société, 1ère Conférence Intercontinentale d’Intelligence Territoriale, October, Gatineau, Canada. pp. 11, INTI-International Network of Territorial Intelligence, available at: https://halshs.archives-ouvertes.fr/halshs-00960909/document.

AfDB, OECD and UNDP (2014), *African Economic Outlook 2014: Global Value Chains and Africa’s Industrialisation*, OECD Publishing, Paris, http://dx.doi.org/10.1787/aeo-2014-en.

Breisinger, C. et al. (2012), *Beyond the Arab Awakening: Policies and Investments for Poverty Reduction and Food Security*, Food Policy Report, International Food Policy Research Institute, Washington DC, http://dx.doi.org/10.2499/9780896295452.

Bureau of the Committee of the Regions (CoR) (2012), “Maroc: Fiche technique – Répartition verticale des compétences”, Europe 2020 Monitoring Platform, available at: https://portal.cor.europa.eu/arlem/Documents/Morocco%20-%20Fact%20Sheet%20No%201%20FR_8%20May%202014.pdf.

CCR (2011), “Mission”, www.regionalisationavancee.ma.

Conseil général du développement agricole (2009), “Atlas de l’agriculture marocaine”, Conseil général du développement agricole, Rabat, Morocco, www.agriculture.gov.ma/pages/publications/atlas-de-lagriculture-marocaine.

Département de la Pêche Maritime (2014), “Stratégie Halieutis”, Ministère de l’Agriculture et de la Pêche Maritime, www.mpm.gov.ma/wps/portal/PortalI-MPM/ACCUEIL/StrategieHalieutis/Projets/!ut/p/b1/04_SjzQyMDc3MTO3MDDSj9CPykssy0xPLMnMz0vMAfGjzOIN3Nx9_I0MzAwswsIsDDzNTQM8PT2dDd3djfRzoxwVAeAaVa8!.

Economic Commission for Africa (2012), “La sécurité alimentaire en Afrique du Nord: Analyse de situation et réactions des états face à l’instabilité des marchés agricoles”, presented at the 27th session of the Comité intergouvernemental d’experts (CIE), Economic Commission for Africa, Office for North Africa, Rabat, Morocco, available at: http://repository.uneca.org/pdfpreview/bitstream/handle/10855/22372/b10789674.pdf?sequence=1.

FAO, Ministry of Agriculture and World Bank (2006), “État des lieux de la mise en œuvre de la Stratégie 2020”, available at: www.fao.org/3/contents/4ad27601-5cc5-59f9-b82e-5518b78f0711/k1461f00.pdf.

Ghanem, H. (2015). “Agriculture and rural development for inclusive growth and food security in Morocco”, *Global Economy & Development Working Papers*, No. 82,

February, Global Economy and Development at Brookings, Brookings, Washington DC, available at: www.brookings.edu/~/media/Research/Files/Papers/2015/02/agriculture-rural-development-inclusive-growth-morocco-ghanem/Agriculture_WEB_Revised.pdf?la=en.

Haut-Commissariat au Plan (2012), "Comptes régionaux: Produit intérieur brut et dépenses de consommation finale des ménages 2012", available at: www.hcp.ma/Comptes-regionaux_r209.html.

Haut-Commissariat au Plan (2009), "Cartographie 2007", available at: www.hcp.ma/Cartographie-2007_r138.html.

Harrigan, J. (2012). "The political economy of food security in North Africa", *AfDB Economic Brief*, African Development Bank, available at: www.afdb.org/fileadmin/uploads/afdb/Documents/Publications/Economic_Brief_-_The_Political_Economy_of_Food_Security_in_North_Africa.pdf.

IFAD (2009), "Rural poverty in the Kingdom of Morocco", Rural Poverty Portal, International Fund for Agricultural Development, Rome, www.ruralpovertyportal.org/country/home/tags/morocco.

IMF (2013), "Morocco: 2012 Article IV consultation and first review under the two-year precautionary and liquidity line", *IMF Country Report*, No. 13/96, International Monetary Fund, Washington DC, available at: www.imf.org/external/pubs/ft/scr/2013/cr1396.pdf.

INDH (2014), "Organisational chart", Initiative Nationale pour le Développement Humaine, Rabat, Morocco, www.indh.gov.ma/index.php/en/gouvernance-et-financement/organes-d-appui.

Lazarev, G. (2013), "La nouvelle approche des plans communaux de développement: Une démarche porteuse encore à valoriser", *GéoDév.ma*, Vol. I, available at: http://revues.imist.ma/?journal=GeoDev&page=article&op=view&path%5B%5D=615.

Mansour, S. and V. Castel (2015), *Morocco 2015*, African Development Bank.

Mansour, S. and V. Castel (2014), *Morocco 2014*, African Development Bank.

Ministère de l'Agriculture et de la Pêche Maritime (2010), "Stratégie de développement des zones oasiennes et de l'arganie".

Ministère de l'Économie et des Finances (2014), *Projet de Loi de finances pour l'année budgétaire 2015: Rapport économique et financier*, Direction des Études et des Prévisions financières, Ministère de l'Économie et des Finances.

Ministère de la Santé (2011), "La stratégie nationale de la nutrition 2011-2019", Ministère de la Santé and UNICEF, Rabat, Morocco, available at: www.unicef.org/morocco/french/Strategie_Nationale_de_Nutrition_.pdf.

Annex 5.A1.
"Territorialisation" and the institutional framework of food security and nutrition in Morocco

The alignment of national policies at sub-national (territorial) level is likely to lead to strategies and programmes that aim to generate increased income opportunities in rural areas, which in turn contribute to improved food security and nutrition (FSN). The following tables outline the relationships between different management models and levels of intervention to address food security and nutrition at various territorial levels.

Table 5.A1.1. **Management model to address food security and nutrition at all territorial levels in Morocco**

Territorial level	Economic situation	National food security situation		Management model
		Secure	Insecure	
National	Supply capacity	Supply > demand	Supply < demand	Supply Distribution Production Stock
Regional/local				Distribution management
Family/household	Consumption capacity	Consumption > need	Consumption < need	Household level consumption management
Individuals	Purchasing power	Consumption > need	Consumption < need	Living standards (individual)

Table 5.A1.2. **Government measures, levels of interventions and departments involved in addressing food security and nutrition at the national, regional/local, family/household and individual level in Morocco**

Territorial level	Government measures	Food security dimension	Level of intervention	Departments involved
National	Macro-level measures	Availability	National production	Agriculture
			Foreign imports	Foreign commerce
		Stability	Basic infrastructure	Infrastructure
			Support policies	Public affairs
Regional/local	Guarantees	Availability	Production and processing	Commerce and industry
		Access	Storage capacity	Public affairs/agriculture
			Access to domestic markets	Interior
		Quality	Health and safety norms	Agriculture
Family/household	Management	Hygiene	Food safety	Health
		Accessibility	Purchasing power	Employment/finance
			Market access	Interior
	Consumption	Permissiveness	Choice of food	Agriculture
Individuals	Purchasing	Access	Market price	Agriculture/public affairs
			Price/quality	–
	Consumption	Habits	Habituation	–

In terms of co-ordination of FSN policies at the national level, the functional relationship (indicative) between the different government departments involved in FSN policies is presented in Figure 5.A1.1.

Figure 5.A1.1. **Departments responsible for food security in Morocco**

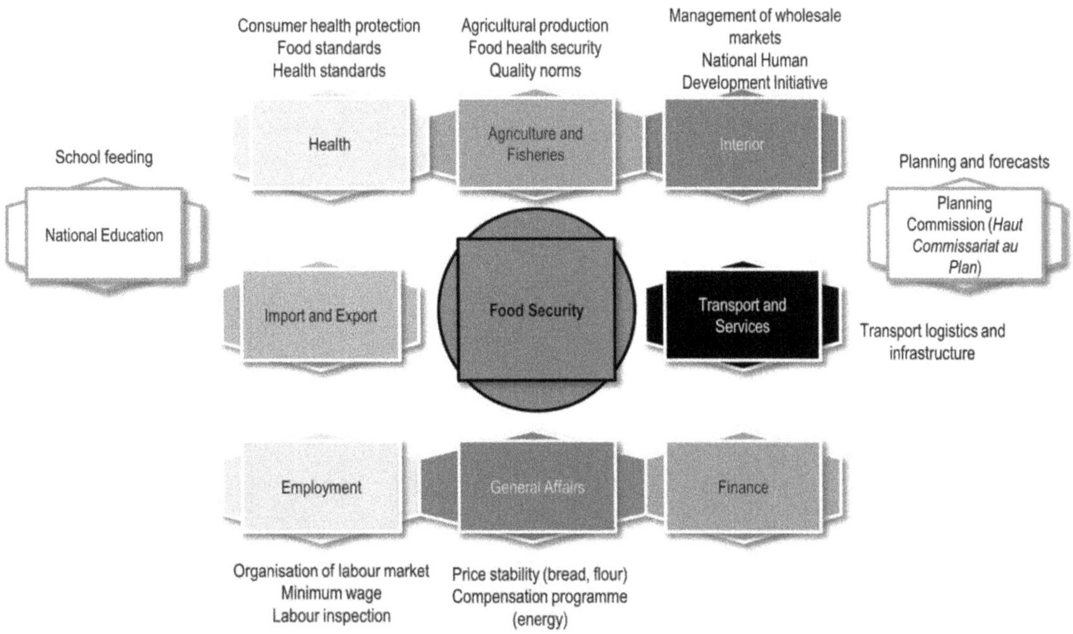

Source: authors' elaboration.

To implement a territorial approach to FSN policies successfully, the following elements need to be considered:

- national-level engagement to ensure the investment capacity in FSN
- integration of nutrition into national strategies and agricultural development
- improved targeting of FSN programmes, to maximise their impact
- further co-ordination of actions undertaken by different government departments and stakeholders, to create the synergies needed to increase efficiency
- social mobilisation at territorial level, acknowledging FSN as a common concern
- mobilisation of human and financial resources.

Chapter 6.

A territorial approach to food security and nutrition policy: The case of Peru

Peru has made great progress in terms of reducing poverty and improving food security, both due to sustained economic growth and the pivotal role played by the Ministry of Development and Social Inclusion and its "Include for Growth" policy. One particularly innovative pilot programme promotes peer-to-peer learning among smallholder farmers to enhance their productivity, hence indirectly improving food security through increased production and incomes. While this development shows promise, some key challenges must be resolved with regards to food security and nutrition in the country. Remote, mountainous areas, as well as those associated with ethnic minorities, remain the most exposed to FSN challenges. Despite the availability of data, territorial information has not been adequately used to support the formulation of pro-growth policies.

Key findings

Sustained economic growth and the implementation of numerous large-scale social and economic programmes – including conditional cash transfer programmes – have lifted more than 20% of Peru's population out of poverty and reduced the prevalence of food insecurity.

Issues of food security and nutrition (FSN) do, however, exist and are especially pronounced in Peru's rural regions. The delivery of programmes and policies to address FSN in rural regions has been hampered by several factors. Among them are a lack of information to inform strategic planning processes, capacity constraints at the local level and generally weak regional governments that are often unable to scale up policies and provide public goods.

Peru's FSN policy has achieved some success. That said, the adoption of a territorial approach to FSN will be essential to develop policies and programmes that reflect the needs and potential of Peru's communities, to encourage co-ordination across these initiatives and, ultimately, to address issues of FSN across all of Peru.

Features of food insecurity and malnutrition in Peru

The territorial dimension of food insecurity and malnutrition in Peru

Peru has achieved considerable economic growth over the past decade. Its economy has expanded at a rate that exceeded both the Latin American and world average and, perhaps more importantly, growth has been relatively inclusive, contributing to a 20% reduction (2000-2013) in the national poverty rate (Figure 6.1). That said, a not insignificant percentage of the population remains in poverty and is, thus, likely to be exposed to issues of FSN. In 2014, for example, 15% of children aged 5 and under suffered from malnutrition.

Figure 6.1. **Average annual GDP per capita growth rates in Peru, 2000-13**

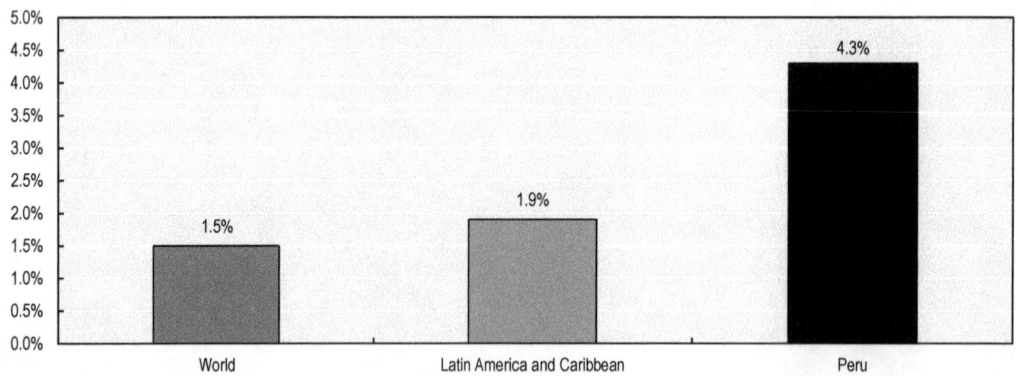

Source: World Bank (2015).

There is considerable inter-departmental variation in the incidence of food insecurity and malnutrition. Issues of FSN are largely concentrated in Peru's poorest departments, and in poorer departments like Huancavelica, Cajamarca, Huánuco and Apurimac, They are comparable to those of severely underdeveloped economies. In Huancavelica, for example, 35% of children aged 5 and under suffered from chronic malnutrition in 2014. Similarly, in 2012, 42% of households in Cajamarca were at risk of caloric deficits.

Table 6.1. **Selected indicators of food insecurity in Peru, department level, 2012 and 2014**

Department	Index of vulnerability to food insecurity, 2012[1]	Children below 5 suffering from chronic malnutrition (%), 2012-14[2]	Households with a deficit in calories, 2012[3]	Poverty rates at the department level (%), 2013
Huancavelica	0.7163	35.0	23.7%	46.6
Cajamarca	0.5688	32.2	42.0%	52.9
Huánuco	0.5549	24.8	34.6%	40.1
Apurímac	0.5183	27.3	42.1%	42.8
Amazonas	0.5117	30.8	27.3%	47.3
Ayacucho	0.5075	26.3	38.1%	51.9
Puno	0.4865	17.9	33.6%	32.4
Cusco	0.4358	18.2	22.8%	18.8
San Martin	0.3948	16.0	22.1%	30.0
Pasco	0.3522	24.9	55.7%	46.6
Loreto	0.3124	24.6	30.1%	37.4
Piura	0.2962	21.7	22.9%	35.1
Ancash	0.2898	20.5	29.2%	23.5
Junín	0.2696	22.1	34.4%	19.5
La Libertad	0.2436	19.9	25.3%	29.5
Ucayali	0.2061	26.1	6.7%	29.5
Lambayeque	0.1589	14.3	15.0%	24.7
Moquegua	0.1281	4.2	19.7%	8.7
Madre de Dios	0.1002	9.8	7.7%	3.8
Arequipa	0.0931	7.3	26.6%	9.1
Ica	0.0869	6.9	8.7%	4.7
Tacna	0.0825	3.7	14.5%	11.8
Tumbes	0.0815	8.3	17.2%	12.7
Lima	0.0270	4.6	17.2%	14.3
Callao	0.0138	7.0	15.0%	13.7

Sources: 1. Normalised for population; Ministerio de Desarrollo e Inclusión Social (MIDIS) and Programa Mundial de Alimentos (PMA) (2012). 2. INEI – *Encuesta Demográfica y de Salud Familiar* (ENDES). 3. *Encuesta Nacional de Hogares* (ENAHO).

Rural communities are more exposed to food security and nutrition challenges

Rural communities – especially those in mountainous areas and those associated with Peru's ethnic minorities – are among the most exposed to FSN-related challenges. In 2014, less than one-third of the country's population lived below the national poverty line. The national rural poverty rate, however, was greater than 50%. Certain rural regions are especially impoverished. In rural Sierra, for example, 17% of the population was considered extremely poor in 2014. The poorest Peruvians are found in the arid Andean highlands that are home to a large majority of the indigenous *Quechua* and *Aymara* peoples, many of whom live below the poverty line (IFAD).[1]

Rural poverty is not an inevitability. Opportunities for economic growth exist in rural areas that, if exploited, could contribute to the eradication of poverty and issues of FSN. However, the absence of good governance systems and policies has constrained rural development. In the department of Cajamarca, for example, resource competition between the agricultural and mining sectors has impeded economic growth and compromised the provision of public goods to local communities.

Cajamarca is home to approximately 1.5 million people (2013 estimate). Agricultural and mining activities constitute the base of its economy. The agricultural sector employs 430 000 people across a myriad of smallholdings, making it the department's primary source of employment. The mining sector, on the other hand, employs relatively few people (approximately 14 000). The department is, however, endowed with vast reserves of gold and copper, with great potential for the expansion of the sector.

Figure 6.2. **Distribution of poverty in a selection of urban and rural areas in Peru, 2004-14**

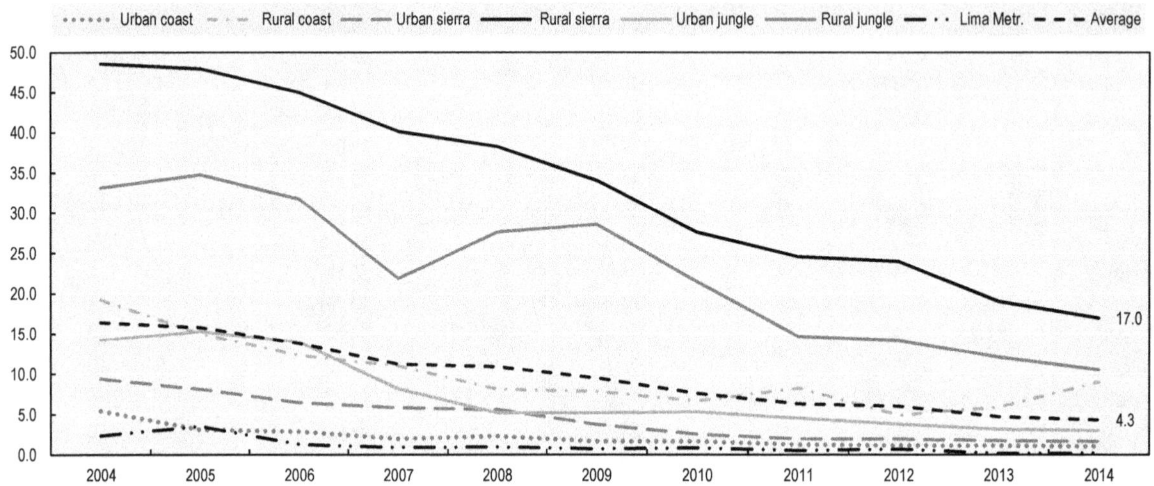

Source: INEI, *Encuesta Nacional de los Hogares* (2004-2014).

Tensions between the agricultural and mining sectors have been detrimental to economic growth in Cajamarca. Competition for scarce water resources, for example, is intense. Agricultural productivity has suffered from the water-grabbing practices of mining development and many agriculturally dependent households have been forced into poverty. New mining development is therefore subject to considerable local opposition.[2] Somewhat paradoxically, local farmers have also opposed the public development of larger water basins from which they were likely to benefit. The opposition is founded on fears that mining developments would use their economic and political influence to hijack the developments and would become the sole beneficiaries of the basins. Farmers would rather suffer from an endemic lack of water, despite the effect it will inevitably have on their productivity. In short, conflict and a lack of trust between the agricultural and mining sectors have stalled potential for economic growth and forced residents of Cajamarca to live just above subsistence level.

Cities, including Lima, are not immune to issues of food security and nutrition

Peru's urban population is also afflicted by issues of FSN. The existence of food insecurity and malnutrition are linked to two related factors:

1. A lack of access to basic services, including health care and education, in rural areas has led to rural-urban migration, primarily to Lima. The capital has not been able to immediately accommodate the influx of people has resulted in large informal settlements (*asentamientos humanos*) on its outskirts and to a host of negative externalities associated with rapid urbanisation.[3] This has, in turn,

increased rural migration to Peru's secondary cities, including Arequipa and Cuzco.

2. Urban areas, in part due to rural-urban migration, have inadequate service delivery and a lack of economic opportunities for migrants from rural areas. Rural citizens living in urban areas struggle to enter the formal labour market. The challenges they face finding formal employment are linked to both the inadequacy of their skill sets as well as high transport costs – many of them live in *asentamientos* far from the city centre.

Many urban residents are exposed to food scarcity and food-related anxiety. Vargas and Penny (2009), for example, note that the highest family food insecurity scores are found in Lima, even though the percentage of food-insecure families in Lima is relatively low by comparison with the rest of the country. This finding is probably attributable, at least in part, to the urban families' lack of access to land and their inability to engage in agricultural activities. Vargas and Penny (2009) also found that all food-insecure families in Lima expressed concern that they would not have enough food to feed their families. This was not the case in rural areas. In rural areas, families maintain food reserves large enough to last for several months. In urban areas, on the other hand, families tend to live from day to day, without any such back-up.

The governance of Peru's food security and nutrition policy

Several agencies are engaged in FSN-related issues in Peru, and numerous policies have been employed to address them. This is a reflection of the multidimensional nature of FSN, which is understood to depend on the availability of, access to, utilisation of and stability of food. Peru has also added an institutional dimension to the conceptualisation of FSN that relates to the integration and co-ordination, as well as to the *ex post* monitoring and evaluation of actions and programmes to promote FSN.

FSN policies pursued in Peru should reflect this multidimensional approach and benefit from a holistic and territorial approach to FSN issues as they are uniquely manifested in Peru's heterogeneous regions.

Food security and nutrition related polices and institutions in Peru

The Multisectoral Commission for Food Security and Nutrition. This commission was responsible for the formulation of Peru's main FSN policies: the National Strategy for Food Security and Nutrition 2013-2021 and the National Plan for Food Security and Nutrition 2015-2021. The commission is composed of representatives from nine ministries, sub-national governments and civil society under the leadership of the Ministry of Agriculture and Irrigation.

The National Plan for Food Security and Nutrition 2015-2021 contains the action lines and strategic activities for implementing the National Strategy for Food and Nutrition Security 2013-2021 and aims to promote co-ordination between relevant actors and policies. The plan integrates FSN into other national strategies, including *Mi Riego* (the national policy for irrigation), the National Strategy for Family Agriculture (the national agricultural policy) and the National Strategy for Development and Social Inclusion ("Include for Growth").

The Roundtable Against Poverty (*Mesa de Concertación para Lucha contra la Pobreza*). The roundtable is not a member of the Multisectoral Commission for Food

Security and Nutrition, although it does participate in its meetings. It co-ordinates the 150 sub-national roundtables responsible for monitoring of public sector capacity to deliver policies for the poor.

Vaso de Leche. This is a policy aims to provide supplementary food for children aged 7 and under (Box 6.1). It also provides assistance to nursing mothers and families with young children. The policy has been implemented in 1 608 municipalities, all of which receive earmarked transfers from the Ministry of Finance. The policy is extremely popular with poor households, and attempts to phase it out have failed thus far.

Box 6.1. The *Vaso de Leche* policy

The *Vaso de Leche* policy was set up by the mayor of Lima, Alfonso Barrantes, in 1984. It was originally conceived as a policy to provide breakfast to poor children. By the end of 1984, it provided 600 000 children with breakfast, rising to 1 million by March 1985. The policy was extended to cover the entire country in January 1985. Today, the policy affects 3 million people.

Since 1996, the policy has been managed directly by municipalities. The central government transfers USD 125 million a year to districts and provincial municipalities to fund the policy. Each municipality is responsible for setting up a local administrative committee to manage the policy. This is composed of the mayor, a municipal agent, a representative from the Ministry of Health, a local representative of farmers and three representatives from the committees of beneficiaries. The local administrative councils are tasked with selecting beneficiaries and planning, co-ordinating and executing the policy. The latter involves the distribution, selection and sourcing of products, as well as its general oversight and auditing. Ninety percent of the products distributed must be produced in Peru, and all must meet certain nutritional requirements. The delivery of the programme is assisted by grassroots organisations.

The central government has criticised the management of the *Vaso de Leche* programme, citing corruption stemming from a lack of accountability. A study conducted in 2009 by the Consorcio de Investigación Económica y Social, a research centre in Peru, revealed that more than 1 million beneficiaries of *Vaso de Leche* do not match the requirements of the policy. The policy has also been plagued by several product procurement-related scandals. Vásquez Huaman (2012) has therefore suggested that the programme be restructured to reflect the multidimensional nature of poverty.

Attempts by the central government to cut or reduce funds allocated to the policy or to reform the programme have encountered strong opposition from citizens' associations, which argue that the *Vaso de Leche* policy is a useful tool to fight childhood hunger and malnutrition, and by organisations with a vested interest in maintaining the programme.

Juntos. This is a large-scale conditional cash transfer programme that provides money to poor households (Box 6.2). Its focus is to disrupt the vicious circle of poverty, ill-health and illiteracy. The programme is not *per se* an FSN initiative, although poverty and issues of FSN are intimately related, and an initiative designed to eradicate poverty may therefore be expected to address issues of FSN as well. The programme has had some success and has helped reduce extreme poverty across the nation.

The Ministry of Agriculture and Irrigation. The Ministry of Agriculture is a pillar of Peru's FSN governance system. Its engagement with FSN is threefold: first, it participates in inter-ministerial commissions dealing with poverty and food security and presides over the Multisectoral Commission for Food Security and Nutrition. Second, it has developed the National Agricultural Policy, co-ordinating several programmes – including those linked to FSN – and provides guidance to sub-national governments. Third, it is active in programmes like *Mi Riego* that promote access to water for irrigation, through infrastructure. Access to water is inevitably tied to issues of FSN. *Mi Riego* employs a holistic approach to water management to tackle challenges related to water availability, a lack of relevant infrastructure and water usage. The leadership of the Ministry of Agriculture and Irrigation in programmes like *Mi Riego* and others has facilitated their integration into National Agrarian Policy, thereby increasing their sustainability and the political support they receive.

Box 6.2. The *Juntos* programme

Founded in 2005, the *Programa Nacional de Apoyo Directo a los más Pobres* (*Juntos*) is a conditional monetary transfer programme. Its overarching objective is to break the vicious cycle of poverty by providing education and health care to children in Peru's impoverished communities. The programme is managed by the Ministry for Development and Social Inclusion and is implemented by a network of deconcentrated agencies.

The *Juntos* programme is not active in all Peru's territories. A territory's eligibility for the programme is assessed according to five criteria: 1) the presence of *Sendero Luminoso*, or "Shining Path", the Peruvian terrorist organisation; 2) level of poverty as measured by the number of households with basic unmet needs; 3) poverty rates; 4) number of children exposed to chronic malnutrition; and 5) prevalence of extreme poverty. Only households with children, teenagers or expectant mothers are eligible for the programme. Households must also be validated by the community prior to enrolment in the programme.

The programme allocates USD 60 to households every month on condition that they fulfil three obligations: 1) pregnant mothers must attend health centres for prenatal testing; 2) children aged 36 months and under must be taken to health centres for developmental check-ups; and 3) children must attend school. Households are enrolled in the programme until their children have either completed secondary school or have turned 19. All households receive USD 60, regardless of the number of children they have. As of 2014, the programme was active in 1 150 districts spread across 15 departments. In 2014, 800 000 households received transfers. *Juntos*' budget in 2015 was increased to USD 340 million.

Figure 6.3. **Districts and household enrolment in *Juntos*, 2005-15**

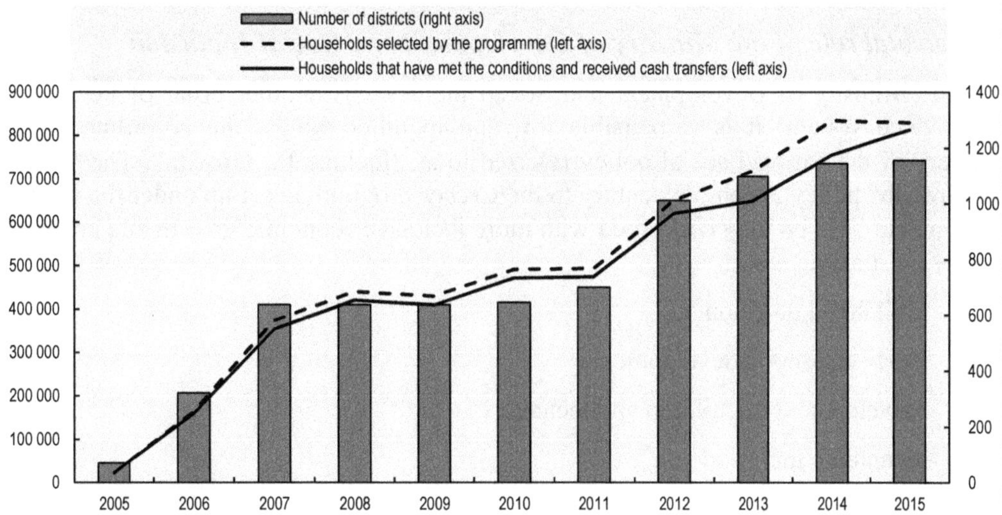

Source: INEI (2015).

The programme has had some notable successes:

- improved schooling in households participating in the programme
- improved access to health care for pregnant women and infants

Box 6.2. **The *Juntos* programme** (*continued*)

- increased use of banking and financial services (i.e. debit cards)
- increased percentage of the population with national identity documents and health insurance
- increased empowerment of women
- 43% greater average income of beneficiary households
- increased food expenditure and non-food consumption in beneficiary households, by 15% and 54%, respectively (World Bank, 2009)
- decreased poverty and extreme poverty rates in beneficiary districts, of 14% and 19% respectively (between 2005 and 2009)
- households that have received benefits from the programme for a year or more have a greater chance of reducing poverty and increases in consumption
- children in beneficiary households are 11% less likely to get sick
- *Juntos* provides beneficiary households with approximately 15% of their income, which is lower than in many other Latin American countries, including Colombia (30%) and Mexico (30%).

It should be noted, however, that the programme has not increased vaccination rates or school enrolment rates, nor decreased the prevalence of child labour.

The Ministry of Agriculture has also developed a series of projects as part of its AGRORURAL programme that are designed to develop the capacities and incomes of agricultural producers in rural areas, both of which are linked to issues of FSN. These include Project Sierra y Selva Alta, Project Sierra Sur, ALIADOS, and others.

The pivotal role of the Ministry of Development and Social Inclusion

The Ministry of Development and Social Inclusion is another pillar of Peru's FSN governance system. It is responsible for, among other things, the co-ordination and delivery of the national social policy referred to as "Include for Growth". The "Include for Growth" policy is complementary to the *Crecer* programme set up under the previous government. It is broadly concerned with more inclusive economic growth and covers the following strategic areas:

- childhood nutrition
- early childhood development
- development of children and teenagers
- economic inclusion
- the older population.

"Include for Growth" includes a series of programmes that provide support to citizens at various stages of their lives. These include:

- *Cuna Más* and *Juntos*, which address infant nutrition (0-3 years of age)
- *Qali Warma* and *Juntos*, which address early childhood development (3-5 years old)

- *Qali Warma* and *Juntos*, which address childhood and adolescence (6-17 years old)
- *Mi Chacra Emprendedora* (also known as *Haku Wiñay*) and other programmes delivered by a deconcentrated body of the Ministry of Development and Social Inclusion referred to as *Foncodes* (*Fondo de Cooperación para el Desarrollo Social*) which addresses economic inclusion (of people 18-64 years old)
- *Pensión 65*, which addresses protection of the older population (65 and older).

Of these programmes, those that directly tackle food security are *Qali Warma* and *Mi Chacra Emprendedora*. *Qali Warma* is a large-scale programme that aims to address childhood food insecurity and malnutrition. It has so far equipped close to 50 000 primary schools with a kitchen and provided fresh food to more than 3 million children. The programme also includes education initiatives to teach children about healthy eating. *Qali Warma* was launched in 2012 and is now, in terms of budget allocation, the Ministry of Development and Social Inclusion's largest programme. It has an inclusive governance system assigning an important and active role to local stakeholders. For example, each school must establish a Purchasing Committee composed of public officials and parents, responsible for buying foodstuffs, and a School Feeding Committee of teachers and parents, responsible for monitoring the quality of the food and delivering the food to students. Interviews with national stakeholders indicate that the programme has successfully addressed health issues and enhanced children's learning. The programme is to be extended across Peru over the coming years.

The *Mi Chacra Emprendedora* programme focuses on increasing the productivity of small holdings. It is run by *Foncodes*, which has regional offices in most of Peru's departments. *Foncodes* was founded in the early 1990s with the mandate to develop Peru's primary and secondary road networks. In 2012, however, it was brought under the control of the Ministry of Development and Social Inclusion and has since focused on issues of FSN.

The *Mi Chacra Emprendedora* programme promotes agricultural innovation, and the resulting increase in productivity, through the maintenance of networks of local leaders and systems of peer-to-peer learning. It has been particularly successful in the Andean region. In the department of Cajamarca, for example, local leaders provided assistance and knowledge to small-scale farmers to help them cultivate new profitable and exportable crops, including quinoa and *aguaymanto*. Benefits of the programme for small-scale farmers include increased incomes and enhanced FSN.

The *Mi Chacra Emprendedora* programme is, very much in its infancy and a pilot programme, and its geographic coverage is limited. In Cajamarca, it has only been implemented in 5 of the department's 12 districts. However, there are plans to scale up the programme and expand its coverage.

Challenges for effective food security and nutrition policy in Peru

Sustained economic growth and the implementation of numerous large-scale social programmes – including conditional cash transfer programmes – have lifted more than 20% of Peru's population out of poverty and reduced the prevalence of food insecurity. However, issues of FSN remain and are especially pronounced in Peru's rural regions. Up to 17% of rural children aged 5 and under are malnourished and many suffer from stunted growth. It has proved difficult to implement effective policies in programmes in rural areas for a number of reasons. Among them are a lack of information to inform strategic planning processes, capacity constraints at the local level and generally weak regional governments that are often unable to scale up policies and provide public goods.

The *Mi Chacra Emprendedora* programme is an example of a programme that should be scaled up and implemented in food-insecure rural regions. The peer-to-peer learning systems boost agricultural innovation and diversification into new, more profitable crops. The programme also helps establish a relationship between the central government and rural communities. This allows communities to articulate their needs and priorities to decision makers at the national level and could also conceivably lead to the more efficient delivery of public services in underserved communities. Better provision of public services could, in turn, stem the outflow of rural citizens to urban areas.

Peru's various FSN policies and programmes are insufficiently co-ordinated. The Ministry of Agriculture and Irrigation and other ministries are responsible for the country's FSN policy. Despite Peru's commitment to multidimensional approach to FSN , FSN-related policies and programmes have focused solely on the immediate relief of hunger, rather than the underlying reasons for food insecurity and malnutrition. The recent National Plan for Food Security and Nutrition may offer an opportunity to implement a FSN governance system with strong leadership, a clear vision and greater co-ordination of policies and programmes.

Finally, Peru's social programmes are largely detached from the country's competitive agenda, which focuses on the creation of employment and income-generating opportunities. The Ministry of the Economy and Finance and the Ministry of Transport do not, for example, participate in the country's Multisectoral Commission for Food Security and Nutrition. The same disconnect is evident at the sub-national level and in NGOs. Participation of citizen organisations and the engagement of the business community is minimal. Mobilisation of all public, private and third sector actors will be essential to address the nation's FSN challenges.

Concluding remarks

Evidence from the field in Peru indicates that a territorial approach for dealing with food insecurity and malnutrition in an integrated fashion is a viable option. In particular, a territorial approach would enhance: 1) integration between social policies and pro-growth policies at the micro level; and 2) transition from a large number of individual programmes to an integrated policy.

Information collected in social programmes could boost a pro-growth agenda

As discussed above, the government – through the *Juntos* programme – provides direct support to approximately 1 million households (2014). This organisational effort could be put to good use for a successful pro-growth strategy. The programme collects a large amount of information on poor households and requires the involvement of local communities to designate beneficiaries (see Box 1). In addition, local governments provide health care and education, which beneficiaries are required to subscribe to if they are to receive the cash transfers. The information and institutional networks they require could also be used to guide a pro-growth policy that promotes the creation of job opportunities in poor regions.

Institutional sustainability could help Peru shift from programmes to FSN policy

While Peru is trying to design a national strategy to deal with FSN challenges (the national plan 2015-2021), hunger and malnutrition are being handled by a series of unrelated programmes. Different constituencies within the government have generated several programmes that deal with different aspects of food insecurity and malnutrition in different territories (mountains, jungle and coastal areas). Some of these programmes, such as *Mi Chacra Emprendedora,* although it is still limited in scope, appear to work well and provide poor rural communities with relief and the tools to generate income. The current attempt to organise programmes into a national framework — a national plan for FSN —goes in the right direction, but the government faces the challenge of scaling up investment and networks. The relative absence of international stakeholders, such as donors and international organisations, may prove to be an advantage in this sense. If the government is not forced into a fast-paced transition from programmes to policies, it can set its own priorities without the influence of international players. Territories do not as yet need to absorb the large, yet sporadic, investment of international donors. As a result, there is time for programme/policy improvement and capacity building based on learning, experience and institutional continuity or "sustainability".

Box 6.3. Project Sierra Sur

The objective of the Project Sierra Sur, which is co-financed by the International Fund for Agricultural Development (IFAD), is to enhance the human, natural, material, financial, cultural and social resources of men and women engaged in small agricultural and non-agricultural activities, to improve their income.

The first phase of this project was conducted from 2005 to 2011, and the second phase from 2011 to 2014. This project has benefited more than 30 000 families in the regions of Apurimac, Arequipa, Cusco, Puno, Moquegua and Tacna, with a budget of approximately USD 40 million.

The project takes into consideration initiatives of organised producers, who present their proposals, and the funding is allocated after approval by the Local Allocation Committee Resource (CLAR is the Spanish acronym). A co-financing scheme by the organisations and strong co-ordination with the local governments helps to promote community participation.

Among the lessons learned from the project are:

- considering the demands of local organisations results in better buy-in
- the development of rural areas should not only be related to agricultural projects
- local governments must be given an important role, to ensure continuity and strengthen leadership.

Notes

1. Van de Poel, O'Donnel and van Doorslaer (2007) found a very large rural-urban disparity in rates of stunted growth: in 2000, the proportion of children under 5 who suffered from stunted growth was 0.47 in rural areas and only 0.18 in urban areas. Peru displayed the greatest rural-urban disparity in stunted growth rates of the 47 developing countries considered in the study.

2. In 2010, a USD 4.8 billion mining project in the Conga area of Cajamarca was, for example, subject to vehement opposition by the local population. The project was anticipated to yield 200 tonnes of gold and 180 000 tonnes of copper per year. The central government approved the project. Local communities, however, elected to strike, with the support of the department's governor. In 2011, the strikes escalated into rioting that caused several deaths and was declared a national political emergency. The project has since been blocked.

3. One-third of Peru's population lives in the capital city of Lima. This spatial concentration has led to several negative externalities. Land, for example, is in short supply. The most recently developed *asentamientos* are located far from the centre of the city and, as consequence, suffer from a lack of access to water and electricity.

References

INEI (2015), "Peru: Statistical overview 2015", Instituto Nacional de Estadística e Informática, Lima, available at: www.inei.gob.pe/media/MenuRecursivo/publicaciones_digitales/Est/Lib1292/libro.pdf.

INEI (2014), Encuesta Demográfica y de Salud Familiar (ENDES), available at: https://www.inei.gob.pe/media/MenuRecursivo/publicaciones_digitales/Est/Lib1211/pdf/Libro.pdf

INEI (n.d.), *Encuesta Nacional de los Hogares* (ENAHO) (2004-2014), https://www.inei.gob.pe/biblioteca-virtual/boletines/condiciones-de-vida/3.

Ministerio de Desarrollo e Inclusión Social (MIDIS) and Programa Mundial de Alimentos (PMA) (2012), "Mapa de vulnerabilidad a la inseguridad alimentaria", available at: http://es.wfp.org/sites/default/files/es/file/mapa_de_vulnerabilidad_a_la_inseguridad_alimentaria_2012_web.pdf.

Van de Poel, E., O. O'Donnel and E. van Doorslaer (2007), "Are urban children really healthier?: Evidence from 47 developing countries", *Tinbergen Institute Discussion Paper*, No. 035/3.

Vargas, S. and M.E. Penny (2009), "Measuring food insecurity and hunger in Peru: A qualitative and quantitative analysis of an adapted version of the USDA's Food Insecurity and Hunger Module", *Public Health and Nutrition*, Vol. 13/10, pp. 1 488-1 497, http://dx.doi.org/10.1017/S136898000999214X.

Vasquez Huaman, E. (2012), "El Perú de los pobres no visibles para el Estado: La inclusión social pendiente a julio de 2012", *Documento de Discusión*, DD/12/04, Centro de Investigación de la Universidad del Pacífico.

World Bank (2009), *World Bank Annual Report 2009: Year in Review*, The World Bank, Washington, DC, available at: http://siteresources.worldbank.org/EXTAR2009/Resources/6223977-1252950831873/AR09_Complete.pdf.

World Bank (2015), database, http://data.worldbank.org/indicator/NY.GDP.PCAP.CD.

Annex A. Evidence from Mali and Niger

Evidence from Mali

A workshop entitled "Territorial Approach to Food Security and Nutrition Policies" was held on 31 March 2016 in Bamako (Mali) to discuss the diagnostic study undertaken in the framework of the joint Food and Agriculture Organization (FAO), OECD and United Nations Capital Development Fund (UNCDF) initiative by the Commission for Food Security (CSA). The study focused on: 1) territorial disparities; 2) how the country addresses the multidimensionality of food security and nutrition (FSN); 3) the issue of multi-level governance and vertical and horizontal co-ordination; 4) the sectoral or multisectoral approach to FSN adopted by the country. This multisectoral commission is responsible for food security and nutrition policy in Mali. The workshop was attended by central and local government stakeholders from all the sectoral ministries, the Prime Minister's Office and various mayors. Donors also attended the event, including USAID, the UN World Food Programme, the UN Development Programme, Belgium Co-operation, Swiss Co-operation, domestic banks, agricultural development banks and non-governmental organisations.

The main causes of food insecurity in Mali

As emerged in the other case studies, the causes of food insecurity in Mali are closely correlated with poverty. Strong territorial disparities in the country persist, in particular between rural and urban areas. The incidence of poverty in Mali in 2010 was 43.6%, but reached 51% in rural areas, as opposed to 31% in urban areas and 10% in Bamako (*Cadre Stratégique de Croissance et de Réduction de la Pauvreté*, or CSCRP, 2012-2017). The three main factors contributing to food insecurity were identified as:

1. The climate challenges to which the country is constantly exposed, including drought and floods, strong winds and wide fluctuations in temperature that weaken production systems and create conditions that favour the proliferation of pests and diseases.
2. Land conflicts and civil strife. Mali has an agro-pastoral vocation, and land issues are far from being settled. In addition, the recurrent armed conflict is a major challenge for FSN.
3. Price volatility is a challenge for food consumption, which can cause the sale of key assets (e.g. livestock) and the rise of inequality.

The policy and institutional framework for food security and nutrition

In Mali, FSN falls under two main policy frameworks: the National Strategy for Food Security of Mali (NSH, 2002) and the National Policy for Nutrition of Mali (ANC, 2011), whose objectives and key challenges are to: 1) increase and diversify agricultural production; 2) improve income levels of the population through better organisation of the basic food markets; 3) ensure adequate food for all residents, especially for people living in marginal areas.

In 1981, a progressive shift towards some elements of a territorial approach to FSN began, to ensure the consistency of the National Food Security Framework and the implementation of the government's decentralisation and reform policy.

These policies have had two main outcomes: 1) improving the conditions for the prevention and management of recurrent crises in relation to food security; and 2) improving the capacity of institutional actors and of the governance of FSN.

Despite this progress, many challenges exist in the implementation of the food security and nutrition policy

There is still a strong dependency on external aid in implementing FSN policy (with projects and programmes financed mainly by external donors), as well as the persistence of a project-basis approach, which has limited geographic and social impact.

FSN policies and programmes face a lack of co-ordination, as well as weak monitoring and evaluation of the results, at both the national and local level.

The lack of technical and financial capacity, both nationally and locally, prevents the development and implementation of sustainable FSN solutions. This is strongly correlated with the lack of capacity-building programmes for FSN actors at different levels.

The diagnoses and discussions during the workshop identified some possible solutions, through the effective implementation of a territorial approach to FSN:

- improving the governance of FSN at the national and local level, by setting up policy and institutional frameworks that can help co-ordinate local actors in planning, implementing and evaluating FSN policies
- developing an inclusive FSN national policy that mainstreams the territorial approach
- establishing funding mechanisms (including public-private) under the Malian government's leadership of its national FSN policy
- strengthening technical and institutional capacity at all levels, in particular those of local authorities, to implement FSN
- strengthening private sector contributions for financing investments for FSN
- improving and strengthening resilience of local food systems, with socially viable FSN investments that can sustain both food supply and value chains and prevent land degradation
- promoting and scaling up the experience of successful programmes that use the territorial approach to FSN (this includes chiefly the UNCDF/Belgian Fund for Food Security Programme in the districts of Nioro du Sahel and Nara).

Evidence from Niger

A workshop on the "Territorial Approach to Food Security and Nutrition Policies" was held on 7 April 2016 at the *Palais de Congrès* in Niamey (Niger). The diagnostic study and workshop were conducted under the leadership and guidance of the High

Commission for the 3N Initiative (Nigériens Nourish Nigériens), the reference framework for implementing food security and nutrition policy in Niger. The diagnostic study focused on the same issues as in Mali. These include: 1) territorial disparities; 2) how the country addresses the multidimensional nature of FSN; 3) the issue of multi-level governance and vertical and horizontal co-ordination; 4) the sectoral or multisectoral approach to FSN adopted by the country. The workshop was attended by central and local government stakeholders (three vice ministers, the Prime Minister's adviser on food crisis, heads of districts and mayors). Donors also participated in the event, including USAID, the World Food Programme (WFP), the United Nations Development Programme (UNDP), Swiss Co-operation, the private sector, International Crops Research for the Semi-Arid Tropics (ICRISAT), agricultural development banks and non-governmental organisations.

The main causes of food insecurity in Niger

Niger is a landlocked country facing major human and natural challenges. Demographically, it has the highest growth rate in the world (3.9% according to the 2012 *Recensement Général de la Population*). Its population doubled between 1988 and 2012, from about 7.2 million to 15.2 million. This represents a major challenge for food security in the country.

In terms of climate, only 1% of the country receives more than 600 millimeters of rain per year, and arable soils are 80% dunes. The country faces recurrent droughts and food crises (1973, 1984, 2001, 2005, 2010). While it had surpluses of cereal in the 1960s, by the 1990s it was suffering from structural shortages. Climate hazards and the degradation of productive assets have caused shortages of food cereals for decades.

Land conflicts and rebellions of the 1990s have exacerbated conflicts over assets for agro-pastoral production. Price volatility is another cause of food insecurity, with a resulting drop in food consumption.

The policy and institutional framework for food security and nutrition

Four major periods demarcate the political and institutional development of FSN:

1. From 1960 to 1973: promotion of cash crops. A purely sectoral approach to support cash crops for export.
2. From 1974 to 1983: a concept of food self-sufficiency, based on the support of agricultural producers, input subsidies, large productivity projects under full control of the central government.
3. From 1984 to 1992: FSN was addressed through structural adjustment, with the mobilisation of food aid, the liberalisation of prices and removal of subsidies.
4. From 1992 to 2010: development of major framework documents, including the *Programme Décennal Pour le Développement Rural* (PDPDR; 1992), *Stratégie Opérationnelle de Sécurité Alimentaire* (SOSA; 2000), *Programme Complet de Sécurité Alimentaire* (PCSA; 2000), National Strategy for Food Security of Mali National Strategy for Food Security of Mali (NSH; 2001), *Programme Régional de Sécurité Alimentaire* (PRS; 2002) and *Stratégie de Développement Rural* (SDR; 2003) with reference to FSN policy, economic growth and poverty reduction.

The High Authority for Food Security (HASA) was created in 2010, launching the strategic 3N Initiative "Nigériens Nourish Nigériens" in 2012, which became the reference framework for all FSN interventions. This is an ambitious programme based on a strong political commitment to "have the Nigerian people free from hunger and to guarantee the conditions for full participation in national production and to improve their income".

Recent initiatives consonant with a territorial approach have been adopted, including:

- In the framework of the 3N, the *approche commune de convergence* is implemented in a multisectoral framework involving different groups of institutional actors. The limits are in defining roles and mechanisms for the consultation of stakeholders, co-ordination of interventions, funding operations, and monitoring and evaluation of local actions.
- The "house of the farmers" is a set of infrastructure and diversified services set up at the municipal level to help producers and agribusiness improve their performance. This approach has limitations in the way it addresses the four dimensions of food security: the access and stability dimensions are somewhat overlooked.
- The FSN Investment Fund (FISAN) is a financing tool of FSN across public and private investments. Its operational limit is in the capacity of key actors to play their roles both in terms of FISAN governance and in terms of funding mechanisms.
- The Support Programme for Local Development (PADEL), developed and implemented by the UNCDF and its partners in Mayahi, aims to strengthen the capacity of local stakeholders for FSN projects and investments, implementation and management by municipalities. The Support Programme for the Implementation of Decentralised Entities in the Dosso region (PAMED-II) is implemented by the Belgian Development Agency (BTC), with support from the Belgian Food Security Fund.

Difficulties in implementing food security and nutrition policy remain

First, a lack of awareness of the multidimensional nature of FSN and the persistence of a sectoral (agricultural) approach to FSN make it difficult to take full advantage of the opportunities offered by the off-farm rural economy.

As emerged in the other least developed countries analysed, FSN policy in Niger relies heavily on external aid, which results in the fragmentation of the projects and programmes and a project-based approach.

Another effect is a lack of coherence in the interventions overall. Poor co-ordination of the different programmes for addressing food insecurity is another big challenge for the country, as is the lack of a solid monitoring and evaluation system for FSN projects and programmes.

Finally, insufficient capacity at the territorial level, in particular at the municipal level, is an issue, as is the absence of plans and capacity-building programmes for FSN actors all levels of government.

The diagnostic study and the discussions during the workshop identified possible solutions, using a territorial approach to food security and nutrition

Adopting a territorial approach could help address food insecurity challenges in the country. Possible interventions include:

- Improving FSN governance to facilitate the co-ordination of local actors for planning, implementing and managing public and private investment in FSN. This will help improve local governance of FSN.
- Improving inter-sectoral co-ordination and ensuring the functionality of existing institutions, including the regional, district and communal committees of the 3N Initiative.
- Strengthening the capacity of human resources at all levels, in particular of local authorities. Raising awareness of the multisectoral nature of FSN and the importance of adopting a holistic approach. Promoting effective transfer of skills and competences in the decentralised context to implement the territorial approach.
- For FSN financing, promoting private domestic financing, public-private partnerships (PPP) and unlocking domestic resources to design, finance and implement FSN policy.
- Strengthening the resilience of local food systems, by promoting economically and socially viable FSN infrastructure and investments that prevent land and environmental degradation.
- Integrating the land dimension into national policies and enhancing the authority of land commissions (COFO) to mitigate land disputes and ensure sustainable FSN.

OECD PUBLISHING, 2, rue André-Pascal, 75775 PARIS CEDEX 16
(42 2016 16 1 P) ISBN 978-92-64-25709-2 – 2016

www.ingramcontent.com/pod-product-compliance
Lightning Source LLC
Chambersburg PA
CBHW061217240926
51846CB00006B/1251